Sport Marketing

Paul Blakey

With special thanks to John Mitchell, University of Chester, for his continued inspiration and critical insight and to Ravi Chavan, Sport und Markt, for his effusive sport marketing spirit.

For Lily

First published in 2011 by Learning Matters Ltd
British Library Cataloguing in Publication Data
A CIP record for this book is available from the British Library
ISBN: 978 0 85725 090 2
This book is also available in the following ebook formats:
Adobe ebook ISBN: 978 0 85725 092 6
EPUB ebook ISBN: 978 0 85725 091 9
Kindle ebook ISBN: 978 0 85725 093 3
The right of Paul Blakey to be identified as the author of this Work has been asserted by him in accordance with the Copyright, Designs and Patents Act 1988.
Cover design by Toucan Design
Text design by Toucan Design
Project Management by Swales & Willis Ltd, Exeter, Devon
Typeset in Garamond Premier Pro by Swales & Willis Ltd, Exeter, Devon
Printed and bound in Great Britain by Short Run Press Ltd, Exeter, Devon
Learning Matters Ltd
20 Cathedral Yard
Exeter
EX1 1HB
Tel: 01392 215560
E-mail: info@learningmatters.co.uk
www.learningmatters.co.uk

THE HENLEY COLLEGE LIBRARY

Contents

Chapter 1
Introduction to sport marketing

Learning Objectives

This chapter is designed to help you:

- define sport marketing;
- distinguish between 'marketing *of* sport' and 'marketing *through* sport';
- appreciate the special nature of sport marketing;
- identify the constituents of the sport marketing industry;
- recognise the key stages of the sport marketing process;
- identify the components of *marketing myopia*.

Introduction

Understanding, and being able to skilfully apply, the principles of sport marketing is an essential part of the professionalism required of organisations operating in the sports industry today. Whether representing a sports star, working for a Premier League football club, engaging with sponsors at a sport events, managing your own sport business, developing merchandising opportunities for national sport governing bodies or producing insightful sport marketing reports for key clients, each role requires the use of practices employed within sport marketing. Increasingly, new technologies are generating new opportunities to engage with the consumers of sport on an individual level, and technological 'natives' will be at the forefront of presenting sport to new audiences.

Defining sport marketing

The concept of sport marketing needs clarification. A definition enables clearer thought and a more specific consideration of the key concepts, ideas, principles, tools and techniques of sport marketing. Without determining such a boundary, the study of sport marketing could become unwieldy, confusing and overly complex. This appears to be the intention of many sport marketing, and generic marketing, textbooks written by scholars or sport professionals with a desire to maintain their authority in the business world! This textbook will explode the myths, simplify the concepts, and apply the principles to aid your understanding and appreciation of sport marketing.

Sport marketing or sports marketing

You will note that this textbook uses the term *sport* marketing rather than *sports* marketing. This is because *sport* is viewed as encompassing all activities performed within the world of sport, some of which may not be related to individual sports. So, for example, *sports* refers directly to the organisations whose business relates to the practice of sports, such as England Netball, the FA and so on, whereas *sport* reflects all additional bodies that associate themselves with sport, such as VISA and the Co-operative. Furthermore, 'sports marketing' is a term coined in the United States and is less suitable for a UK-focused text such as this.

Sport marketing as a matching process

Sport marketing is a matching process – the matching of sport products and services to the demands of sport consumers and customers. It helps to bring supply and demand into balance. Sport consumers (i.e. those who use sport services) and customers (i.e. those who buy them) require sport products and services to satisfy the needs and wants they have in life. The need to exercise produces sports clothing and footwear demands; the need for affiliation leads to a need or desire to support and follow a football team or to participate in a five-a-side football league; and the want of fun and excitement may be satisfied by attendance at a motorsport event. Needs and wants lead to demands that the sport industry is able to satisfy. However, many potential consumers and customers of sport are unaware of their own personal needs and wants. There is, therefore, an opportunity for sport marketing to reach out and tap this latent and unexpressed demand by creating demand, e.g. 3D TV, Wii Sports and the option of betting live on the next goal scorer, all from inside your own front room!

Communication is at the heart of sport marketing. Communication between a sport product/service provider and a sport consumer/customer is a bedrock component of sport marketing when matching supply to demand. Sport marketing, therefore, can be defined as the means by which the demands of consumers/customers are satisfied by sport products and services. Without expressed demand, sport products and services would have no reason to exist. However, we live in commercial times and the necessity to encourage consumption of sport through the development of new sport products/services is as integral to the growth of the sport industry as it is to any other industry sector. Furthermore, sport marketing has applications across all sectors of the economy and is not viewed simply as a transactional, consumption-based concept. This fact is an important consideration in maintaining the integrity of the processes and practices of sport marketing within an ever more critically minded sport consumer marketplace.

Reflection Point 1.1

Consider your most recent sport product/service transaction: what need or want did it satisfy in you? Could any of these needs or wants have been satisfied in other ways?

Approaches to sport marketing

Sport products and services require the application of marketing principles to communicate their message directly to identified target segments. In recent years, sport has been used by non-sport-related organisations as a vehicle to reach many of the same target segments with messages about their own non-sport-related products and services. This distinction has created two approaches to sport marketing:

1 marketing of sport;
2 marketing through sport.

Marketing of sport

This approach centres on the efforts to encourage consumption of the products and services of sport. These include competitive contests (e.g. Khan versus Mayweather or Manchester United versus Chelsea); sport events (e.g. London 2012, the Commonwealth Games or the Youth Games); and sports equipment (e.g. Slazenger tennis rackets). Sports teams and clubs of all sizes, at all levels of their sport and in all sectors of the sports industry will engage in marketing activities that present their products and services to the market in a favourable manner – it simply is not an option *not* to!

Marketing through sport

As sport as a business has developed in recent years, we have seen a plethora of non-sport-related companies using sport as a medium to reach out to sport enthusiasts with their products and services. Sponsorship has been the dominant approach to gaining rights to access this market: naming rights to Premier League football stadia (e.g. Arsenal's Emirates stadium), or professional cycling teams (e.g. Team Sky); product endorsement (e.g. Sir Chris Hoy and Kellogg's Bran Flakes); or as official supplier/partner (e.g. BMW or Holiday Inn to the British Olympic Association (BOA)).

A note of caution: sport has encouraged an unquestioning investment from companies that has necessitated changes to UK law in some instances, such as to rid the communication of an unhealthy message through the sponsorship of sports events or sports teams by tobacco companies: what will be next – alcohol, gambling?

> ## Reflection Point 1.2
>
> Identify five non-sport-related products/services that you have purchased which have created an association with sport. Why do you think these products/services chose to ally themselves with sport?

Much of our conscious thought about sport revolves around professional sport. It is carried across so many media platforms that it is difficult not to take note. However, the elite level of sport does pose an interesting environment for sport marketers to manipulate and use as a context to reach the broader sport market (see Figure 1.1).

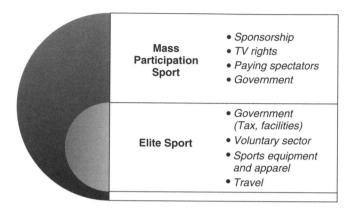

Figure 1.1 The sport market (adapted from Gratton and Taylor, 2000)

The special nature of sport marketing

At the professional level, sport is entertainment; where hard cash and chunks of our time are exchanged for a suspension of our real lives. Consumption of sport at this level is an investment in a special human experience. Professional sport has special characteristics that create unique experiences for each sport spectator, as identified by Mullin et al. (2007):

* *An intangible, ephemeral, experiential, and subjective nature*: sport is live not bottled; sport is open to interpretation and debated; sport trades on memories; the benefits of sport are difficult to consume.
* *Strong personal and emotional identification*: sport fosters high levels of passion and commitment from its supporters. Team and player attachment emerges once a passion for sport takes hold.
* *Simultaneous production and consumption*: seats that are not sold for a live sport event are lost forever, so pre-sales are very important. This perishability means that creative ways to 'sell out the stadium' are vital to generating revenues.
* *Dependence on social facilitation*: how frequently do you practise sport or go to a sport event alone? Sport brings people together in a public setting and generates interaction which enhances enjoyment of the activity.
* *Inconsistency and predictability*: the outcome of the game is always in doubt right up until the end of the game (well almost). Competitive sports leagues try to engineer this element, but weather, rivalries, crowd response, injuries, refereeing decisions and form can all create uncertain outcomes which result in an enhanced level of excitement for the crowd.
* *Core-product control beyond sport marketer's hands*: sport creates winners and losers, but who wants to see a losing team perform each week? Making rule/safety changes to sports shows a minimal level of control if it results in excitement gains, but it is a major challenge to present an entertainment experience in an activity where there can only be one winner.

The special nature of professional sport provides the focus for most sporting output that is viewed through the variety of media channels that exist today. Sport can consume people's lives and much of it feeds from professional sport. Sport enthusiasts (just one of several sport consumer segments) want to emulate their heroes as well as to participate for health and social reasons. Participation sports now align themselves with elite performers. For example, mass-start running events such as the Virgin London Marathon include both elite professionals and amateur enthusiasts. The sport marketing industry has developed as a result of these factors and to cater for these needs.

Case Study
The Virgin London Marathon

The 2010 Virgin London Marathon received over 120,000 applications for the 45,000 places on offer. Runners of all standards from elite performers through club runners to those running for charity, many in fancy dress, all line up to tackle the 26.2 miles distance. Sir Richard Branson has called the London Marathon 'an epic and inspirational event … the single biggest fundraising day on the planet'. In fact the London Marathon has raised over £400 million since its inception in 1981, but its key objectives include:

- *to improve the overall standard and status of British marathon running by providing a fast course and strong international competition;*
- *to show mankind that, on occasions, the Family of Man can be united;*
- *to raise money for the provision of recreational facilities in London;*
- *to help London tourism;*
- *to prove that when it comes to organising major events, 'Britain is best';*
- *to have fun and provide happiness and sense of achievement in a troubled world.*

(www.virginlondonmarathon.com)

Learning Activity 1.1

Visit the website of the Virgin London Marathon to identify ten different sport/non-sport/participant groups or organisations who have some input into the event.

For one of these groups/organisations, explain how you think they attain one or more of the objectives of the sport event. In particular, consider the benefit(s) they receive from the media coverage available.

The sport marketing industry

Shank's (2009) simplified model of the consumer–supplier relationship in the sports industry (see Figure 1.2) outlines the key sub-sectors of producers of sports goods and services in the sport marketing industry. This helps us to appreciate the range of sport organisations engaged in the practices of sport marketing. It also helps to signpost career options available in sport marketing-related organisations.

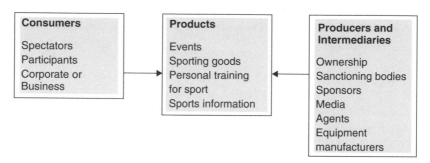

Figure 1.2 Simplified model of the consumer–supplier relationship in the sports industry (Shank, 2009)

The advent of the sport marketing sector is usually dated from a handshake between the American sports lawyer Mark McCormack and the golfer Arnold Palmer in 1960. The resultant creation of International Management Group (IMG) fathered modern approaches to athlete representation, event and TV production, and sponsorship negotiation, initially in tennis and golf. The corporate acceptance of the potential of sport as a commercial platform emerged from the Los Angeles Olympic Games in 1984 when brands such as McDonald's and Coca-Cola were pleased with the return on their sponsorship investment in the event (Sports Marketing, 2009). Latterly, the creation of superbrands such as Real Madrid and Manchester United, a sports sponsorship market in the UK worth £486 million in 2008 (Picasso Enterprises, 2010), the need to feed 24-hour sports news channels and a voracious internet market has meant the development of a sport marketing sector in its own right.

Sport Business (2009) broadly concur with the *producers* and *intermediaries* categories identified by Shank (2009), but also offer additional insight with more specific sub-categories of the sport marketing sector by listing names of companies for each one as shown in Table 1.1.

The categories in Table 1.1 simply give a flavour of the spread of organisations operating within the sport marketing sector. As is the case in the broader sport industry, networks of relationships exist between companies to connect producers of sport products and services to sport consumers. In most circumstances, national or international federations are the rights holders of sports properties, such as leagues and competitions, and of the associated commercial and broadcast rights for individual sports. However, in order to bring the excitement of a sport to the consumer, a host of intermediary companies are required. These are organisations such as those which broadcast images (e.g. the BBC), provide corporate hospitality packages (e.g. Sportsworld), provide sport event tickets (e.g. Keith Prowse), bring sponsors into sport (e.g. Synergy) and are licensed (plus some who are not) to sell branded merchandise (e.g. Kitbag Limited, through its F1 Store). Additionally, the athletes, teams, administrators, venues, travel operators and so on all play a role in synchronising the sport we consume.

Category	Exemplar organisation
Advertising, PR and sales promotion	WPP www.wpp.com
Brands	Castrol www.castrol.com
	Ford www.ford.co.uk
Conference, exhibitions and venues	Wembley Stadium www.wembleystadium.com
Consultancy	IMG www.imgworld.com
Data and information supplier	Sportsmedia Broadcasting Ltd www.sportsmedia.co.uk
	TV Sports Markets www.tvsportsmarkets.com
Event management and corporate hospitality	Olympic Delivery Authority (ODA) www.london-2012.co.uk/ODA
	IMG www.imgworld.com
International federations	Association of Tennis Professionals (ATP) www.atpworldtour.com
	International Automobile Federation (FIA) www.fia.com
	Union Cycliste Internationale (UCI) www.uci.ch
Leagues	English Premier League (EPL) www.premierleague.com
Local government	Wigan Leisure and Culture Trust www.wlct.org
Media owners	Datateam Publishing Ltd www.datateam.co.uk
New media	Octopus Media Technology www.octopusmt.com
Sponsorship	Generate www.generatesponsorship.com
	Sport Driven www.sportdriven.co.uk

Table 1.1

Case Study
Dorna Sports

Dorna Sports is the exclusive holder of all commercial and TV rights of the MotoGP World Championship. This private company also participates in the management, marketing and distribution of other motorsports properties. Dorna provides a vast array of products: advertising exposure, promotional and corporate activities, merchandising, commercial rights, corporate hospitality, overseas freight, TV rights, TV production, live feeds, post-produced programmes, OnBoard technology, graphics for live broadcast, internet webcasts, online results and video streaming amongst them.

These services require the use of the latest technology and a permanent concern for quality and evolution, fulfilling the extreme demands of a highly competitive environment. Dorna uses a multinational team of professionals with knowledge and expertise in advertising, sports TV, media, technology, information technology and law. Currently around 150 full-time employees work for the company, with a further 200 part-time contracted professionals operational during racing peaks.

The company also markets 'Ad-Time', a rotating advertising system for sports events, in several countries.

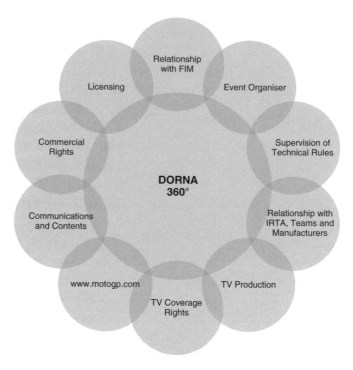

Adapted from Dorna Sports, 2010

Dorna Sports is an example of a sport organisation that provides a range of services to the governing body of motorcycle racing, the Federation Internationale de Motocyclisme (FIM). Their expertise enables the thrills and spills of MotoGP to be consumed live at the racetrack or on TV. Companies such as these are omnipresent in the sports world, acting as key links in the chain between production and consumption of elite level sport. Other companies that provide a similar function include IMG with the World Matchplay Golf Championship and as commercial rights holders to the Wimbledon tennis tournament and Nova International with their Great Run and Swim series.

So, having provided an insight into the sport marketing industry, and having hinted earlier at some of the concepts and ideas used in sport marketing, the fundamental components that constitute the sport marketing process will now be considered.

The sport marketing process

Sport marketing may be thought of as a philosophy that should permeate through the entire sport organisation. The marketing function of any sport organisation (in the public, private or voluntary sector) cannot be separated from other business functions such as financial planning and human resources management, but its principle of identifying and satisfying the needs and wants of sport consumers must run throughout the business. The 'public face' of the sport organisation is represented through the sport marketing function as it communicates its sport products and services to its target markets.

Sport marketing comprises a logical, structured process that considers the environment within which the sport organisation operates to help it make decisions and move forwards. In its simplest form, the sport marketing process has four phases: 1) analysis; 2) planning; 3) implementation; and 4) control (see Figure 1.3).

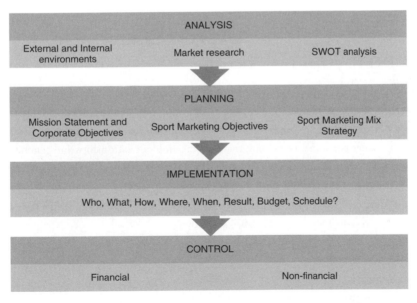

Figure 1.3 The sport marketing process

Information is the bedrock of any sport organisation, and the analysis stage gathers the data necessary for the later phases – information relating to the external business environment, internal organisational performance, and market research. The SWOT (Strengths, Weaknesses, Opportunities and Threats) analysis condenses, summarises and enables identification of key issues for the sport organisation to address in the planning phase of the process.

The planning phase considers the direction of the whole sport organisation when determining its specific marketing objectives – the desired achievements of the marketing function within the sport organisation. Sport marketing strategy outlines the broad approach towards the fulfilment of each sport marketing objective, both in the short-term (up to 12 months) and longer term (two to three years). It is the implementation phase which puts the components of the sport marketing mix into action, and the control phase which ensures that the sport marketing activities being used ultimately achieve the sport marketing objectives as stated. If discrepancies occur, then the control phase can assess where remedial action is required and what actions should be implemented.

Learning Activity 1.2

Each phase of the sport marketing process will be outlined in much greater detail in Chapter 4. However, two authors worth investigating are McDonald, M. (2007) *Marketing Plans: How to Prepare Them, How to Write Them,* 6th edition, Oxford: Butterworth-Heinemann, and Shank, M. (2009) *Sports Marketing: A Strategic Perspective*, 4th edition, Upper Saddle River, NJ: Prentice Hall. See (a) what differences you can find in the way they present sport marketing diagrammatically and (b) what underlying similarities there are in the way they conceptualise the process.

Marketing myopia

A sport organisation might accept the philosophy of the sport marketing process, but there will be little benefit if its *implementation* is hampered. If a sport organisation is not careful, it can fall into the trap of *marketing myopia*. A world-leading community sport system needs marketers who understand how to attract customers, change consumer behaviour, manage stakeholder relationships and generate further investment, sponsorship or revenue (Sport England, 2009). This is true of all sport organisations, but unfortunately many do not engage fully with the sport marketing process.

Levitt (1960) described this condition as *marketing myopia*, the symptoms of which have been identified in sport marketing (Mullin et al., 2007) as follows:

- focus on producing and selling;
- reliance on winning;
- confusion between promotions and marketing;
- short-term focus;
- lack of research.

These factors lead to organisations failing either to understand the key characteristics of sport target groups or to focus on the desire to satisfy the needs and wants of sport consumers. Furthermore, any hope of retaining sport customers is compromised by an inability to utilise the full range of sport marketing tools and techniques available. The passion and excitement enabled through sport can be lost if there exists such a fundamental oversight of the sport marketing process. The knock-on effect for sport organisations can be serious with the need for strategy re-alignment, resource re-distribution, and product and service re-positioning. Sport organisations beware!

Chapter Review

This chapter has established the basis of sport marketing as a process designed to facilitate the successful communication between the products and services offered by a sport organisation and the consumers/customers most likely to satisfy their sporting wants and needs. The overview presented in this chapter is designed to provide a foundation knowledge upon which the remaining chapters will broaden and deepen. By engaging with the learning activities and the wider reading a further exploration of the principles of sport marketing becomes possible.

Further Reading

Beech, J. and Chadwick, S. (2007) *The Marketing of Sport*, Harlow: Prentice Hall/Financial Times.
     A particularly insightful textbook that provides both depth and breadth to the study of sport marketing. Authoritatively constructed, well written and good cases used throughout.

Mullin, B.J., Hardy, S. and Sutton, W.A. (2007) *Sport Marketing*, 3rd edition, Champaign, IL: Human Kinetics.
     A US-based text, but covers the fundamentals of sport marketing and more complex components such as branding, public relations and legal aspects of sport marketing.

Smith, A.C.T. (2008) *Introduction to Sport Marketing*, Oxford: Butterworth-Heinemann.
     This textbook gives a solid foundation to students of sport marketing by covering all the main principles and concepts in an applied manner. Examples are provided from a broad range of international sport contexts, and further study options assist the interactivity with the subject matter.

www.sportbusiness.com
     An essential website for up-to-date news of sport marketing issues, and others, in the sport industry. Subscribe for automatic daily updates.

Chapter 2
Research for sport marketing

This chapter is designed to help you:

- appreciate the importance of information collection as a basis for decision-making in sport marketing;
- recognise the environments from which information can be derived;
- identify the factors that impact upon decision-making in sport marketing;
- identify key conceptual components for research in sport marketing.

Introduction

Information is the basis of sound evidence-based sport marketing decision-making. Sport organisations require information about sport consumers, their competitors and the sport market so that they can understand and consider the factors that influence behaviour in their marketplace. Sport marketers talk about 'environments', the internal environment and the external environment, the macro environment and the micro environment; all they are really doing is investigating different places from which any organisation needs to collect information. This is a research task. However, the information derived also must be synthesised into a coherent form, analysed and utilised in a systematic and logical manner. This process of research helps to provide reliable information that acts as the heartbeat of sensible decision-making in all situations. It is the fundamental component of all sport marketing decisions.

Analysis stage of the sport marketing process

The sport marketing process gives structure and direction to the collection, synthesis, analysis and utilisation of sport marketing research information (refer back to Figure 1.3). Sport organisations need to enable this process by focusing upon their internal activities and on external conditions that impact upon their business. Knowledge of the wider business environment is crucial in order to appreciate likely implications for the sport industry and all sport organisations operating within it. For a sport organisation to satisfy the demands of its customers, the formal stage of analysis begins with an environmental analysis (often also referred to as a situational analysis). This constitutes the external environment (both macro and micro, including PESTEL (political, economic, sociological, technological, environmental and legal), competitor and stakeholder analysis) and the internal environment of the organisation. Market research captures specific information about sport consumers, their desires and expectations as well as their responses to communication stimuli. All information derived is distilled down to manageable proportions through the SWOT analysis. The key findings of the SWOT analysis can then guide the next phase of the sport marketing process – planning.

Environment/situational analysis

The collection of information upon which decisions about how sport products/services are presented to the marketplace starts here. The environment/situational analysis considers potential options available to a sport organisation in the sport marketplace, the positives and benefits that can be brought into the sport marketplace by a sport organisation, the activities of competitors, and the real desires of sport consumers. All aspects of the analysis are inter-related and should be brought together to consider their impact(s). In effect the environmental/situational analysis considers the controllable and uncontrollable factors that affect a sport organisation during the delivery of its marketing function as part of its business operation. The uncontrollable factors relate to those variables that influence the marketing practice of a sport organisation and form the external environment analysis. Subsequently, the internal environment of the sport organisation is investigated to determine the benefits it is likely able to bring to the sport marketplace, and its limitations. These are the controllable factors; those variables that the sport organisation has some influence over and form the internal environment analysis of the sport organisation. The internal environment analysis is often referred to as the internal marketing audit.

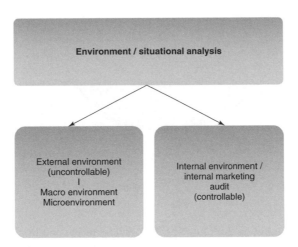

Figure 2.1 Environments in sport marketing

External environment – the macro

Sport organisations need to be aware of events in their own sport sector, the sport industry more generally, and the wider business and societal contexts. Each of these contexts must also be considered from a local/regional, national and international perspective. Such spheres of influence can have important effects upon any sport organisation and so a process of on-going monitoring is necessary to deliver the information inputs to inform marketing-related decisions and actions. The uncontrollable nature of these factors present unforeseen circumstances that can result in disappointment for sport consumers. For example, the restricted movement of elite sport performers and cancellation of sport events due to the formation of a volcanic ash cloud in European airspace in April 2010 grounding hundreds of flights and thousands of people. For example, the Carnegie Challenge Cup Rugby League fixture between Widnes Vikings and Lezignan fell victim to the volcanic ash cloud after the French club's flight to England was cancelled.

The predominant marketing concept utilised to consider information in the external macro environment is the PESTEL analysis – political, economic, social, technological, environmental and legal. Each element presents challenges and possibilities for a sport organisation, for example through changing policy initiatives brought about by a change in national government (political) or of a slowing birth rate or ageing population (social).

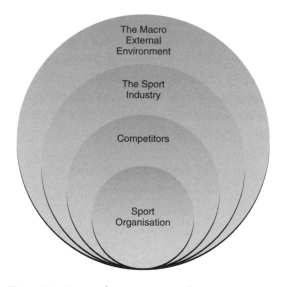

Figure 2.2 External environments of a sport organisation (adapted from Smith, 2008)

PESTEL analysis

These factors (a development of the PEST or STEP analysis) present conditions that affect the operational environment of the sport organisation. A successful sport organisation will be able to understand existing factors and potentially forecast effects, thus take advantage of the information it has received. Don't forget that the sport organisation has no direct control over these factors and so can only respond to them in their sport marketing approaches.

Political

Political factors can create opportunities yet place obligations on sport organisations. European Union and national government policies must be considered here, including:

- political stability – of coalition governments and developing nations;
- pricing regulations – for example, the wholesale price of Sky TV to its competitors;
- taxation – personal, including inheritance and capital gains, and business;
- wage legislation – minimum wage;
- market regulations – work permits for non-EU nationals or the Bosman ruling in Association Football.

In summer 2010 the UK government announced plans to increase sports' share of lottery funding from 16 per cent to 20 per cent; structural reform of UK Sport, Sport England and the Youth Sport Trust; and for school sport to focus more sharply on competitive activity through an Olympic- and Paralympic-style competition across England. Such political initiatives will impact upon the delivery of new or upgraded sport products/services and will require the sport marketing discipline to encourage sport participation through its communication function.

Economic

National and global economic factors affect all organisations, not just sport organisations. The economic climate dictates the behaviour of sport consumers, suppliers and other stakeholders. In recession an economy will likely have higher unemployment, lower spending power and lower stakeholder confidence. Conversely, an economy in growth will have lower unemployment, higher spending power and higher stakeholder confidence. Economists categorise those factors that relate to the broad economy (e.g. employment levels, business economic life-cycle stage and exchange rates) as macroeconomic and those factors that relate directly to organisations or consumers (e.g. income levels) as microeconomic. The sport industry will expand or contract in accordance with these economic influencers, but spending on sport products and services does not always follow a logical pattern of spending as sport consumers increasingly consider sport purchases as important as everyday living costs, becoming essentials rather than luxuries. More specifically these include:

- government intervention in free markets – the UK being a mixed economy with government regulation at 'arm's length';
- efficiency of financial markets – the UK being a key international financial centre;
- exchange rates – approximately US$1.51 and €1.20 to £1 sterling;
- business cycle stage – prosperity, recession, recovery;
- unemployment rate – currently 7.9 per cent in the UK and rising;
- inflation rate – currently above 3 per cent in the UK;
- interest rate – currently 0.5 per cent in the UK;
- skill level of workforce – the development of a knowledge society in the UK is indicated in part by the increased numbers participating in higher education.

The UK government views the London 2012 Olympic and Paralympic Games as 'an economic stimulus package … to develop and open up new markets for UK businesses' (DCMS, 2010, p. 3). However, in response to the worldwide economic downturn from 2008 efficiency savings in the £9.325bn budget were identified as necessary and between January and May 2010 £130m worth were set in motion (DCMS,

2010). This is an example of a direct effect of the macroeconomic situation on the sports industry. However, this one-off sports mega event bucks the trend of rational action as the Olympic site in East London requires 11,000 workers to complete construction works – the highest number of any time during the whole project. This is at a time when the construction industry in general is struggling and shedding jobs. For those engaged on the Olympic project, their income level is likely to be unaffected by the wider economic malaise and so they will still be able to spend money on sports products and services if desired.

Social

Social forces such as family, friends, work colleagues and the media affect the attitudes, interests and opinions of us all. The social experiences we are exposed to affect the way we view the world, the thoughts we have and, therefore, our behaviour and, ultimately, our purchases – sport being no exception here. Social factors to consider include:

- demographics – the appeal of a sport product/service according to an age band, social class category or gender (check out weekday evening five-a-side leagues);
- education – the content of the National Curriculum for Physical Education, and time the individual spends in full-time education, e.g. going on to university;
- culture – sport fans' use of technology, e.g. blogging on their forum to express their views of the game);
- attitudes – these endure for Nike who faced criticism in the 1990s for using child labour in Cambodia and Pakistan in factories it contracted to manufacture footballs;
- interests – are facilitated by the internet as it facilitates a sport enthusiast's ability to receive the latest news, follow the match 'live' on fan-sites, and interact with other like-minded people;
- class structure – some sports attract different echelons of society, e.g. golf and equestrian rather than football or basketball), despite the protestations!

Sport marketers who establish real insight into people's lifestyle and behaviour can develop complementary sport products and services that can generate demand and grow market share. An awareness of population dynamics (a pattern of an ageing population in the UK), of cultural norms and values (the traditional sports in the UK of football and cricket), and of an acceptance of the need for a healthier lifestyle can create a scenario where sports with a long heritage can target and encourage particular segments to continue to participate in sport. For example, rugby union actively encourages older players – veterans (over 35s) and golden oldies (over 50s) – through promotion of leisure rugby. Training and competitive games occur weekly and thus realise fitness gains that foster team spirit which is developed further through well rehearsed post-game activities.

Technological

Technology is used today by all age groups and by sport organisations and sport consumers. This may be technology infrastructure such as the internet, technology hardware such as mobile phones, laptops, iPhones and iPads or technology software such as Mac OS X or Microsoft Windows – both known as system software – or application software such as web browsers (e.g. Apple's Safari) or media players (e.g.

Quicktime and iTunes), plus CRM databases and performance analysis tools (e.g. Hawkeye or Prozone's Post Match Analysis).

The pace of technological change and the diffusion of technological usage has created a faster exchange of information between stakeholders, but means extra pressure for businesses as they are expected to deliver their products and services far more quickly. Further technological factors include:

- technology's impact on product offering – improved quality and channels of distribution;
- impact on cost structure – initial investment costs that increase efficiencies in production;
- impact on value chain structure – improved logistics;
- rate of technological diffusion – increased acceptance of innovation across the sport marketplace.

Computer and mobile means that sports information is at your fingertips 24/7 and it is expected that this information be constantly updated and accurate. The BBC's online stream of England versus Slovenia at the 2010 football World Cup peaked at 800,000 viewers/listeners with another 15.4m watching live on TV (Glanville, 2010). Sport organisations should ignore the impact of technology on sport consumer habits and expectations at their peril.

Environmental

The geographical features and climate of a region impacts upon the type and nature of sports participation performed. The type and nature of built facilities also makes up a key element of the sporting environment. The eventual necessity for the redevelopment of centre court at Wimbledon SW19 to include a sliding roof was a result of the frequent inclement June weather in London affecting the world's premier tennis tournament. The severe winter weather of 2009/10 meant great conditions for skiing in Scotland with Aviemore in the Cairngorm mountain range reporting increases of 500 per cent in numbers of skiers (Collinson, 2010).

Increasingly, issues of sustainability have assumed a greater focus in the sporting environment. The building of new facilities for sports events such as the Olympic Games and major football tournaments or the redevelopment of stadia facilities such as Landsdowne Road (now Aviva Stadium) in Dublin has required carbon footprint impact to be addressed. The 2006 Football World Cup in Germany was one of the first sports events to set a 'Green Goal' to limit its carbon impact. The event organisers utilised standard approaches to energy efficiency – for example, efficient lighting technology and public transport initiatives – but added to these by harvesting rainwater to re-use on the pitches and using returnable drinking beakers. Interestingly, the 2010 World Cup in South Africa was estimated to have a carbon footprint of six times that of Germany, due mainly to the necessity for large-scale building works and internal transport distances between host cities (www.energy-savingnews.com). The 'green' message seems likely to be a major challenge for the hosting of sports events into the future and will require a delicate handling of the message through all communication channels.

Legal

The sporting world is bound, increasingly, by the legal environment of the macro external environment. Age discrimination and disability discrimination legislation, health and safety legislation, employment and competition laws affect the sport providers obligations and costs, and as a result, the provision of sport products and services. Furthermore, sport governing bodies regulate their own sports and have jurisdiction over all competitors. Increasingly, sport bodies are liaising with broader legal powers to overcome difficulties in sport, e.g. the BALCO drugs scandal in athletics in the USA with the outcome of jail terms for some individuals. Similarly, price fixing by English football clubs and sports retailers resulting in significant financial penalties for those involved.

Political	Economic	Social	Technological	Environmental	Legal
Stability	Government intervention	Demographics Education	Impact on product/cost/ value chain	Geographical e.g. climate	Age/ disability/ health and
Taxation	Interest rates	Culture	Rate of diffusion	Built facilities	safety legislation
Wage legislation	Unemployment rate	Attitudes		Sustainability	Employment/
Market and price regulation	Exchange rates	Interests			competition laws
	Business cycles	Class structure			
	Skill levels				
	Market efficiency				

Table 2.1 Key PESTEL factors

One important point to note is the inter-relatedness between PESTEL categories as issues can cross categories (see Figure 2.3). Political decisions in particular have a major impact upon the economic factors, e.g. a government's degree of willingness to control interest rates, inflation and funding of government departments can have an impact on jobs and, therefore, consumption of sport products and services. Governments, through international agreements, have also made decisions about limiting the impact of climate change by setting sustainability targets. These are considered in new sport projects from the design phase, through construction to operation. You might consider the position of events such as Formula 1 (and its fuel consumption) if more stringent 'green' regulation of sport events was introduced. This is particularly pertinent if we see rationing of fuel at the time of a future fuel crisis.

Sport organisations must also identify which PESTEL factors have the most relevance and greatest impact on their business and consider these more fully in their planning. A sport organisation with redevelopment plans would need to take account of interest rates if a bank loan was to be sought. Funding of new projects may be available if benefits to sport consumers can be identified, e.g. sports events that

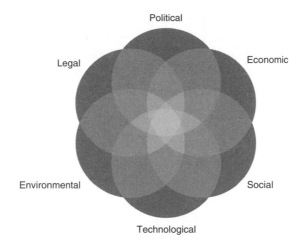

Figure 2.3 The inter-relatedness of the PESTEL analysis

provide health benefits for young people are often supported by the local Tesco or Sainsbury's supermarket providing refreshments.

For large companies such as Nike it is necessary to perform a PESTEL analysis in each of its territories. Nike would apply the concept to each of its subsiduary companies (e.g. Converse Inc. and Hurley International LLC) in relation to the customer segments served by these brands.

The nature of our globalised world has also meant the PESTEL analysis can be considered along geographical lines, locally, nationally and globally, thus subdividing each category accordingly and creating the acronym LoNGPESTEL. This is pertinent for sport organisations as so much production of sports apparel and equipment now occurs in the Far East. This can have impacts upon the retail price of goods at your local sports outlet once transport costs, exchange rate fluctuations and potential increases in wage costs are factored in.

Learning Activity 2.1

In order to encourage you to adopt the position of the sport marketer and to view the sport experience as it exists at the interface of the sport provider, try answering the following:

Which element(s) of the external environment relate to the following sport consumer behaviours and transactions?

a) Four football supporters sharing a car to cross London to an evening match at West Ham. Think about the use and operation of the stadium, car sharing, potential use of a GPS navigation system, and the banter in car.

b) An 11-year-old Asian female signing up for swimming lessons at her local swimming pool. Think about pool management, staff accreditation, and possible conflict with older generation of her family.

External environment – the micro

The environment specific to the sport industry presents particular influences for any sports organisation. The micro external environment involves factors dealt with regularly from the key stakeholders of the organisation, e.g. customers, employees, suppliers, shareholders, the media and competitors. Developing relationships with these groups is very important as the costs, quality, strategy and the overall success of the sport business can be affected without mutual co-operation. For each stakeholder issues for the sport organisation include the following.

Customers – business survival is based on providing benefits to customers that satisfy their needs, wants and demands. A process of monitoring customer requirements and anticipating those of the future helps guide action towards the satisfaction of these desires. Information to aid this process is far more available today as a result of the use of technology. In the sport industry membership is a well-used practice to govern access to the golf club, the leisure centre and to a seat at the football match. This enables a sport organisation to build a picture of the behaviours performed by those members who can be contacted and encouraged to attend more often. Swipe cards provide invaluable information to organisations and appear to be used to reward loyalty. Despite customers having great bargaining power in the sports marketplace due to the phenomenal level of choice available when making a purchase, sport does encourage great loyalty in its enthusiasts. Relationship building and maintenance is crucial for sport organisations to effect loyal behaviour.

Employees – key to organisational performance, particularly in the sport industry where direct contact with customers is so prevalent, recruiting and retaining motivated employees is of high importance. Training and development is an on-going process as organisations move to flatter management structures and increase the responsibilities of staff. The sport sector suffers from transience due to many jobs being part time, short term, lower paid than other industry sectors and relying heavily upon volunteers. Many sport events would not occur were it not for committed volunteer helpers. High-quality employees are very important to customer-facing sport organisations and many organisations strive hard to provide rewarding experiences and training towards appropriate qualifications for their employees. Construction and security workers on the Olympic venues for London 2012 are offered the opportunity to complete related professional qualifications (e.g. NVQs) in order to develop their workforce skills and enhance their long-term employment prospects once the Olympic site is completed (DCMS, 2010). It is worth noting that this sort of development makes a contribution, in the form of enhanced employability, to the social legacy left behind after the Games.

Case Study
Job prospects of London 2012

Hackney resident Sarah M. Salem has got involved in volunteering with the help of Hackney's 2012 Unit, and it's done a lot for her skills and confidence. In her words, 'When I decided to volunteer in 2007 I did not anticipate what was to follow.'

Sarah was unemployed and suffered from health problems. Whilst on a training course, she met with Cuthbert Jack, a tutor on the Personal Best volunteering programme. He recommended that she get involved with volunteering for 2012. Sarah enrolled onto the programme having already completed some volunteering at the Homework Club and Queensbridge Primary School.

Her first 2012 experience was at the 'Get Set Hackney' jobs fair in March 2008 at the Ocean on Mare Street. Over 2,000 people signed up for training and jobs at the Olympic site, and Sarah was part of the welcoming and registration team. 'I thoroughly enjoyed my time with the team and meeting people. As a disabled person I was very much aware of people with disabilities' needs and reacted sensitively to these. I have a fond memory of that event', Sarah says about the experience.

She has had training in market research, the role of stewards at events and assisting people with sight impairments, organised by the 2012 Unit. She has volunteered at the Learning Trust and got involved in the New Age Games, winning a javelin event.

She took part in the launch of the Legacy Masterplanning Framework event, talking to people and finding out what they thought about the benefits the Olympic Park could bring Hackney when the Games are over.

(Source: www.hackney.gov.uk)

Suppliers – the quality of goods provided at a satisfactory price is paramount here along with the ability to supply sufficient volumes and flexibility to fluctuations in supply and demand. Pricing decisions for the finished product or service can be affected by suppliers that then impacts upon sport consumers who are particularly price sensitive. *Lusso* is a cycling apparel brand based in Manchester that boasts the tagline 'Handmade in the UK'. This production association with its key customer market clearly has patriotic advantages for the company and may provide a sense of quality in its garments. The values of the company are also communicated through this statement and this can translate into a competitive advantage in the marketplace.

Competitors – different markets have varying levels of competition in existence. Organisations gauge their level of market share in comparison to their competitors and this can influence pricing decisions and the quality of product/service offered. A market share of more than 25 per cent is considered to be a monopoly position in the UK and regulation exists to challenge companies that achieve such positions to ensure that they do not unduly increase prices for consumers. The dominance of the satellite broadcaster BSkyB in the UK sports market is a good example of a monopolistic position in relation to Premier League football. EU legislation has been enacted to limit the company's power in the marketplace by forcing competition between broadcasters through a bidding process for live rights and ensuring that one company cannot have sole rights to all live matches. The manipulation of regulation and legislation in sports broadcasting is an on-going situation to try to enable fairer competition. This ultimately brings benefits for sport consumers.

Media – the positive or adverse portrayal of a sport organisation in the media is internally monitored to assess the impact it may have for its key markets. Managing the media is a crucial activity for most organisations and specialist staff are recruited to aid the process. The high profile of sport across all media platforms means that a sport organisation could be subject to media interest on a frequent basis, therefore, actively managing the media is a key PR function. You only have to mention the names of Tiger Woods, Lewis Hamilton, Northern Rock or the FA to conjure up an image and opinion based upon information derived from the public domain. The attitudes of the sport consumer may thus affect their purchase decision.

Shareholders – all businesses are legal entities with ownership rights held by individuals, organisations or government. Shareholders (or stockholders) are granted rights to influence the decisions made by an organisation and to share the distribution of its income. Sport organisations span the variety of business ownership models, but high-profile shareholder activity has surrounded sports such as F1 and sports teams such as Manchester United and Team Sky cycling. In the case of the latter, the team is owned by Tour Racing Limited, comprising two board members from BSkyB and two from British Cycling, but owned and funded by BSkyB. Confusing perhaps, but nonetheless important to understand, as it is likely to identify the direction an organisation might pursue through its business intentions.

Competitors

Understanding the type and nature of competitor activity in your chosen marketplace is an information gathering process of paramount importance. Competition exists for all sport organisations in all markets and so information about the strengths and weaknesses of competitors can be used to inform new business possibilities, threats posed, and insights for one's own direction. Considering your competitors' reaction to your own strategies and tactics is also a valuable approach in order to consider the power and influence that a particular competitor might wield over yourself.

Competition in the sport industry takes on a dual format. The object of sport is to win, competition is inherent, but sport requires co-existence between players and teams for it to continue. Underlying business competition between teams operating in the same sports league is moderated because unsuccessful business performance could mean the loss of a club through financial difficulties. A number of professional sports teams have suffered relegation due to off-field irregularities, the most high profile being Portsmouth AFC in the 2009/10 football league season. It could be argued that the governance of the game itself is partly to blame for such failures. Furthermore, disparity in the financial performance of sports organisations in the same sector can lead to match day performance gaps rendering the outcome of the game known in advance, thus diminishing the spectacle of the sports event. Significant financial profit and loss figures have been observed in English cricket with Durham CCC reporting a profit of almost £200,000 as opposed to Essex that recorded a loss of £216,000 for 2009 (www.cricinfo.com). Rugby League has instigated a policy originating from the United States sports leagues such as the NBA, NFL and MLS. This regulates spending on salaries by limiting expenditure to a specified formula applied to the characteristics of each team in the league. This has the effect of sustaining an organisation's existence and creating greater performance parity on the pitch.

Competition exists in different spheres – directly and indirectly (see Figure 2.4). Direct competition exists between sport organisations producing the same products and services and who operate in the same sport sector, e.g. a private health club such as David Lloyd and the local leisure centre, despite their different ownership models. Substitute competition exists between sport organisations producing different products and services that have sufficient similarities to be used in multiple scenarios, e.g. Tacchini Zip Polo short sleeve tennis apparel can be used when playing golf. Finally, indirect competition exists between those organisations from different industries, e.g. attendance at a rugby union match or going to a restaurant – each satisfies a different need, but each could be undertaken within the same timeframe at the same time of day and the chosen option accounting for the (similar) customer spend.

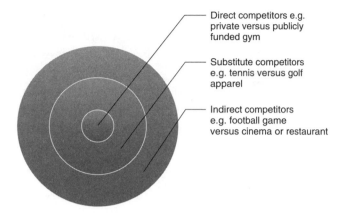

Direct competitors e.g.
private versus publicly
funded gym

Substitute competitors
e.g. tennis versus golf
apparel

Indirect competitors
e.g. football game
versus cinema or restaurant

Figure 2.4 Competitors in the sport industry

Competitor analysis

Accounting for competitor activity in the sport marketplace needs to be performed logically and systematically. Such an analysis will consider: the key forces at play in the competitive environment; the underlying forces and whether these will change or stay the same into the future; the strengths and weaknesses of competitors; and whether strategy can utilise or overcome these competitive forces. The most commonly used tool applied to the competitive environment is Porter's (1980) Five Forces Analysis, and applied to the sport industry by Smith (2008).

However, whilst Porter's model considers information about competitors that exist currently and may exist in the future, it does not predict competitor behaviour. To this end, Porter's (1980) Competitor Analysis Framework (see Figure 2.5) focuses upon four key aspects of a competitor:

- competitor's objectives;
- competitor's assumptions;
- competitor's strategy;
- competitor's capabilities.

Objectives and assumptions give purpose to the organisation and strategy and capabilities identify the things that competitors can do. For example, whether the competitor's current performance is achieving the objectives set or whether a change of strategy is required. Further investment requirements and non-financial objectives, that is, sustainability/conservation concerns, can also be indentified. The identification of sport target market segments, the nature of the strategy (quality, price, brand image-based) and the capabilities of management, marketing, innovation, production and finances enables reactions to one's own sport marketing strategy to be gauged. The reaction could be certain retaliation perhaps via aggressive price discounting, a failure to react due to being in an established sport market, a specific reaction perhaps price-based only, and an inconsistent reaction therefore being completely unpredictable.

Ultimately, the sport organisation has to judge itself and its competitors within the conditions of the sport marketplace it is operating. Customer analysis and segmentation also inform this part of the process, and is the focus of the next chapter.

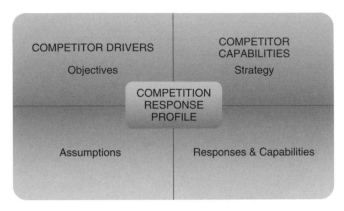

Figure 2.5 Competitor analysis framework (adapted from Porter, 1980)

Learning Activity 2.2

Identify a sports organisation with which you are familiar, and for its most immediate competitor identify the following:

- product characteristics
- strengths
- weaknesses
- opportunities
- threats
- current market share
- current action in the market
- probable response to your actions.

Internal environment

All sport organisations must also focus internally to undertake a comprehensive evaluation of their own performance and operational processes affecting the sport marketing function. These are the factors that the sport organisation can control (in contrast to the uncontrollable factors of the external environment). This is not an easy process for any organisation to perform as it involves a range of information about current and past sport marketing performance. For example: size, growth and trends of current sport market(s); sport customer satisfaction; sport marketing planning and organisational efficiency and effectiveness; sport marketing function (application of the sport marketing mix). It can include an assessment of broader organisational practice. For example: organisational culture, structure and image; and internal resources – people, finance and equipment.

For an established sport organisation each of these elements already exists, therefore, an objective reflection on each is required to feed into this information collection phase to help guide future direction.

The broader organisational influences are likely to be embodied in strategic documents that already exist such as the *Corporate Plan*. Elements of such a document will provide points of useful reference, e.g. the mission/vision statement, perhaps core values, and the organisational objectives. The mission/vision of a sport organisation states the purpose of its existence – what it does, how it does it, to whom, and where it sees itself in the future. Thus the mission/vision statement provides a guide to the development of a sport marketing strategy that is also consistent with the organisational objectives – the measurable statements of achievement desired by the sport organisation. However, mission statements can sometimes be quite subjective and aspirational, so need to be viewed with caution. For a new sport business, each of these elements is required to ensure that it approaches the sport marketing function in a structured way, in line with conventional business practices.

Most sport marketing textbooks provide little detail on this important phase of the sport marketing process, leaving you, the student, without a full appreciation of the type and nature of information necessary for collection. The following case study will provide a greater level of insight for you.

Case Study
Company analysis – Nike
Strengths and weaknesses of the corporate/business level
Strategic managers

- *Board of Directors – consists of both management directors and independent directors. This combination can assist the overall board in thinking 'outside the box' (strength). However, Nike's lack of younger members of the board who could bring a new perspective to the company and assist in achieving Nike's goals (weakness).*

Environmental analysis

- *Internal – Nike's management analyses its internal environment and makes decisions based on that analysis. Nike's marketing research allows the company to be more fashion savvy. As a result of product and pricing research, Nike has decided to continue to focus on the high-end market while increasing its market share in the middle and low price ranges to broaden Nike's product spectrum (strength).*
- *External – Nike's failure to foresee problems in relation to labour and factory conditions have now been rectified, but resulted in bad publicity and declining sales as society and consumers call for more 'socially responsible' companies (weakness).*

Strategy formulation

- *Mission – 'To be the world's leading sports and fitness company.' Nike's mission statement resembles a vision statement. It is not specific as to the products and services provided and the mission statement also omits any mention of distribution channels and customers (weakness).*
- *Corporate objectives – Nike has no published corporate objectives in relation to the overall company. However, it has established corporate objectives in relation to perceived corporate responsibility. The objective is to 'lead in corporate citizenship through programs that reflect caring for the world family of Nike, our teammates, our consumers, and those who provide services to Nike' (weakness).*

- *Grand strategies – Nike utilises innovation to produce top-quality athletic footwear and apparel (strength).*
- *Competitive strategies – marketing strategies and product offerings through product differentiation (strength).*

Strategy implementation
- *Corporate culture – Nike has created a corporate culture rich with employee loyalty and team spirit. Employees are called 'players', supervisors are 'coaches' and meetings are 'huddles' (strength).*
- *Leadership – Nike's top management's leadership style can be characterised by the team management approach. Top management leadership consists of a committed group of executives all bringing together vast experience and knowledge (strength).*
- *Motivation – employee morale remains a challenge to the company (weakness).*

Strategy control
- *Establishment of standards – a comprehensive establishment of profitability standards has assisted Nike in its evaluation of individual performance as well as a comparison to other competitors (strength).*
- *Evaluation of performance – Nike thoroughly examines and compares the aforementioned performance standards to the actual results that have occurred as a result of implementing strategies to meet or exceed performance standards (strength).*

Strengths and weaknesses of the functional level
Marketing
- *Market share – (strength)*
- *Distribution through e-commerce – (strength)*
- *Advertising and promotion – (strength)*
- *Products – (strength)*
- *Marketing research – (strength)*

Production
Location of facilities – Nike's facilities are located throughout Asia and South America. The locations are geographically dispersed which works well in its mission to be a truly global company (strength).

Research and development
Focus – Nike conducts continuous, basic research that benefits numerous facets of the sports and fitness industry, with the primary focus directed towards applied research.

Human resources
Human capital – weaknesses still exist in regard to labour policies in overseas locations, but Nike has committed to goals to better the problems.

(Adapted from www.condor.depaul.edu)

Learning activity 2.3

- Why is Nike so successful in the sport market?
- Which elements of its business could it do better?

Go to www.nike.biz.com to identify its financial performance for 2009–10.

To provide some semblance of order to the data derived during the internal environment analysis, Drummond and Ensor (1999) identified two key components of organisational capability to which the information could be assigned:

1 Organisational assets.
2 Organisational competencies.

Organisational assets include financial, physical, operational, human and information systems. Further assets are customer-based (sport brand image and reputation, market leadership), distribution-based (size and quality of distribution), internally based (cost structure, innovation culture) and alliance-based (access to markets, exclusive agreements).

Organisational competencies relate to the skills and abilities of the sport organisation at three decision-making levels – strategic (management skills), functional (finance, marketing) and operational (implementation of functions) – and three structural levels – individual, team and corporate.

This sport organisation-wide process identifies the competencies that can assist the sport marketing function directly, but it must be supplemented by more detailed information about a Strategic Business Unit (SBU), e.g. TaylorMade-adidas golf or specific sport products/services. Auditing tools such as portfolio analysis are used to reflect current performance and to identify strengths that can help generate an appropriate strategy. The Boston Consulting Group (BCG) growth share matrix is perhaps the best-known portfolio model. The fundamental basis of the model is quite straightforward as it is concerned with the generation and use of cash by the SBU or sport product/service (see Figure 2.6).

Relative market share predicts the capacity to generate cash and market growth predicts the need for cash investment. Therefore, a 'Cash Cow' is a market leader in a low growth market, so does not need much investment yet is highly profitable (e.g. Nike Air Jordan's); a 'Star' is a market leader that generates cash, but needs investment due to operating in a rapid growth market (e.g. Nike+); 'Question Marks' are not market leaders thereby not generating much cash, but also need investment (e.g. Nike watches); and finally, 'Dogs' fall into a low growth and low market share position that may produce cash, but equally could be divested (e.g. Nike cycling).

One crucial decision across all sport products/services in the range is to consider how best to use the cash generated by the 'Cash Cow' to support the development of 'Question Marks' into 'Stars' and onwards to becoming a 'Cash Cow' in their own right.

The BCG is often criticised for over-simplifying the factors affecting market growth and market share such as developing competitive advantage, the sport PLC and other financial measures (e.g. ROI and

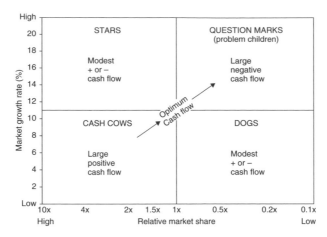

Figure 2.6 The Boston Consultancy Group (BCG) growth–share matrix

market size). Nevertheless, the principle of identifying the potential success of sport products in the range is sound. Other matrices have been established to give a greater level of insight (e.g. the General Electric multi-factor portfolio matrix), but these are dependent upon internal data (often subjective judgement), and their weighting. This type of information is commercially sensitive and is not made available to us. (See the further reading section at the end of this chapter for more sources of information about portfolio analysis techniques.)

The culmination of this data-deriving phase of the sport marketing process is the summary tool the SWOT analysis. The *strengths*, *weaknesses*, *opportunities* and *threats* analysis reduces and filters the information collected via the internal and external analysis phase into a more structured and useable form that helps to determine subsequent strategic sport marketing direction. It is a much used, much referenced, simple and effective sport marketing tool.

SWOT analysis

The most important point to remember about the SWOT analysis from the outset is that the strengths and weaknesses are derived from the internal environment analysis and the opportunities and threats are derived from the external environment analysis. Remembering that the sport organisation has control over its internal environment, but no control over its external environment, the SWOT analysis brings this information together in a four quadrants framework (see Figure 2.7) to help guide subsequent decisions. Appreciating the sport organisation's current situation enables strengths to be exploited, weaknesses to be confronted, opportunities to be identified and threats to be avoided. In effect the SWOT analysis gives a clearer idea of:

- what the sport organisation does well and what it needs to improve on (strengths and opportunities);
- where the sport organisation has competition which can be defended (strengths and threats);
- where the sport organisation needs to change to protect itself from outside influences (weaknesses and threats);

- where the sport organisation needs to focus on its priorities (weaknesses and opportunities) (New South Wales Sport and Recreation, 2010).

Furthermore, a SWOT analysis should conform to several basic rules:

1 Be realistic about the strengths and weaknesses of the sport organisation.
2 Distinguish between where the sport organisation is placed today, and where it could be in the future.
3 Always analyse in relation to the competition, that is, better than or worse than.
4 Be short and simple, not overly complex.
5 Be specific.

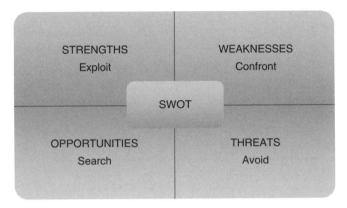

Figure 2.7 SWOT analysis

The example in Table 2.2 provides actual evidence relating to the provision of sport in north western England. It makes every effort to fulfil the criteria for a SWOT advised in this section, by focusing internally on the controllable factors and externally at the uncontrollable factors in the sport environment.

Strengths	Weaknesses
• Strong infrastructure of major sport venues and professional clubs • Strong football presence – Premier League and Championship clubs • Impressive reputation for hosting major sport events • Ability of professional sport clubs to deliver community programmes – contribution to wider socio-economic agendas • Importance of history and heritage	• Under-developed cluster, limited coordination, B2B networking and collaborative work • Public perceptions of clubs in relation to community engagement • Under-representation in rugby union • High dependence upon (discretionary) leisure • Spend among smaller professional clubs • Limited understanding of, and success obtaining, public and private sector funding

···▶

	Lack of 'middle-sized' venues
	Sector diversity – small and difficulty coming up with common solutions

Opportunities	Threats
• Innovative funding • Acceptance of the need, and willingness, to network and collaborate in the future • Willingness to work more closely with the public sector and to take a long-term view • Broad, cross-sector recognition of economic value of major event • RDA involvement in, and facilitation of, improved knowledge transfer and best practice • Potential growth of key sports (e.g. basketball) • Growth potential in Far East – particularly football	• Negative perception of London 2012 and the detraction from the profile of the NW • Reliance on casual/low-skill labour • Decline in public sector spending and capacity to invest • Slowdown in the UK economy

Table 2.2 SWOT analysis of major sport venues and professional sport clubs in the northwest region (www.nwda.co.uk)

Learning Activity 2.4

For each of the statements listed in the four quadrants of the SWOT framework, identify the relevant component from either the internal (i.e. capabilities, assets) or external environment (i.e. PESTEL).

Strengths
- Strong financial base.
- Fast-paced and exciting sport format.
- Appealing to live spectator audience, including TV.
- Support from local businesses and politicians.

Weaknesses
- Diminishing number of new members.
- Difficulties recruiting volunteers.

Learning Activity 2.4 continued

- Lack of advertising/sponsorship revenues.
- Expensive ticket prices.

Opportunities
- Renewed focus on team sports by national government.
- International/national interest in sport, e.g. effect of London 2012 Olympic Games.
- Desire for association by 'green' business organisations.
- Corporate social responsibility initiatives for community sports activities.

Threats
- Economic recession effects.
- 'In the home' sport/leisure activities, e.g. social networking.
- Other sport organisations with better facilities.
- Time related issues, e.g. longer working hours, working parents.

NB: despite its ability to co-ordinate a large amount of information into a more manageable form, the SWOT analysis tool tends to oversimplify the ease of distinguishing into which category each environmental factor fits as some factors may appear to correspond with more than one. Nevertheless, the sport organisation is made aware of these factors and can develop competitive advantages in its strategic direction as a result.

The sport marketing research process

The evidence-based sport marketing decision-making process requires a systematic approach to the collection, analysis, interpretation and implementation of information. The sport marketing research process establishes the need to gain insights into sport environments, sport competitors and sport consumers – the foci of this chapter and the next. Data from these sources is required regularly and should be a formal, proactive and integrated gathering, storing, analysis and use of the information.

The process necessitates a database system, often referred to as a Marketing Information System (MIS) to co-ordinate matters – don't forget that this process seeks to understand all the information that is considered by the brain of the sport consumer during their decision-making. The key information requirements (Mullin et al., 2007) therefore are:

- Who – are the sport consumers, specific sport segment profiles, or the sport consumers of competitors?
- What – are the benefits sought by sport consumers, factors influencing demand, the sport products/ services of competitors?
- Where – is the sport purchase decision made, sport purchase made?

- When – is the purchase made?
- Why – do sport consumers buy?
- How – is the sport product/service used, much do sport consumers buy?

The MIS should seek to capture information from all the 'touch points' a sport consumer has with a sport organisation. The use of information technology means that our sport purchases and purchase intentions can be tracked. Profiles of our activities can be created upon which sport communication messages to encourage sport consumption are based, e.g. Road Runner Sports uses personalisation by sending an email to any sport consumer who adds an item to their on-line basket but who does not complete their transaction. This approach is an attempt to convert purchase intention into actual sport consumption.

The basis of a good MIS, rather than a GIGO ('Garbage In – Garbage Out') system is the management of the data flow. Mullin et al. (2007) suggest the five steps of data flow as:

1 Collect data from a wide range of sources – e.g. ticket buyers, groups, sport participants, e-newsletter subscribers.
2 Process the data including merging, purging, cleaning and de-duplicating.
3 Create one single data repository.
4 Use the data for all sport marketing activity.
5 Track campaign effectiveness.

The MIS is both an internal and an external information co-ordinating device. The principal internal resources accessed to inform the MIS includes sales records, enquiries, account holders (e.g. season-ticket holders or corporate sponsors), personal details of complainants or commendation providers. External resources relate to sport market reports, census data, sport media coverage and primary data about the specific characteristics (demographic, geographic, behavioural, psychographic) of the sport market segment. Figure 2.8 provides a diagram of the basic process performed by a MIS.

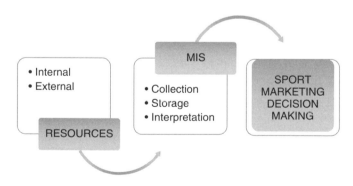

Figure 2.8 Marketing Information System model

The primary research route is one all sport organisations must involve themselves with during this planned data collection phase. Engaging directly with sport consumers can be a costly activity to perform, and requiring specialist skills, therefore, a third party agency (e.g. Performance Research) is often contracted to undertake this form of research. Primary research is necessary at pre-, iterative and post-sport event/campaign stages to gauge the fullest effect of the decisions to be made, and those implemented by sport marketers. Primary research is an involved process of answering a specific question/ issue by generating sport research objectives, devising and implementing a suitable research methodology, and analysing, interpreting and reporting the findings. Applied sport research investigates a specific issue that faces a sport organisation and is an accepted tool in the sport marketing and management field. Examples abound, including: 'Customer Viewpoints of Corporate Sponsorship of Sport in the Current Economic Crisis', 'Brand Image and Awareness of Sponsors in Formula 1' or 'The European Football Jersey Report'.

Discussion about the necessity for a qualitative or a quantitative methodological approach and the need to address issues such as reliability, validity, sampling and means of analysis I will leave to your sport research methods class. These are crucial determinants for successful sport marketing research and the information derived should be fed into the MIS to aid sport marketing decision-making. A detailed discussion and application of these approaches and techniques can be followed up through the resources detailed in the further reading section of this chapter.

Chapter Review

Information is the bedrock of evidence-based sport marketing decision-making. The necessity for a sport organisation to focus on information sources internal and external to the organisation means that the factors that can be controlled by the sport organisation and the factors outside the control of the sport organisation are accounted for in this process. It is a very involved process that requires specific tools (e.g. a MIS and the SWOT analysis) to co-ordinate the data that has been generated. These tools help to identify the most crucial components for the sport marketer to consider in the planning phase of the sport marketing planning process.

Further Reading

Mullin, B. J., Hardy, S. and Sutton, W.A. (2007) *Sport Marketing*, 3rd edition, Champaign, IL: Human Kinetics.

Chapter 5 'Data-based marketing and the role of research in sport marketing' provides valuable information about the constituents of a MIS and of ways of collecting primary data through surveys and questionnaires etc.

Shank, M. (2009) *Sports Marketing: A Strategic Perspective*, 4th edition, Upper Saddle River, NJ: Prentice Hall.

Chapter 4 'Research tools for understanding sports consumers' considers the entire sport marketing research process, including several of the issues mentioned in the earlier section here.

Andrew, D. and Pedersen, P. (2010) *Research Methods and Design in Sport Management*, Champaign, IL: Human Kinetics.

This book is also available as an e-book and explains research design, implementation, analysis, and assessment criteria with a focus on specific procedures unique to the discipline of sport management.

Chapter 3
Sport consumers

This chapter is designed to help you:

- appreciate the concepts of customer analysis and consumer behaviour in identifying the sport consumer;
- identify a range of factors by which the sports market can be segmented;
- consider the application of sport market research.

Introduction

Sport consumers are the focal point of the sport marketing function and the reason that sport organisations exist. A good understanding of the sport consumer – be they spectators, participants, or other stakeholder (e.g. a sponsor or corporate guest) – is required to enable a more targeted sport product offering and, ultimately, a more satisfied customer. It is necessary to gauge both the internal and the external influences that have an effect upon the decision process of sport consumers, to recognise the need for sport market research, and to consider the process of analysis to help guide the use of this information in the sport marketing planning process.

This chapter is influenced by the work of Matthew Shank, an eminent sport marketer in the United States. In one single diagram you will appreciate the decision-making process that sport consumers go through when making sport consumption decisions, and consider many of the influencing factors that we are all subject to when making those decisions. We will concentrate on sport participants and sport spectators, leaving other stakeholders for another day. With only a few exceptions, which will become apparent, sport participants and sport spectators make decisions in very similar ways and are often the same people, so there is no reason to treat them as separate groups. If you are anything like me, you will believe that you are Wayne Rooney or Frank Lampard when kicking a football about in the park or garden, Victoria Pendleton or Bradley Wiggins when out on the bike, or Mo Farrah when out for a run (and Usain Bolt in the last 100m!). Where possible I want to go to Old Trafford, Alpe d'Huez or Crystal Palace stadium to watch the stars in the flesh, and if that is not possible, I will watch them live on TV. Furthermore, I want to wear the same kit – a replica shirt, Reebok football boots, Bont cycling shoes, adidas running shorts, and maybe even grow my sideburns like Bradley! These are some of the influences elite sport can have on the sport consumer. The result is increased sales of equipment and apparel required for participation in sport at all levels, and in encouraging attendance at sport events or for consumption of sport via electronic means – TV, PC or mobile. So what are the other influences on our sport consumption decisions, many of which may be outside our consciousness?

Sport consumption behaviour

Figure 3.1 is the focal point of the first part of this chapter. Sport consumer behaviour is the basis of the decision-making process and will enable you as a sport marketer to understand why, how, when and where sport consumers make their decisions to consume sport. An appreciation of these factors will enable you to better satisfy their sporting needs and desires. The Model of Participant Consumption Behaviour (Shank, 2009), which I have re-classified as the Model of Sport Consumer Consumption Behaviour, also informs the remainder of the strategic sport marketing process by ensuring that you have a clear appreciation of the activities and actions of sport consumers.

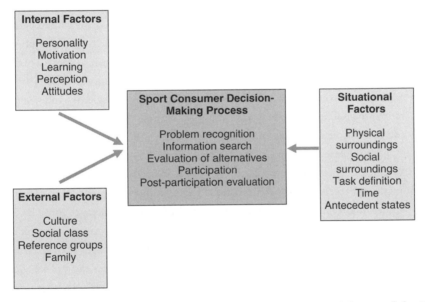

Figure 3.1 Model of Sport Consumer Consumption Behaviour (after Shank, 2009)

The model appears complex – it is not. The amount and type of information that exists about sport consumers is vast and often complicated, but this model can help to simplify and provide insight into the thoughts and actions of specific sport consumer groups. Yes, it is a generic framework that may not apply to all situations in exactly the same way, but it provides sport marketers with a way to think about their key sport consumer markets. One way for you to appreciate the value of the framework is to apply your own sport purchase behaviour to it – you will be encouraged to do this throughout this section.

Actually there are only two components to the model:

1 The sport consumer decision-making process at the core (something we all follow when making any decision in life).

2   The influencing factors on our sport consumption decisions – internal, external and situational (again all our decisions in life are influenced by many things, sport is no different).

These will be explained in more detail in the following sections.

The sport consumer (participant and spectator) decision-making process

All sport consumers are capable of making individual consumption decisions, and they do. It just so happens that many other individuals make the same decision (and for a variety of their own personal reasons). For example, 45,000 individual decisions to participate in the Great North Run; 75,123 individual decisions to go to Old Trafford to watch Manchester United versus Liverpool; and 11,000 individual decisions to participate in the London Triathlon.

The decision-making process makes sense of the cognitions occurring inside the mind of the individual sport consumer: their thinking, their processing of information, and their judging of the options. The process begins when the sport consumer realises that they have a need to consume sport; a realisation termed *problem recognition*. It is a desire that is sufficiently important to require an action (the instigation of the decision-making process) to ensure satisfaction. To illustrate this, consider the following cognitive process: I have wanted to go skiing for several years now, only having skied on snow once before. I run and bike frequently and love the outdoors, but I need a different activity that can give me a challenge, as well as some mental and physical relaxation time – skiing can provide this.

Thinking strategically, sport marketers could identify seasonal peaks and troughs of activity as key decision points in sports that are closely related. They would do this in order to target a group of sport consumers who might have a similar state of mind. Promotional packages could be designed to offer activities and events to eliminate the sports consumer's 'problems'. Immediately you can identify how many of the concepts and ideas of sport marketing begin to develop into a coherent whole – for example, the need for sport marketing research and the ability to access and use secondary and primary sources of data, followed by the co-ordination and structuring into a package through the components of the sport marketing mix to encourage positive consumption behaviour. Think about the various components of sport marketing wherever possible as you move through the chapters of this textbook.

The natural inclination of a sport consumer to satisfy a desire for sport consumption is to seek out information upon which the decision can be made. There are two types of useful information: 1) *internal sources*; and 2) *external sources*. Internal sources are predominantly memories from previous experience and/or exposure and a resultant attitude formation, and are heavily related to the internal factors that influence the decision-making process. External sources are personal sources – for example, friends and family, and sport marketing sources – and are heavily related to the external factors of the decision-making process. Perceived risk (in a number of contexts) is a major factor here in determining the extent of the information search. Expensive purchases, dangerous activities, and ability levels all lengthen the search. A skiing holiday can fall into all three of these and so can involve a lengthy search for information upon which to base a decision. Sport marketers need to know from where sport consumers seek information and ensure an effective sport promotional strategy to get the right information out there in front of potential skiers with a range of aspirations and intentions.

In all situations a variety of possibilities exists that will satisfy the initial desire. An evaluation of alternatives is performed, first through the broadest range of possibilities before these are narrowed to an evoked set (the final few possibilities). The evaluative criteria are the important characteristics of the initial desire and this guides the final decision. My skiing desire is actually for the cross-country variant – no cable cars required. So the *information search* takes a different turn as most skiing holidays are geared towards downhill locations. I have some internal data sources available as I have witnessed cross-country skiing in Switzerland; I have checked websites in the past and know that France has several venues; and whilst walking in Scotland I have seen marked cross-country skiing routes in the Cairngorm mountain range. This is a start. I need good snow conditions, a range of routes, and comfortable accommodation in a small town or village near the ski tracks. Sport marketers need their sport product/service to become part of the evoked set, therefore, an understanding of the evaluation criteria is crucial. Just to reiterate, market research should have established these factors.

Suddenly the decision has been made and *participation* in the sport consumption experience takes place. More specific factors will have played a part in the final selection, e.g. the influences of the other members of the party, equipment and apparel requirements, après ski options. As a sport marketer it is necessary to maintain an on-going dialogue with the sport consumer to ensure all their needs are met. Without this sport consumers can question their own decisions as they perform *post-participation evaluation*. We all do this with many purchases we make – a reason why consumer law enables goods and services to be returned to the sales outlet within a specified time, no questions asked. This is cognitive dissonance – a mismatch between need and purchase decision. As sport consumers we consider all aspects of the purchase and decide if it satisfied all our initial needs and desires, and if not, why not. I decided to go to Sparenmoos near Gstaad in Switzerland as it ticked all the boxes I required. The trip got off to a bad start when the flight was delayed for several hours and a half-day of skiing was lost. Everything else was fantastic, a little pricey but that was to be expected. Sport marketers need this kind of feedback so that improvements can be made to the individual components of the sport product/ service to ensure that word-of-mouth communication, increasingly through social networking sites, is positive. Future participation by those on the trip and others who come to know about it is affected directly by such evaluative insight.

The cross-country skiing scenario exhibits the need for an extensive problem-solving decision of considerable duration. It necessitated an initial consumption need requiring a heavy internal and external information search to present several alternatives. The complexity of the decision can trigger post-purchase dissonance and comprehensive post-purchase evaluation. Nevertheless, it is possible that if a similar desire were perceived in the future, a more limited problem-solving decision process would be required. For the equipment and apparel decisions there would be a need only for a limited external search as most criteria could be satisfied internally from knowledge and experience. Experience, both of sports information gathering and of the sport itself, dramatically reduces the range of suitable options next time around. To put it another way, as the activity becomes more familiar, fewer options need to be considered and habitual problem-solving occurs, taking account of only internal sources. Decisions are routinised and alternatives are not considered, although this can be difficult to achieve in many sport product/service purchase decisions as new and improved products supplant those that already do the job well!

Learning Activity 3.1

As a sport marketer you should be able to appreciate how a sport consumption decision is made by considering your own actions and the reasons for them. Therefore, consider an extensive problem-solving sport product/service consumption decision you have made by considering the following:

- The fundamental need/desire.
- Internal and external information sources accessed.
- List the evoked set of alternatives that were available.
- Identify five important elements of the need/desire that you wanted to satisfy.
- Did you suffer any cognitive dissonance?
- Was complete satisfaction attained – if not, why not?

I hope you agree that the Model of Sport Consumer Consumption Behaviour (Shank, 2009) is providing a great deal of insight into the mind of the sport consumer; the influencing factors upon the process will now be considered.

Influencing factors on the sport consumer decision-making process

Internal factors

These are psychological elements such as personality, motivation, learning, perception and attitudes. These elements have become increasingly important in sport marketing in recent years, as the bases of sport market segmentation (more to follow in this chapter) have placed a greater emphasis on using such lifestyle and behaviour characteristics to profile and select target groups. Again, all sport consumers have each of these characteristics – yes we all have a personality, however flawed!

Sport consumers are drawn to sport activities, sport events or other sport products/services that reflect their own inner self. *Personality* traits represent a person's skill, belief and attitude responses to their environment (Feldt et al., 2007). There are many words to describe personality characteristics, e.g. extrovert, introvert, emotional stability, orderliness and intelligence. It could be pre-supposed that participants in individual sports have a greater tendency towards introversion – that is, reliable and thoughtful characteristics – whereas team sport players are more more extroverted – that is, outgoing, energetic and spontaneous. Research evidence is mixed in that Dobersek and Bartling (2008) observed introversion in volleyball team players whilst Eagleton et al. (2007) observed individual sport players to be reserved, passive and controlled, all traits of introverts too. Freestyle snowboarders appear to hold a mixture of traits such as sociability, self-confidence, optimistic, emotionally stable with low rates of stress and anxiety (Mueller and Peters, 2007).

These assumptions need a greater level of evidence in the range of sports available, and across sport product/service offerings before sport marketers can link personality profiles to sport communication approaches in a strategically, coherent way.

Case Study
The UK sportswear market

*The UK sportswear market (sport clothing and sports footwear) is a major crossover market
serving sport as fashion as well as sport as function (T-shirts, trainers, even swimwear). Designer
brands such as K Swiss have permeated the market, although it is dominated by Nike and adidas.
Specialist brands such as NBX (a sub-brand of New Balance) target serious runners and Skins is a
hit with its technologically advanced 'bio-acceleration' and 'reduced lactic-acid build-up' clothing.*

*But the sportswear market is saturated and rife with intensive price competition between the
main retailers. Sport consumers are pursuing general fitness activities rather than competitive
sports and seeking crossover kit, footwear especially. Sportswear (not swimwear) is bought by 36
per cent of adults, more generally men, younger and of higher social grade. Swimwear is bought by
25 per cent of adults, biased towards women aged 35–44 years old. Sports footwear is purchased
by half of all adults annually – 75 per cent of 15–19 year olds, declining to 66 per cent of 35–44 year
olds, with no gender or social grade bias.*

*Attitudes of adults towards sports goods revealed 69 per cent were concerned about sweat shop
production; 47 per cent dislike going to social occasions in sports wear; and 36 per cent thought
Nike or adidas offered better quality than other providers; 26 per cent were wearing sportswear
at that moment and the same percentage buy sportwear but never take part in sport or exercise;
50 per cent bought sportswear specifically for sport, while 35 per cent used it as 'fashionable
leisurewear'.*

(Fenn (2008) *Keynote Sports Market Review*)

Learning Activity 3.2

Ask questions of your colleagues to reveal the profile of their sportswear consumption. Do you
generate the same findings regarding brands purchased, crossover use, sports footwear statistics,
and attitudes to manufacturers and quality of sportswear as the Keynote Sports Market Review?

It would be good practice for one or two people in the class to act as spokesperson(s) and to
co-ordinate the findings for the whole group up at the front of the classroom.

Motivation 'directs behaviour toward the fulfilment of needs' (Shank, 2009, p. 136). Sport satisfies
needs, be they personal improvement – for example, mastering a new skill such as improving your
tennis forehand – sport appreciation, or social facilitation within a sport (Milne et al., 1996). All sport
consumers have a motive for their consumption behaviours that can be termed either *motive direction* or
motive strength. Motive direction can mean a positive move towards being actively competitive in a sport
and controlling nutritional intake to benefit training requirements. Motive strength is observed via the
degree of sports involvement. Compare two gym users, one trains everyday whilst the other goes to the

gym about twice a month. When involvement is high, sport marketers can determine strategies that target the receptiveness of sport fanatics. Similarly, the more casual sport consumer can still feature in the sport marketers 'offer'.

Perception is 'the complex process of selecting, organizing and interpreting stimuli' (Shank, 2009, p. 140). We all hold perceptions about sports people, sport brands and sports themselves, garnered from many sources such as friends, TV and magazines. These dictate our thoughts, and ultimately our sport consumption decisions. Sport marketers try extremely hard to influence the perception of the sport products and services they serve through the sport promotion element of the sport marketing mix (see Chapter 7). However, we all suffer from (or benefit from) *selective attention* meaning much of the sport marketing stimuli around us is filtered out, and we concentrate on satisfying the sport needs we have brought to us via the most eye-catching messages. Individualised/personalised communication, predominantly via email or newsletter sign-up, is one means of penetrating an individual's selective process.

We all also suffer from selective interpretation. For example, it is very easy to assume that boxing is a painful sport, therefore, I do not want to participate in the sport as I prefer to impart pain on myself through the sport activities I do rather than have someone else determine the level of pain for me. Sport consumers also have *selective retention*, another filtering mechanism so that only key elements are remembered, e.g. the elation of victory or a personal best time. Perception is reality, so my perception is my reality. The portrayal of image is closely associated and this can be shaped by the sport marketer to good effect through the communication messages presented to the target market.

Learning is 'a relatively permanent change in response tendency due to the effects of experience' (Shank, 2009, p. 141). Sport consumers learn in three ways:

1   Behaviourally through information stimuli – these elicit a positive or negative feeling or behaviour response. Swimming your first length of the pool provides a reward for the effort and a motivation to swim further and more often. However, a very young child getting splashed in the face could mean an adverse early water experience. Sport marketers of course focus on presenting the reward experience to encourage involvement.
2   Cognitively through problem-solving – where a performance goal is set to drive consumption of the sport activity such as the completion of a marathon. Sport magazines, websites or GPS/HRM products can play a part in providing information for the sport consumer to achieve their goal.
3   Socially by learning through other people's actions. Sports are good for this as they have rules and guidelines that govern behaviour and a punishment system if these are breached. Role models in sport (sometimes controversial, but frequently used by sport marketers) also have the potential to effect participation and spectator sport consumption behaviour.

Attitudes 'are learned thoughts, feelings and behaviours toward some given object' (Shank, 2009, p. 143), and have three components:

1   Cognitive – beliefs held.
2   Affective – feelings/emotional reactions.
3   Behavioural – actions.

Past experiences and the influences all around us (external factors) create our attitudes about sport, specific sports, sport products/services, and of situations in life more generally. So what do you think about the sport of netball?

- It is a fast-moving team sport (cognitive).
- Netball is played mainly by school girls (cognitive).
- Not appropriate for boys to play (affective).
- I prefer basketball (affective).
- It helps to be tall (cognitive).
- I don't play netball (behavioural).
- I watch my girlfriend play for the school team (behavioural)

Sport marketers have increasingly undertaken attitudinal surveys to assess thoughts and feelings towards a sport product/service ahead of creating sport marketing strategies to change/improve such attitudes. For example, Quester and Lardinoit's (2001) assessment of global and local sponsors' impact on sport consumer attitudes and purchase intentions at the 2000 Sydney Olympics.

Again image plays a big part in the portrayal of sport products/services and their reception by targeted sport markets (more to follow in Chapter 7).

External factors

These are sociological elements existing in society such as culture, social class, reference groups and family. These elements interact with the internal factors to make each one of us act as we do. *Culture*, for example, 'is the set of learned values, beliefs, language, traditions, and symbols shared by a people and passed down from generation to generation' (Shank, 2009, p. 145). All those things actually which many people in the UK, and further afield, suggest are being lost from society as homogenisation of culture continues (read American cultural dominance via TV, music, politics, etc.) through globalisation (or mondialisation in France). The author Thomas L. Friedman refers to this phenomenon as the world becoming flatter through technological advances that have meant fewer cultural and geographical boundaries, thus enabling business activity to occur wherever it is most efficient and effective, e.g. China for production and India for technical and customer services.

Nevertheless it is still the case that different cultures have different traditions and ways of doing things, including sports, e.g. the big four sports in the United States – basketball, American Football, baseball and ice hockey – do not have the same sense of attachment in Britain. Similarly, cricket, rugby, and even F1 do not travel well across the Atlantic. We learn about the skills, knowledge and attitudes required for sports through the process of socialisation. As children we are subject to guidance from parents, teachers, friends, the media etc. from whom we learn about one or more sports, watching or playing (or indeed inactivity) and the degree of involvement to be afforded. Fewer people horse ride than play football due to a basic lack of opportunity, be that geographical availability, cost or lack of knowledge about entry into the sport. Some sports have many access issues (barriers to entry) that prohibit potentially talented and effusive individuals becoming involved.

Values underpin beliefs in society and again determine cultural differences. To what extent does the UK population value sport and want to benefit from the fitness benefits it offers or the diversion opportunities it presents? Why does England have almost twice the proportion of its youth (11–16) overweight compared to the Netherlands (Janssen et al., 2005)?

Social class 'is the ... division of people in a society sharing similar values, lifestyles, and behaviours that can be hierarchically categorized' (Shank, 2009, p. 147). Occupation, income and education pre-determine the sport consumer hierarchy which results in the residents of deprived neighbourhoods not having an equal chance to get involved in grassroots sport: most British sports ignore their talents and their needs (StreetGames, 2006) and is one of the simpler determinants of likely decision-making used by sport marketers in their planning activities.

Reference groups 'are individuals who influence the information, attitudes, and behaviours of other group members' (Shank, 2009, p. 148). These groups can be friends or work colleagues who encourage sport participation or purchase. Remember the inherent element of human interaction in sport that means other people influence us all through our engagement with sport. Similarly, sport celebrities have this power too. I wonder how many young footballers wanted to 'bend it like Beckham?'

Finally, *family* influence perhaps carries the greatest sense of gravity. Family members influence each other, children on parents and parents on children. Who got you interested in sport? But modern family structures suggest that the dynamic in encouraging sport participation is different where there are single or divorced parents, dually employed parents with kids, and of extended families, such as grandparents. The simple necessities of taking children to sports opportunities, meeting the costs of participation and providing encouragement and support underpin family influence (Kay, 2009).

Situational factors

These are temporary factors and include physical surroundings, social surroundings, time, reason for participation, and antecedent states. They occur at a particular time or place and can affect sport consumer decision-making immediately. *Physical surroundings*, for example, include climatic conditions, of which we are so fond of discussing in the UK and Ireland. The weather has a real impact upon our sport consumption decisions, often stopping us getting out for a run, ski or ride. Why do you think that Centre Court at Wimbledon and the Millennium Stadium in Wales both have a sliding roof?

Social surroundings have increased numbers signing up to mass participation events such as cyclo-sportives, half marathons, and open water swimming. The motivation from participating with hundreds of other people is key to engagement in such events. The broader social opportunities afforded to golfers or rugby players likely prove to be a pull-factor for participation.

Time is possibly the most crucial factor in determining sport consumption decision-making. Leisure time has actually increased in recent years as white goods have saved time spent on everyday chores. We have, however, decided to spend more time at work, or at least the feeling that we do; then there is the daily commute and suddenly time, and energy, for sport is diminished. Why do you think Twenty20 cricket was packaged as a two-hour game targeting families and starting at 5.30 pm? Also do you think the 40 minute six-a-side evening soccer match is an alternative to the 90 minute weekend version for a 'man in a hurry'?

Reasons for participation are many, but the seriousness with which a sport is engaged with determines the need for sports equipment and apparel. Frequency of involvement is one determining factor for likely sport consumption decision-making, that is, greater involvement equals greater sport consumption.

Finally, *antecedent states* (or psychological state) can motivate sport consumption or vice versa. Activity can rejuvenate a tired body or an individual can excuse himself or herself as being 'too tired'. The socially interactive nature of sport can help to motivate when you feel a lack of energy. Or perhaps this can be replaced by Lucozade energy drinks as the adverts seem to suggest. On the other hand, whole body workout programmes such as yoga and pilates are available when such states are evident.

To complete this section of the chapter, I want to draw upon the factors that Shank (2009) suggests, additionally, influence our attendance at live sport events. Millions of visits to live sport events occur each year, but these are undertaken by a lower percentage of the population than you might think: only 12 per cent of respondents to the General Household Survey in Scotland had been to a live sport event in the preceding four weeks (ONS, 2010). For many live sport spectators there is also the desire to emulate elite level sport stars by visiting or using venues when sport events are not actually happening there, e.g. the Aintree Experience (home of the Grand National horse race), or a track day at Silverstone or Oulton Park race circuit in Cheshire. Mad Sunday is a famous occasion at the Isle of Man TT motorcycle races when the actual race circuit is open to the public and thousands of motorbikes tour round at various speeds just to say they emulated the stars of the sport with this privileged access. I have never stepped on the turf at Wembley Stadium, Old Trafford or the Keepmoat Stadium as the privilege is not often extended that far, but I have cycled on the Manchester Velodrome in the wheel tracks of Chris Boardman and Sir Chris Hoy and run on the track at Gateshead Stadium in the footsteps of Tyson Gay.

Learning Activity 3.3

- Which venues have you received privileged access to, and for what reason?
- How did you feel following in the footsteps of the stars?
- Did you recreate a specific past event (your own action replay)? Where were you at the time, and with whom?
- Was a particular moment more significant than others?
- Did you have a favourite celebrity in mind?
- Can any of these be represented in merchandise that would appeal to you?

Discuss your responses with those of a colleague in your class to identify similarities and differences.

We are attracted to live sport events for several reasons:

- *Fan motivation factors* such as self-esteem enhancement, diversion from everyday life, entertainment value, eustress, economic value, aesthetic value, need for affiliation and family ties (Wann, 1995).
- *Game attractiveness* based upon the likely quality of the contest usually increases attendance levels.
- *Economic factors* prevailing in the wider society reflect the desire to watch sport. As reported in Chapter 2 about the effects of the recession, sport businesses have at least considered the value provided to

sport consumers, and in many circumstances maintained, or sometimes reduced, prices. For example, Watford FC had to review their financial plans as a result of selling 2,000 fewer season tickets for the 2010/11 season than the year before; this despite up to 20 per cent reductions in price (Smith, 2010). This is evidence of sport consumers questioning the necessity of their sport consumption behaviours and the sport industry reacting to try to encourage continued patronage.

- *Competitive factors* between live and televised (which can be live, self-recorded or highlights) sport are heightened now that wider access to sport on TV, PC and mobile technology has permeated the sport industry. It is increasingly difficult to sell live sport events that are broadcast simultaneously, and a key reason why season ticket and corporate hospitality packages are encouraged so much.
- *Demographic factors* such as age, gender, education etc. still play a key role in determining spectator profiles. See the next section on market segmentation for more details on their importance for sport marketing.
- *Stadium factors* including seating comfort, stadium accessibility, perception of crowding, and layout accessibility have increased in magnitude in recent years. Two reasons: 1) sport consumer expectations have increased, partly as a result of having the option of watching from home in a comfortable armchair; and 2) the Hillsborough disaster led to the Taylor Report (1990) and subsequent legislation to create all-seater football stadia, and which has permeated into stadia expectations in other sports.
- *Value of sport to the community* be that community solidarity enhancement, health awareness or as a business opportunity (Zhang et al., 1996).
- *Sports involvement* tends to speak for itself, e.g. greater consumption of sport products/services such as newspapers, TV, magazines, fan forums, phone-ins, on-line and merchandising sales from sport consumers with higher levels of involvement and interest in sport.
- *Fan identification* through personal and emotional commitment runs in parallel with sports involvement. Affiliation characteristics with friends and family (reference groups) and activity characteristics, be they social or more fanatical.

A lot of research has focused on fan behaviour or 'fandom', and has identified the characteristics of a number of categories pertinent to individual sports. Wann et al. (2008) investigated fan motives across a range of sports. Greater levels of eustress, self-esteem, group affiliation, entertainment and family were observed in team sports fans as opposed to aesthetic movement being important in individual and non-aggressive sports such as gymnastics and golf. One key point to make is that sport marketers can concentrate their efforts on the most likely prospects – the fundamental underpinning of sport market segmentation.

Sport market segmentation

Sport market segmentation begins the process of distilling down the information available about sport consumers. In most circumstances the total sport consumer market is split into smaller groups that have similar characteristics that can be targeted with a specific campaign message to encourage their consumption of a given sport product/service. Sport market segmentation is a planned activity that precedes target market selection and the development and implementation of the sport marketing mix.

Specifically, sport market segmentation identifies groups of sport consumers who have common needs and requirements. It is the task of the sport marketer to identify these sport consumers and encourage their patronage. The previous section of this chapter outlined the key processes that sport consumers pursue when making sport consumption decisions, and the factors that influence these decisions. Sport market segmentation draws these elements together and gives direction to the phases of the strategic sport marketing planning process that follow.

There are four basic bases for segmentation of the sport market: 1) demographic segmentation; 2) geographic segmentation; 3) psychographic segmentation; and 4) behavioural segmentation.

Demographic segmentation

You can tell a lot about a person from their demographic information such as age, gender, ethnic background, and stage of the family lifecycle. Additionally, income, education, and occupation are often separated into a socio-economic category – no need really as it is all just demographics to me! Much of this information is available in secondary data sources such as census, or national sport governing body member statistics. Demographics are a solid predictor of sport consumption behaviour. Each demographic variable is important in its own right, but sport marketers co-ordinate these variables to develop a deeper insight into the individual sport consumer or sport target group; this co-ordination creates the basis of the sport marketing strategy.

Age is an obvious basis for segmentation of the sport market. Sport is separated into age categories at school level through to early adulthood. Children compete against their own age group to eliminate development issues relating to size and skill level. The early adulthood categories of under-19s and under-23s occur in many sports to encourage fair competition. Senior and veterans categories have witnessed significant growth in participation numbers, and associated sport consumption activity of equipment and apparel, as the average age of sport participants has increased. The Mamil – the middle-aged man in lycra – is an increasingly common sight (yes OK, it includes me too!!). Stories appear in the media of footballers or runners still competing into their 80s; sport is not confined to the under-35s!

Age from a spectator perspective combines with other variables such as gender and income, to pre-determine consumption behaviour. For example, the audience at a Super League netball game is not the same composition as a Premier League football match. This is in part due to differences in ticket prices (income related), fan identification perhaps through cultural socialisation in school (gender related), and these factors help to create the average age profile of sport spectators and participants.

Gender differences are established early in sporting lives (around nine or ten in schools), and are often maintained – how many males do you know who play netball? Actually the International Federation of Netball Association (IFNA) does not sanction netball for males over the age of 11 (www.englandnetball.co.uk). It has been a culturally imposed gender separation in English schools that boys play football and girls play netball in the winter months. Barriers to participation are often viewed from the need to break down obstacles and to encourage female participation in sports. My co-authored paper entitled 'Do boys and girls go out to play? Women's football and social marketing at EURO 2005' (Bell and Blakey, 2010) focused on the marketing activities surrounding the Women's EURO 2005 Football Championship in England in changing perceptions about football for girls and motivating greater involvement. Many sports activities and, very importantly, environments cater to the female sport market, e.g. private sector health club's or women-only sessions at public sport centres. Increasingly, males and females can participate in the same events/activities, e.g. the London Marathon, team adventure racing or spinning classes. Similarly, some sports actively target the female spectator, such as Ladies Day at Royal Ascot, and families, such as Twenty20 cricket.

Ethnic background considers race, religion, and nationality. Britain and Ireland are culturally diverse countries and a touch overly sensitive when considering ethnic variables. I see no barriers to sport along ethnic lines as cultural values and traditions can be incorporated into those of sporting activity where necessary. I had no difficulties stepping into the Pont L'Eveque running club whilst living in France recently even though I did not speak the lingo. Respect and acceptance comes from sharing the hardships of training, and being as good as, or as bad as, the locals! Some sports have developed genuine and worthwhile sport marketing strategies to target ethnic groups, e.g. Yorkshire County Cricket Club through their Black and Ethnic Minority (BAME) development centres in places such as Huddersfield and Bradford. But let us be honest for a minute, sport market segmentation is a process of discrimination, so if you want to target ethnic groups in Ladywood, Birmingham or the Pakistani community in Yorkshire just go and do it. If not, then go find other groups you want to encourage to consume your sport – it's not an issue!

The traditional *family lifecycle* has lost much of its credence due to changes in family structure, that is, more single parents and separated families. This adds a degree of complication into the process of identifying the family market, but adds, potentially, an opportunity as parents seek out sport venues and sport events at which to keep their kids entertained. Ticket pricing, event timing and venue atmosphere are crucial considerations if this sport market is to be explored.

Income, education and *occupation* are often combined; however, the premise that a higher level of education will warrant an occupation with a very desirable income is not altogether effectual. Nevertheless, in Britain the ensuing structures of social class are still evident and used widely as predictors of sport consumption behaviour. Involvement in sport at any level can be costly, bearing in mind the equipment and apparel requirements, even if it is sometimes a case of 'all the gear ... no idea!' However, golf, tennis, sailing and skiing have always been used as examples of sports with barriers to entry linked to the broad features of social class, that is, costs of participation. These have diminished somewhat in recent years as average incomes have increased, meaning greater potential for new members. Nevertheless, you won't get much change out of £200 if a family of four want to go to a Premier League football match – usually the preserve of traditional working folk.

Geographic segmentation

Simple and more complex at the same time. Geographic segments exist across local, regional, national and international territories. Increased mobility means greater access to sport events further afield: I once flew to Girona in Spain to watch the Vuelta a Espana cycle race (the equivalent of the Tour de France). I spent one day in Lloret de Mar watching a time trial stage, and then hired a car to drive 180 kms into Andorra to watch a mountain stage the next day. Runners from over 100 countries participate in the Chicago Marathon each year and international runners from over 40 countries compete in the London Marathon. The sale of Premier League football rights around the world (especially the Far East) indicates that international markets, aided by technology, are considered as important as the local sports fan as a revenue stream for professional sports clubs. 'Glocal' is a term coined to express the reach sport has into global markets, enabling those sport consumers to be as fanatical as local supporters. Sport marketing strategy bends to the specific nature of the sport in question, e.g. Premier League football teams have chased the foreign dollar. How long do you think it will be before a Premier League match (say Chelsea versus Manchester United) is played in Dubai or Bejing? Whereas Rugby League puts a great deal of effort into local community activity to encourage local people to support their local team (see case study below).

Case Study
Warrington Wolves Rugby League Club

Warrington Wolves are a Super League club and current holders of the Challenge Cup (2010). Their home is the Halliwell Jones stadium, named after the local BMW car dealer. The stadium holds just over 13,000 spectators and is usually full to capacity, particularly when the team is enjoying success.

As a super league club the Wolves primary interest is rugby league – not just the elite game but also developing the sport locally at the grass roots. In an attempt to achieve this, hundreds of youngsters have benefited from the Wolves outreach coaching programme. However, sports development activities by the Wolves are not confined to elite-level rugby league and the infrastructure which feeds local talented youngsters into the Wolves Service Area. They have boxing, handball and basketball clubs in their portfolio and, in addition, a physical activity project (Fit Kidz) was delivered in all 72 Warrington primary schools. These activities are reflective of a broad community approach to the promotion of the club.

In relation to the community work of the Wolves, the key structure of the organisation is the Warrington Wolves Community Learning and Sport Foundation, which receives a small percentage of its turnover from Warrington Borough Council. Occupying a floor of the stadium the Foundation's activities include classes in yoga, tai chi, and chair-based exercise. Furthermore, activities of the Foundation extend the 'reach' of the Wolves far beyond sport and physical activity. Wider community outcomes can be identified in the range of projects aimed at achieving non-sport goals. For example, there is a pupil referral unit aimed at achieving higher educational attainment in excluded youngsters.

Similarly, 'Playing for Success', a programme aimed at improving literacy, numeracy and ICT, was delivered to over 2,000 school children. With a specific focus on literacy there was a half-term tour, by the Challenge Cup itself, around all the local libraries, which was intended to promote greater access to the library service. This tour was, in effect, an extension of the Rugby Reading Stars project, in partnership with Warrington Libraries, which involved Super League players nominating their favourite book, local libraries acquiring a copy, children being invited to read it, then meeting the player to discuss it. Finally, the family receive a free ticket to a game. There has also been a healthy lifestyle project based around good diet and nutrition for the family ('Wolf It Up') involving interactive sessions and a chance to cook a meal with one of the players at the stadium. Some 230 young people have undertaken leadership courses and dance, with the 'haka' as a theme, which have been taught in 32 primary schools.

It is unsurprising that such a far-reaching community programme has won a number of national awards.

As is evident, Warrington Wolves deploy a sport marketing effort aimed at social goals (e.g. education, health, nutrition, literacy), as well as financial ones such as increased sales and greater exposure in the local and national media.

(Courtesy of John Mitchell, 2010)

Learning Activity 3.4

Bearing in mind that the Engage Super League Fan Survey indicates that 43 per cent of all Warrington Wolves fans with children have had some contact with the community programme you might like to consider whether both sets of goals (social and financial) are complementary.

Geographic segmentation is not just about where people live, but also where people work. Workplaces can be targeted with individual and group sport packages as the socially interactive nature of sport is encouraged and emphasised. Corporate hospitality sales fall into this category and a range of sports can be patronised, e.g. horse racing, dog racing, basketball, football, rugby union and rugby league. This is potentially profitable and an efficient and effective use of resources if strategised in an appropriate manner.

A more sophisticated development of demographic and geographic segmentation variables is that of *geo-demographic segmentation*. Its basis is that people living in the same neighbourhood may share a lifestyle and demographic likeness. A logical assumption if you consider the incidence of Sky TV receiving equipment on many houses in the same postcode area. MOSAIC is one geo-demographic package used by sport marketers that has two principles: 1) people who live in the same neighbourhood share similar characteristics; and 2) neighbourhoods can be categorised by the characteristics of the population they contain, that is, neighbourhoods in different towns and cities share characteristics. There are ten types of neighbourhood and 15 main socio-economic groups in the UK in this classification system.

Psychographic segmentation

Psychographic or lifestyle segmentation adds a deeper appreciation of sport consumption behaviour. *AIO* dimensions – *activities*, *interests* and *opinions* (Wells and Tigert, 1971) – are the basis for determining why sport consumers make the sport consumption decisions they do. For example, the highly coveted youth sport market (Generation Y, born 1982–2003) has connected with action sports – for example, BMX biking, surfing, wakeboarding and motocross – as they are risky, individualistic and alternative. Their growth is demonstrated by increased media coverage, major events, e.g. X Games, athlete endorsement and corporate sponsorship. Understanding the avid internet surfers, technology savvy and broad media consumption habits of this segment is key for sport marketers to appeal to their athlete, music and interactive lifestyle behaviours (Bennett and Lachowetz, 2004).

Behavioural segmentation

Extremely revealing of the quantity, frequency and specific reason for sport consumption behaviour. Loyalty to a sport brand, sport product/service, sport team or organisation is revealed and sport marketers can consider relationship marketing techniques to foster and maintain an effective communication strategy with sport consumers. How much and how often a sport consumer makes a purchase is monitored through the MIS database (see Chapter 2): remember that every action in life leaves a fingerprint that can be used for information purposes. Think how much information you generate when performing an online sport product/service purchase. Similarly, through the identification of benefits sought by sport consumers, the sport marketing strategy can emphasise their satisfaction, thereby encouraging sport consumption behaviour. For example, Durchholz and Woratschek (2010) identified pricing and prospective promotional approaches ahead of the 2011 FIFA Women's Football World Cup in Germany as important consumption behaviour determinants.

Case Study
Sport England

Sport England has produced a fantastic sport market segmentation resource that is available to each one of us. Building on the Active People Survey and Taking Part Survey, 19 sporting segments have been developed to help us understand the nation's attitudes to top sport and motivations for doing it (or not). Sport marketers can use this information to influence and persuade people to consume sport.

Each of the 19 segments has an individual pen portrait which details how sporty they are and how satisfied they are with their sporting experience, plus what else they like to do and how to reach them with sport communication messages. For example:

- 'Ben' (a competitive male urbanite) aged 18–25, single, employed full-time, no children, social class ABC1, 'works hard – plays hard' being the most sport active of all segments. 'Ben' constitutes 6.4 per cent of the UK population, his preferred information channel is the SMS text and his preferred service channel is the internet. 'Ben' is responsive to brands such as Samsung, Apple, Orange and Diesel.
- 'Helena' (a career-focused female) aged 26–45, single, owns her home, employed full-time, no children, social class ABC1, image conscious with a healthy diet and exercise regime. Helena constitutes 5 per cent of the UK population and lives in Chelsea, Harrogate or Brighton. She prefers telephone communication and is responsive to brands such as BMW and Habitat.
- 'Terry' (local old boy) aged 46–64, married, lives in a council flat, no children living at home, social class DE. Some 68 per cent of 'Terry's' do less than the government guided minimum sport and exercise per week. 'Terry' constitutes 3.45 per cent of the UK population and lives in Sunderland, Mansfield or Dewsbury. He is responsive to TV adverts and is informed through the local newspaper. 'Terry' is responsive to brands such as BetFred, Birdseye and the Racing Post.

The Sport Market Segmentation web tool allows us to find out what people's sporting habits are in a particular street, community, local authority or region. You can download maps, charts and tables *to gain a great insight into sport behaviours. There are also case study examples to show how sport product/service and sport communication intervention helps to increase participation levels within regions in England.*

(www.sportengland.org)

Learning Activity 3.5

It would be a really worthwhile exercise for you to spend time accessing the information available on the Sport England website. You can focus upon your own part of the country to answer the following questions: go to www.sportengland.org/research/market_segmentation.aspx.

- What percentage of 'Ben's, Helena's and Terry's' participate in canoeing and kayaking in your postcode area?
- Who are the main winter sport consumers in your local authority area?
- Which are the main segments in England wanting to participate in an individual sport?

Reflection Point 3.1

It is interesting to note that the British Horseracing Association (BHA) through their Racing for Change initiative have targeted 'Ben' as they shift their customer market focus away from 'Brian' (aka 'Terry') and try to encourage a younger, more lively crowd to the racecourse.

Chapter Review

Human beings can be unpredictable beasts, but actually share many similar characteristics and behaviours. Sport marketers seek to identify the similarities of sport consumers to propose sport products/services that serve these needs. All sport consumers are influenced by internal factors (themselves) and external factors (the environment around them). The decision process that brings these factors together precipitates the sport consumption decision. For the providers of sport products/services, it is the consumption back-drop that requires time and effort to understand so that sport consumers enjoy their sporting experience and return again and again.

Further Reading

Hunt, K.A., Bristol, T. and Bashaw, R.E. (1999) 'A conceptual approach to classifying sports fans', *Journal of Services Marketing*, 13, 6: 439–452.

One of the first sport segmentation studies which identifies temporary, local, devoted, fanatical and dysfunctional typologies, albeit in US sport.

Giulianotti, R. (2002) 'Supporters, followers, fans, and flaneurs: a taxonomy of spectator identities in football', *Journal of Sport & Social Issues*, 26, 1: 25–46.

The article advances four ideal types of spectator identity: supporters, followers, fans, and flâneurs, and suggests a trend away from the supporter model (with its hot, traditional identification with local clubs) and towards the more detached, cool, consumer-orientated identification of the flâneur.

Tapp, A. and Clowes, J. (2002) 'From "carefree casuals" to "professional wanderers": segmentation possibilities for football supporters', *European Journal of Marketing*, 36, 11/12: 1248–1269.

An exploration of football supporters with the objective of identifying segmentation opportunities. A number of new segments were identified, among them 'professional wanderers', 'carefree casuals' and 'repertoire fans'. This work could better inform the marketing efforts of professional sports franchises and indeed all leisure sectors that rely on regular live audiences for their livelihood.

Chapter 4
Sport marketing planning

Learning Objectives

This chapter is designed to help you:

- consider the bases for developing sport marketing objectives;
- identify approaches to determining sport marketing strategy;
- appreciate the process of sport target market selection;
- consider the key elements of sport market positioning.

Introduction

Having collated information about sport consumers and a variety of factors relevant to the sport industry, made sense of this data and identified the most important issues likely to affect the sport organisation, making decisions about the direction of the sport organisation and its positioning for competitive advantage in the sport marketplace is the next stage. The development of sport marketing objectives and sport marketing strategy are the foundation of activity for the sport organisation at this point of the sport marketing process.

Remember the SWOT analysis? The purpose of the SWOT was to identify factors that are likely to impact upon the sport organisation and thereby assist it in making sensible sport marketing decisions based on evidence. Review Table 2.2 and Figure 2.7 to remind yourself that strengths are to be exploited, weaknesses confronted, opportunities searched and threats avoided, and to recall the potential contents of each SWOT segment. This is the point at which these elements are considered and actions established. Too few, if any, textbooks make the link between the data/information derived by the techniques described in the earlier chapters and their utilisation in the later stages of the sport marketing process. Without such an approach, the entire sport marketing process exists in a vacuum: disjointed, difficult to interpret and not implementable!

Two things need clarification first of all:

1 Sport marketing objectives are statements of intention – they identify what is to be achieved.
2 Sport marketing strategy is the approach to be used to achieve each sport marketing objective.

Think of objectives as your holiday destination and the strategy as the travel options for getting there (train, plane, car, etc.) and by which route.

NB: it is important to note that sport marketing objectives are influenced by the wider objectives of the sport organisation (as considered by the SWOT analysis), and that the sport marketing strategy engages the components of the sport marketing mix, each with their own objectives to achieve – much more of which will come later.

Sport marketing objectives

A sport marketing objective will have one of three targets: 1) profit; 2) revenue; or 3) market share. Each objective has an underlying sales imperative – a profit objective considers sales costs; a revenue objective considers product/service potential; and a market share objective considers competitors – but a number of sport marketing objectives are needed, each with their own sport marketing strategy, when targeting a sport consumer market segment. According to Lamb et al. (2009) sport marketing objectives present one of four scenarios:

1 To *build* sales for increased market share.
2 To *hold* sales and market share.
3 To *harvest* sales by allowing sales and market share to fall whilst decreasing costs to maximise profit.
4 To *divest* sales by dropping products from the market.

Sport marketing objectives must conform to several features so that their achievement, or otherwise, can be evaluated/monitored iteratively (on-going) and post-implementation. The features are:

• relevance – to the corporate mission and objectives;
• specific – focused on one specific goal;
• measurable – quantified;
• challenging – difficult, but achievable;
• focused – by time, and on the sport markets and products/services of the sport organisation.

Or as the frequently used acronym SMART suggests: Specific, Measurable, Achievable, Realistic and Time related.

Therefore, an example of sport marketing objectives for the Vancouver 2010 Winter Olympic and Paralympic Games Organising Committee (VANOC) is:

• Domestic sponsorship revenue of $760 million, including sponsorship for the Torch Relays:
   o Establish strategies for maximising domestic sponsorship revenue through the targeting of quality companies in appropriate categories.
   o Execute the plan, estimated to include the completion of agreements with approximately 50 sponsors.
   o Develop and execute a sponsor service plan for both domestic and TOP sponsors to ensure sponsors receive positive returns on their investment.

- Ticket sales revenue of more than $230 million:

    o Establish strategies for optimising ticket sales revenue, including the marketing, allocation and distribution of tickets.

    o Develop and execute strategies to ensure maximum usage of sold tickets to minimise empty seats at all sport events and ceremonies.

    o Acquire ticket agency services as required to ensure the effective sale and distribution of tickets to the public and Olympic Family.

    o Conduct a ticket selling process that is fair and transparent, ensuring a positive experience for ticket buyers.

- Licensing and merchandising net revenue of $46 million:

    o Develop and manage a comprehensive licensed merchandise programme generating royalty revenue for VANOC and a wide range of quality products to consumers.

    o Develop a retail program for VANOC-licensed products for both pre-Games and Games time sales.

    o Develop a coin program (www.vancouver2010.com).

Learning Activity 4.1
International Olympic Committee (IOC) marketing documents

There really are some great sport marketing documents available on the IOC website. Go to www. olympic.org/en/content/Footer-Pages/Documents/ and take a look at the reports available from a range of Olympic Games. Then click on the Marketing Fact File and seek out the over-riding Olympic marketing objectives and those for sponsorship.

- What other sport marketing-related objectives can you see in this document?
- Why are the foci for the objectives so important to the IOC?

Sport marketing objectives tend to relate to only a few key categories, e.g. customer satisfaction, awareness and perception of the sport organisation or the sport product/service, and spectator and participation levels. Innovative strategic solutions as a result are provoked to achieve them.

Sport marketing strategy

Sport marketing strategy is the route taken to achieve the stated sport marketing objectives. They express the broad approach to be taken in engaging the sport marketing mix ahead of the detailed first-year implementation plan established in the sport marketing plan. Several tools, techniques and frameworks exist to guide strategic thinking, most notably the Ansoff matrix (see Figure 4.1).

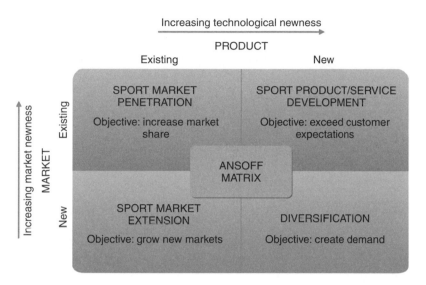

Figure 4.1 The Ansoff matrix

This diagram is used so often in textbooks that in time it will become second nature to you as an indicator of sport marketing strategic options. Each quadrant proposes a likely effect as follows:

- Sport market penetration – encourages additional sales of existing sport products/services from the existing sport consumer market through increased use or brand switching. This is the least risky method of achieving growth, and is often related to pricing decisions, e.g. Sky Sports showing highlights of the Ashes series.
- Sport product/service development – higher sales from the existing sport consumer market through an improved product offering, frequently due to technological improvement, e.g. carbon fibre use in bikes, boats, hockey sticks, fixing a sail to a surfboard.
- Sport market extension – a growth in sales due to a move into a new sport consumer market with an existing sport product, the realisation of untapped sport market segments, e.g. GPS technology for cyclists and runners, insole moulding transferred from ski footwear to running shoes, goretex fabrics transferred from mountaineering to cycling, running and golf wear.
- Diversification – sales resulting from creating new sport products for new sport consumer markets (new sport market entry), e.g. Wii Fit. This is the most risky method of achieving growth as the sport organisation is moved outside its core competence (the things it knows and can do well).

Case Study
Virgin

I often tell the story of the Virgin brand and Sir Richard Branson's beginnings as a student entrepreneur selling vinyl records in the 1970s (Virgin Records). The brand developed through a process of diversification (although able to cross-sell the brand to current customers) into transatlantic aviation (Virgin Atlantic), the cinema industry (Virgin Cinemas), the financial sector

(Virgin Money), the mobile phone sector (Virgin Mobile), the soft drinks market (Virgin Cola), and rail transportation (Virgin Trains). The brand has featured in the sport industry through sponsorship of the Virgin Mobile British Superbike racing team in 2001 and, as mentioned in Chapter 1, the Virgin London Marathon. However, few people remember the brand venturing into the wedding market with Virgin Brides. It is true, go check!!

Learning Activity 4.2

- Why do you think Virgin associate the brand with sport through sponsorship?
- Can you think of any other non-sport brand that uses an association with sport to achieve its corporate/marketing objectives?

Examples of a sport marketing strategy emanating from each of the quadrants of the Ansoff matrix would be:

- *Sport market penetration* – combining of competitive pricing strategies, e.g. inclusive gym membership package, advertising, sales promotion and perhaps more resources dedicated to personal selling. It is possible to restructure a mature market by driving out competitors, but this would require a much more aggressive promotional campaign, supported by a pricing strategy designed to make the market unattractive for competitors. A market penetration marketing strategy is very much about 'business as usual'. The sport organisation is focusing on sport markets and products/services it knows well. It is likely to have good information on competitors and on sport consumer needs. It is unlikely, therefore, that this strategy will require much investment in new market research.
- *Sport product/service development* – new competencies may need to be developed and the modification of existing sport products/services, e.g. street sports, to appeal to existing markets. This strategy is particularly suitable for a sport business where the product/service needs to be differentiated in order to remain competitive. A successful product development strategy places the marketing emphasis on:
  - research and development and innovation;
  - detailed insights into sport consumer needs (and how they change);
  - being first to market.

- *Sport market extension* – there are many possible ways of approaching this strategy, including:
  - new geographical markets, e.g. exporting the product/service to a new country;
  - new sport product dimensions or packaging;
  - new sport distribution channels, e.g. moving from selling via retail to selling using e-commerce and mail order;
  - different sport pricing policies to attract different sport consumers or create new sport market

segments, e.g. The North Face developing its mass market appeal with a desire to be as successful as Nike.

- *Diversification* – for any sport business to adopt a diversification strategy it must have a clear idea about what it expects to gain from the strategy and an honest assessment of the risks. However, for the right balance between risk and reward, a marketing strategy of diversification can be highly rewarding, e.g. workplace initiatives encouraging physical activity.

For sport product/service development in particular, there is a link to the sport product life-cycle model that formed part of the current sport product offering in the internal environment analysis in Chapter 2, but which is explained more fully in the next chapter. The sport product life cycle (PLC) offers a guide to the sales status of a sport product on its path from inception (market entry) to extinction (divestment or death). McDonald (1994) transposed the components of the Ansoff matrix onto the PLC to further aid marketing strategy development and implementation (see Figure 4.2). The Product/Market Strategy and the PLC model is a helpful tool that indicates the marketing strategy to be implemented at a given point of sales on the PLC. Whilst the PLC is a crude determinant of the specific stage at which a sport product sits at any one point in time, if sales are monitored, then greater pro-activity in strategic manipulation of the sport marketing mix can be instigated.

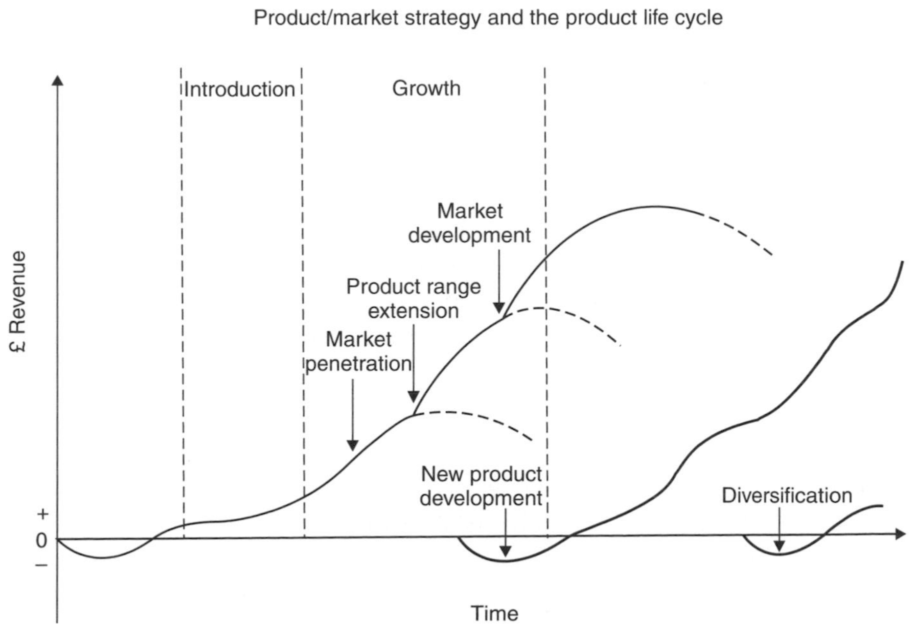

Product/market strategy and the product life cycle

Figure 4.2 Product/market strategy and the sport PLC (McDonald, 1994)

Sport marketing strategic options are also aided by using the SWOT analysis to guide decision-making. Co-ordination of the quadrants is a sensible policy to undertake each of the following strategic options:

- match the strengths of the sport organisation to market opportunities in pursuit of growth;
- match strengths to a threat to reduce vulnerability in the sport marketplace;
- improve a weakness in the sport organisation to become a strength to respond to a market opportunity;
- question the value of staying in a sport market where a weakness and a threat are matched.

In effect, sport strategy generation aims to create opportunities in all situations. Through matching strategies strengths become opportunities, and through conversion strategies threats become opportunities and weaknesses become strengths that are matched with opportunities. In theory every sport marketing strategy is a winner!

Other frequently quoted sport marketing strategy development approaches include market dominance or innovation/growth strategies, but the most frequently cited is Porter's (1984) generic strategies.

The core here is strategic scope (i.e. level of market penetration) and strategic strength (i.e. competitive advantage) in three areas – cost leadership, differentiation and market segmentation. The first two have a broad market scope and are combined with the narrower market scope of the sport segment to be focused upon. So, for example, a cost leadership strategy achieves market share by appealing to cost-conscious and price-sensitive sport customers. The sport organisation must ensure its production costs are minimised, and lower customer loyalty emerges as price-sensitive sport customers quickly switch to lower-priced substitutes. However, this is a strategy followed very successfully by sportsdirect.com. A differentiation strategy creates a unique sport product/service for which a premium can be charged. Brand loyalty appears to lower sport customers' sensitivity to price, certainly evident in English football supporters where a high level of fan loyalty creates a key revenue stream for football clubs.

Target market selection

Once segmentation of the sport market has taken place, sport target markets must be chosen. This is the selection of the group(s) through which the sport marketing objectives aim to be satisfied and, therefore, the basis of the sport marketing strategy. The final decision is based upon the size, reachability, measurability and degree of behavioural variation (Shank, 2009) in the potential sport target market. More specifically:

1   Size – current size and growth potential. The sport target market must not be too large otherwise it becomes undifferentiated and lacks sufficient similarity between its members. Alternatively, it must not be too small otherwise the potential for sales is limited. Niche sports markets, however, can be lucrative as its members have a high level of homogeneity and seek a unique need – how many of you buy *Trail Running* or *Triathlon* magazines, or have purchased (or even used) a hypobaric chamber to improve your oxygen uptake? Niche yes, but sizeable enough demand exists for suppliers to satisfy.
2   Reachability – the ability to communicate with the sport target market. All sport markets are reachable with today's communications technology, but the sport marketing budget can determine how easy it is to reach new sport target markets, e.g. the necessity to use expensive advertising or sponsorship acquisition as a means of initial awareness generation.

3 Measurability – size, accessibility and purchasing power need to be assessed. Crucially, demographic, geographic and behavioural segmentation bases can be measured quite easily by a MIS.

4 Behavioural variation – similarities in behaviour, attitudes and lifestyles are desired in the sport target market. The differences in motivations for attending a live sport event between individual spectators and corporate hospitality clients, e.g. the British round of the Moto GP championship identifies two distinct sport target markets for the same sport event.

Target market selection may equally be based upon distance or drive-time from the sport venue, historical sales records, identified through a market research survey, or from sport industry sales patterns informing indexing methods to identify market potential (especially in sport retail sales). One, or multiple, sport target markets can be pursued depending upon the sport marketing objectives of the sport organisation, that is, to maintain or penetrate sport markets. Again the sport marketing budget will determine the sport marketing strategy to be followed, be it a parallel or staggered programme of sport marketing implementation where multiple sport markets are being targeted.

Sport market positioning

Sport market positioning creates an image of the sport product/service/organisation in the mind of the target sport consumer. Crucially, the image is based on a perception when compared to the competitors in the same sport category. Perception can be influenced positively through strategic actions, but would naturally evolve (positively or negatively) without assistance. Sport consumers will find a place in their mind for all alternative options before making a purchase decision. A successful market positioning strategy creates a differentiated sport product/service that will 'stand out from the crowd' in the sport marketplace. Fundamentally, sport market positioning considers the fusion of sport product attributes and their communication. This 'value proposition' is judged by the sport consumer against that of the competition when making a purchase decision. One important point to remember is that the same sport product/service can be targeted at different sport market segments, therefore, requiring multiple market positioning strategies. For example, the price point of a Slazenger tennis racquet reflects the level of experience of the tennis player – beginner to expert.

Reflection Point 4.1

Think about the 2008 Beijing Olympic Games. From the images that are running through your mind, ask yourself if the hosting of the Games changed your view of Beijing as a city or China as a country in any way. Are you more inclined to want to visit China as a result? If not, why not? Positioning strategy was being implemented by the Chinese government to change the image of the country in the mind of the watching world through the hosting of the Games.

In fact the Beijing Olympics is an example of re-positioning the image of China in the mind of the watching millions. Re-positioning changes the image of existing sport entities relative to competitor products/services (e.g. the Dunlop Volley – see case study below) and de-positioning attempts to change the image of competing sport products/services – often an unedifying approach to sport marketing activity between two competing sport organisations.

Sport market positioning is inextricably linked to sport brands and the sport branding process that will be covered in Chapter 5. But key to the whole concept of positioning is the identification of the attributes of a sport product/service deemed important by sport consumers. Market research can identify the desired level and relative importance of each attribute to enable the positioning strategy to be co-ordinated for the sport consumer target group. So for example,

> In spring 2010, Reebok will introduce ZigTech™, a completely new training shoe for endurance sports like running and agility sports. In product testing, a host of enthusiastic athletes and consumers confirm that ZigTech™ is not only visually striking, but more importantly it addresses an unmet need of fitness runners and athletes. This need is to get more out of their workout and reduce wear and tear – thus allowing them to enhance their lifetime as an athlete. By maximising energy transfer through its zigzag geometry back to the actual running stride, this shoe allows the wearer to train longer, faster and healthier. This is achieved as the unique energy and cushioning system reduces stress on muscles by up to 20%, therefore reducing wear and tear on the runner's body. The introduction of ZigTech™ will be supported by an integrated global marketing campaign 'ReeZig' – featuring key athletes from Reebok's roster – with major launches planned to coincide with global event milestones such as the Super Bowl.
>
> (www.adidas-group.com, 2010)

You can see here the key role played by market research in identifying the main attributes required in a sport shoe and then to communicate those features in the promotional effort. However, a successful sport positioning strategy would be based on several fundamental features of the sport product/service on offer. These include the following, and are illustrated predominantly by reference to Nike +:

- product features – Nike+ running technology;
- benefits, needs or solutions – health and fitness improvements from a 5 km run;
- use categories – sport, everyday leisure;
- usage occasions – TV images of the Great North Run;
- product class dissociation (i.e. what it does not what it is) – Nike+ online running community;
- placing and comparing it relative to another product – Nike+ ability to connect with iPod, unlike Garmin or Polar.

The integrated features of sport products/services are developing as a category in their own right. The 'added value' of cross-over between sport and fashion or between technological devices provides an additional reason for sport consumption, especially at a time when a clash between formats necessitates an upgrade, e.g. VCRs, DVDs, Sky+, HDTV, 3DTV. Confused? You should be a sport consumer! Sport marketers please help by providing timely and helpful advice.

Conceptually, three bases of positioning exist:

- Functional positioning (sport product features solve the needs and problems to provide benefits to sport customers) – it does the job, e.g. Umbro.
- Symbolic positioning (usage occasions, product class dissociation and comparison to competitors can have the effect of self-image enhancement, ego identification, belongingness and social meaningfulness, affective need fulfilment in the sport customer) – prestige and an expression of the user's personality, e.g. Nike.
- Experiential positioning (the sport product features, use categories and usage occasions can provide sensory stimulation and cognitive stimulation in the sport customer), e.g. a Puma strategy to evoke the most passionate response through colour, design, packaging and the retail environment.

Learning Activity 4.3

Click on www.nike.com and go to Nike+. Play the short video and note down how each of these three positions has been considered by the Nike+ running performance monitoring product on offer.

Sport perceptual maps

To visually organise sport market positioning more clearly, perceptual mapping is a technique that displays the perceptions of sport customers. The position of a sport product/service, organisation, or sport brand is displayed on a two-axis diagram alongside each of its competitors in that sport marketplace (see Figure 4.3). The closer together each sport product/service competitor is clustered on the map the greater the competitive level in the sport marketplace. The further apart the positions on the map, a lower level of competition exists, but with the greater possibility of a new competitor entering that sport market. Perceptual maps offer insights about a sport organisations' own products/services, but also their competitors. Differentiation strategies, based upon key attributes, can be determined to ensure a more effective implementation into the sport target market.

Price and quality

The most frequently used dimensions to conceptualise sport market positioning, nevertheless, are quality and price. Pricing of sport products/services is a very sensitive issue (more to follow in Chapter 6). However, the trade-off between price to be charged (high – low) and the perceived quality of the sport product/service on offer (high – low) is a key decision to be judged by any sport marketer. The influence of sport celebrity endorsements (e.g. Tiger Woods wearing the Nike 'flash') encourages self-image enhancement and ego identification in sport customers thus stimulating purchase intention for a specific sport brand at a particular price and quality point. For example, cycling 'weekend warriors' (participants of the sport only able to ride at weekends) aspire to ride the same specification bikes as the professional riders they see in the Tour de France (and likely wear Rapha or Assos clothing rather than dhb). Due to their, often, high level of disposable income, high-specification bikes cost circa £5,000, but can spend a great deal of time in the garage/shed rather than on the road. The quality of such machines is extremely high and no other specification of bike would be considered by this sport segment. Nonetheless, all high-quality manufacturers offer several specification options to cater to a broader range of budgets, and many cycle brands are aimed at the mass market which is only prepared to pay a great deal less, but also has less demanding socially meaningful expectations.

However, Martin (1994) deepened the basis of comparison by identifying six dimensions/attributes of a sport for perceptual mapping purposes. Only two of these dimensions (extremes) can be transposed onto a perceptual map at one time; these include:

- *Athletes only as participants* versus *athletes plus recreational participants*, e.g. the World or Olympic Marathon (which allows only pre-selected elite level athletes to enter) versus the Virgin London Marathon (which mixes ability levels, although elite athletes start at the front to avoid impediment).
- *Skill development and practice primarily alone* (individual sports) versus *primarily with others* (team sports), e.g. tennis, golf, swimming, athletics versus rugby, football, hockey, lacrosse.

The two-dimensional map of these two factors is represented by Figure 4.3. Sports develop a variety of market positioning strategies based upon multiple bases of segmentation through the sport events they conceive. For example, triathlon, swimming and road running all have events that enable elite and recreational participants to compete together. The experience of competing in the same sport event as a world or Olympic champion touches functional and symbolic bases of positioning, and can enhance the desire of sport consumers to sign up to the sport event and to return year after year. A pro-am golf tournament has a similar effect, but is clearly more selective in opportunity to access than a 40,000 participant half marathon.

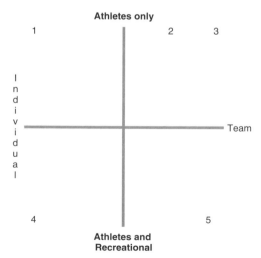

1. World Matchplay Golf Championship
2. Ryder Cup
3. Champion's League Football Match
4. Great North Run
5. London Tri relay.

Figure 4.3 Perceptual map (adapted from Martin, 1994)

Alternatives in developing the sport market positioning strategy are several (Drummond and Ensor, 1999), including:

- Building on the current market position to deepen and strengthen the perception of the sport brand, e.g. maintain premium priced items to act as status symbols – Rapha cycling clothing.
- Identifying an unoccupied market position, e.g. maybe import snow shoes from Finland for the increasingly harsh UK winter conditions.
- Repositioning the brand, e.g. when I was a lad my mum gave me Lucozade when I was ill to 'get you better' she said. Now Lucozade energy and sport products 'get (you) match fit' and 'improve your workout'.
- Identifying, and concentrating on, one unique selling proposition (USP) to become brand leader for that functional component, e.g. Goretex fabric for breathable, waterproof and lightweight clothing.
- Identifying, and concentrating on, one emotional selling proposition (ESP), e.g. the heritage and image of Ferrari in F1.

Sport market positioning has the sport branding strategy at its heart; a very important component within sport marketing. Sport brands will form a fundamental part of the next chapter on sport products.

Case Study
Re-positioning the Dunlop Volley

Re-positioning changes the image and/or perception of a sport product/service in the mind of the targeted sport consumer. One good example is that of the Dunlop Volley, *a rubber-soled, white canvas upper shoe that became very popular as a tennis shoe in the 1970s. For several reasons, but primarily due to the increased profile of competitor products from Nike and adidas as fashion items, sales dipped and the shoe lost credibility and brand recognition. Quite unplanned during the mid-1990s in the Australian market, the* Dunlop Volley *re-emerged as a 'street shoe' and a must-have product in the teen market. Cleverly, Dunlop resisted the temptation to exploit adoption of the shoe through mass market outlets and instead concentrated on developing authenticity in the brand by eschewing traditional sport marketing techniques and allowing a more natural adoption process through consumer product endorsers. Sales escalated, and at the point of the most credible adopters moving on to new products a mainstream strategy was implemented to broaden the sales base and increase profits. This is a clear case of implementing a consumer-led brand re-positioning strategy.*

(Beverland and Ewing, 2005)

Learning Activity 4.4

- Which sports or sport products/services are you aware of that have successfully re-positioned their offering in the sport marketplace?

From your answer, which sport market(s) are now the key sport consumers?

Chapter Review

Sport marketing planning begins the process of sport marketing decision-making and is guided by the corporate aims of the sport organisation. Specific marketing objectives establish what is to be achieved and the sport marketing strategy identifies the 'road map' towards that end. Selecting a sport target market, or markets, creates a focus for the positioning of the sport product/service in the mind of the sport consumer. The communication of the image of the sport brand can determine the successful achievement or failure of satisfying the sport marketing objectives.

Further Reading

Beverland, M. and Ewing, M. (2005) 'Slowing the adoption and diffusion process to enhance brand repositioning: the consumer driven repositioning of Dunlop Volley', *Business Horizons*, 48: 385–391. For further details of case study 'Repositioning the Dunlop Volley'.

Kriemadis, T. and Terzoudis, C. (2007) 'Strategic marketing planning in the sport sector', *Sport Management International Journal*, 3, 1: 27–45.
The purposes of this study were to: (a) examine the strategic marketing planning process, and (b) propose a strategic marketing planning process for the sport sector and analyse its various elements. It concludes by suggesting that if sport marketers follow the proposed strategic marketing planning process, they will be able to handle the complicated sport business environment and deliver high economic benefits.

Chapter 5
Sport products

This chapter is designed to help you:

- explain the sport product/service;
- identify key sport product/service concepts;
- address sport brands and the sport branding process.

Introduction

You will have noted throughout this textbook that I have used the term *sport product/service*. This chapter will address the intertwining of sport products and sport services as, at the customer level, sport products are presented within the envelope (or bundle) of the sport service. Sport product consumption occurs alongside sport service delivery in the package that the sport customer receives throughout the buying process. In most circumstances the two are completely indistinguishable from each other, but are actually manipulated to provide a positive sport customer satisfaction response. Bound within these elements are sport product and service concepts, and the ever increasingly important subject of sport brands and the sport branding process.

The sport product is most frequently the first component of the sport marketing mix to be discussed, as it is the fundamental component of the sport mix. All other sport mix components revolve around the sport product, as there would be no need for them without its existence.

The extended sport marketing mix of *process*, *physical evidence* and *people* consider the process that a sport consumer is required to go through to purchase and access a sport product, e.g. waiting in line at the ticket office of a Npower League 1 football club on match day before queuing again at the turnstiles to enter the stadium. Physical evidence is a direct extension of the sport product through the environment within which the sport product is offered, e.g. the quality of the sound system and scoreboard in a sports venue. *People* refers to the quality of the assistance provided by the human element of the sport service experience. Training is essential to present a consistent level.

However, after a considered period of reading and reflection, I have concluded that the three P's of the extended sport marketing mix are simply a sub-section of the sport product itself. They can, therefore, be considered in this context as part of the sport product/service.

Defining the sport product and sport service

A sport product is a tangible and physical item such as a swimsuit or a pair of ice skates, but can also refer to the service environment within which the sport product is presented. Think about the 'Hi' greeting you get as you walk into one of those far too brightly lit high street sport retailers, along with the lack of genuine knowledge about the sport products on offer. Is that really a place you want to shop? Is that a valuable sport service? You can go get your caps and T-shirts somewhere else if you want to. This is a really important point as the sport product exists in a multitude of places, but can be completely affected by the 'servicescape' surrounding it. But let us step back a pace before developing the sport service angle.

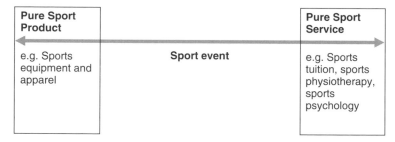

Figure 5.1 The sport product/service continuum

You can see from Figure 5.1 that a sport product/service continuum exists with pure sport products at one end and pure sport services at the other; a combination of the two exists somewhere between. Sport products refer to sporting goods, equipment and apparel (e.g. ski boots, skis and salopettes), whilst sport services refer to the receiving of sport coaching/tuition, sport physiotherapy and, increasingly, sport psychology. The strict difference between a sport product and a sport service lies in five characteristics:

1   Intangibility – you cannot touch, taste, smell, hear or see a sport service. It is an experience that cannot be consumed physically.
2   Perishability – there is a time limit/shelf life for a sport service. If seats are unsold for an Aviva Premiership Rugby Union game, they remain unsold forever. Any potential revenue associated with that unsold ticket is also lost forever, thus a double-whammy to the finances of the club.
3   Lack of ownership – you borrow the sport service for a specified time such as the 45 minutes you spend in the swimming pool which you share with other people.

4   Inseparability – the creation and consumption of the sport product/service occurs at the same time. The person taking your ticket at the gate or serving you a drink at the refreshment stall effects your enjoyment of the game.
5   Heterogeneity (made of different parts) – there can be variability in each of the 'touch points' above giving you a more or less than satisfactory service experience.

As a sport consumer, virtually all sport purchase actions involve an element of service. I have alluded to an experience of high street sports retailing and so now I always attempt to find a specialist retailer for a better fitting service encounter. But do not forget that online purchases also fall into this category, that is, ease of purchase, speed of delivery, returns policy etc. equate to the service experience. Sport events, however, are the classic combination of each of the two ends of the continuum. At Newmarket racecourse, for example, the sporting component of the event is intangible for the sport consumer. You do not take anything home with you, neither a horse nor a jockey, only the excitement and thrill of the races themselves. Placing a bet on a horse enhances this core feature and adds an element of tangibility to the sport event through monetary winnings or losses. The food and drink options, as well as available merchandising, are the tangible elements to the sport event. Sport marketers can manipulate the emphasis placed on these components in their promotional messages, but really need to be aware of each of the layers of a sport product/service and the benefits each can bring to the sport target market.

The three levels of the sport product/service

Sport products/services are a package of features bundled together. The package consists of three layers which seek to satisfy the basic need/desire of the sport consumer and to differentiate the expected product from its competitors by creating attractive reasons to purchase; these are the *core benefit(s)*, the *expected sport product*, and the *augmented sport product* (see Figure 5.2).

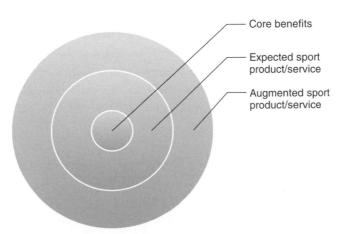

Core benefits

Expected sport product/service

Augmented sport product/service

Figure 5.2 Three levels of the sport product/service (adapted from Kotler, 1997)

The *core benefit* reflects the problem recognition stage of the *Model of Sport Consumer Consumption Behaviour* outlined in Chapter 3. It is the fundamental benefit provided by the sport product/service, be it an implement to hit a ball (e.g. a cricket bat), a support item to aid running comfort (e.g. a sports bra), a night of entertainment to rid yourself of the stresses of the working week (e.g. a ticket to watch a rugby union match), or the feeling of stroke improvement from a tennis lesson.

The *expected sport product/service* comprises the actual components received by the sport consumer. To follow the previous thread, it is the shape, weight, and finish of the cricket bat; the colour, fit and feel of the sports bra; the athleticism and voracity of the players, appropriateness of the venue and its facilities at the rugby game; and the motivation and confidence developed in the tennis swing that ensure the core benefits are satisfied by the sport product/service.

The *augmented sport product/service* presents enhanced features to improve the basic offer. Sport events, both from a participation and spectator perspective, are always augmented in some way. For example, identifying a senior citizen spectator at a football match and offering them the opportunity to take the lift instead of the stairs; offering betting booths in stadia; creating a pulsating atmosphere pre-game with music and pitch-side entertainment; pre-purchase of half-time refreshments; an informative interactive scoreboard; post-game on-pitch player interviews etc. for spectators and pre-registry; safe and dry storage for clothing and valuables; GPS timing devices etc. for participants.

The sport service element can augment the sport product. A very clear and informative website for a sport event can dispel many anxieties for sport consumers in advance. Programmes, merchandise, photos, goody bags etc. are all offered as extra incentives to augment the basic sport product at sport events. Enhancement of the image of the sport product/service via sponsorship or celebrity endorsement is also rife. However, ensuring that the promise matches the reality of the sport product/service experience is key as the manipulation of the basic offer becomes expected, e.g. a giant screen at British horse racing venues so that the action at the far side of the race track can be seen clearly. Sport marketers must improve their sport product/service offer consistently, but credibly, as the target sport consumer may not desire short-termism and price-related incentivisation.

Sport product concepts: sport brands

One key sport product concept that relates to the characteristics of the sport product/service discussed above is sport brands. We are all surrounded by sport brands (e.g. adidas, Manchester United, Hurley, Specialized, Tiger Woods) that help the sport consumer to identify with the sport product/service on offer. Sport branding relates to the brand name, brand logo and trademark whose purpose is to 'stand out from the crowd' in a competitive sport market. Sport branding is verbal, visual and psychological in nature. The sport brand name is the spoken dimension – a word or group of letters – that should be:

- distinctive;
- generate positive feelings;
- easy to remember;
- easy to pronounce;
- translatable through a logo;
- translatable into other languages;

- imply the benefits to be delivered;
- legally and ethically permissible (Shank, 2009).

The sport brand logo is unspoken and, therefore, must be easily recognisable. Creative thought and, frequently, a great deal of research is applied to designing a sport logo, as its distinctiveness alone can become the key to the success of the sport brand. There are many iconic sport brand logos (e.g. the Nike 'swoosh', Puma or the Lacoste crocodile).

The trademark simply identifies that the sport brand/logo has been registered legally to stop counterfeiting and trademark infringement by other sport organisations. Such practice is a necessity in sport marketing as the sport industry becomes ever more competitive.

Learning Activity 5.1

Consider two sport brands (other than those already mentioned), and for each:

- Identify the spoken and unspoken dimensions.
- Considering the perception of these brands in the sport marketplace, which sport consumers are attracted to them, and why?

Sport brands express the characteristics of the sport product/service available. The concept is closely aligned to that of sport product positioning, as it reflects the qualities deemed important by the sport consumer. The attributes desired by the sport consumer could include: 1) a perception of strength, durability, power, reliability, safety or adventure; 2) the culture and values of the sporting organisation; 3) the personality; and 4) user reflection/self-identity. The sport brand triggers images in the mind of the sport consumer, thereby augmenting the sport product/service and creating differentiation in the sport marketplace. This dimension of the sport product/service becomes the equity of the sport brand, built through the sport branding process.

The sport branding process

The aim of stimulating a behaviour response from a sport consumer is assisted through the sport branding process. Distinguishing your sport product/service from those of the competition is the purpose of the process, moving through a series of stages (see Figure 5.3), designed to develop a loyal and repeat sport consumption behaviour pattern in the sport consumer.

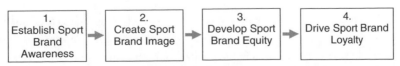

Figure 5.3 The sport branding process (adapted from Smith, 2008)

Sport Brand awareness is the first aim. This is a sport promotion task and is the first stage of the AIDA principle (see Chapter 7). The target sport market must be made aware of the sport brand, and recognise and remember it. Without an awareness of the sport brand, the creation of the sport brand image cannot begin. Here the 'personality' of the sport brand is presented; for example through the sport product/service features, sport product/service performance, its price, its promotion, and the distribution channels used as points of access to the sport product/service (see later chapters for more on each of these).

Crucially, the *sport brand image* exists in the mind of the sport consumer as a set of beliefs about the sport brand, resulting in their attitude towards it. As sport consumers we will have different attitudes to a sport brand based on our allegiance resulting from past experiences and past decisions. Rolex and Timex are both watch makers but each has a very different association with sport. The choice of sponsorship association reinforces the image of power and grace through yachting and equestrian, swimming and athletics but to a different target sport segment. Maintenance of the desired sport brand image is a key role of the sport marketer as the environment in which the sport industry exists is in a constant state of flux.

The next aim is to develop *sport brand equity*, essentially the 'power' of the sport brand itself. This is the added value created by the image of the sport brand. Gladden, Milne and Sutton (1998) suggested that the perceived quality of the sport brand is the key to brand equity, although no credible measure of this dimension has been forthcoming. As you would expect, sport brand equity is influenced by internal and external environment factors such as media coverage, the competitive situation in the sport marketplace, sport product/service packaging and delivery, and the reputation of the sport organisation that owns the sport brand. Positive consequences can occur for the sport brand by enhancing equity, e.g. increased sales of tickets and merchandise, the potential for premium price setting and, crucially, increased brand loyalty – the final stage of the sport branding process.

Sport brand loyalty is a strategic objective for sport marketers as repeat purchase establishes the habitual behaviour pattern of consistent and preferential choice among competing sport brands. Loyalty, however, is a derided concept in British consumption behaviour, so creative strategies have been employed to generate repeat purchase. Loyalty programmes are structured marketing efforts that reward loyal buying behaviour. Their intention is to encourage repeat purchase by offering an inducement to purchase via a reward system. I bet we all have them – Tesco Clubcard, Sainsbury's Nectar card, Boots Advantage Card etc. – but is anyone a Ladbroke's OddsON! punter?

The basis of loyalty is psychological, including perceived quality, trust and satisfaction. Kotler et al. (2009) identified four patterns of behaviour commitment to a brand:

- hard-core loyals – who buy the brand all the time;
- split loyals – who are loyal to two or three brands;
- shifting loyals – who move from brand to brand;
- switchers – who exhibit no loyalty.

Most research on brand loyalty relates to multi-national/high street brands such as McDonald's or Coca-Cola, but in the sport sector fan team loyalty has seen the greatest emphasis. Kotler's (2009) patterns of behaviour commitment have been mirrored in the work of Hunt, Bristol and Bashaw (1999), Tapp and Clowes (2002) and Giulianotti (2002).

The application of the Pareto 80:20 rule suggesting that approximately 80 per cent of sport brand sales/usage is generated by 20 per cent of users (the sport fan) concentrates the mind of sport marketers to identify 'heavy', 'medium' and 'low' users, and to target heavy usage sport fans. The creation and management of membership schemes, supporters clubs, and the principle of the presentation of benefits through these and other points of attachment, centres on driving emotional attachment to the sport brand.

Sport fan loyalty has been exploited where sport brands have applied the concepts of brand extension and brand stretching. Using the equity developed by the sport brand in its current market, brand extension uses the sport brand name on new brands in that market, e.g. Lucozade whereas brand stretching uses the sport brand name on new brands in un-related markets (remember the example of Virgin in the last chapter?).

Case Study
Manchester United Football Club

Manchester United has been described as a global brand; a 2009 report valued the club's trademarks and associated intellectual property at £329 million, and gave the brand a strength rating of AAA (Extremely Strong) (www.brandfinance.com). In 2010, Forbes magazine ranked Manchester United second only to the New York Yankees in its list of the ten most valuable sports team brands, valuing the Manchester United brand at $285 million (16 per cent of the club's $1.835 billion value) (Schwartz, 2010). The club is currently ranked third in the Deloitte Football Money League (behind Real Madrid and Barcelona).

The core strength of Manchester United's global brand has been attributed to Matt Busby's rebuilding of the team, and subsequent success, following the Munich air disaster in 1958, which drew worldwide acclaim. The 'iconic' team included Bobby Charlton and Nobby Stiles (members of England's World Cup winning team), Denis Law and George Best. The attacking style of play adopted by this team captured the imagination of the English footballing public, and its tradition is maintained to this day. Busby's team also became associated with a more liberal Western society during the 1960s; George Best, known as the 'fifth Beatle' for his iconic haircut, was the first footballer to significantly develop an off-the-field media profile.

As the first English football club to float on the London Stock Exchange in 1991, the club raised significant capital, with which it further developed its commercial strategy. The club's focus on commercial and sporting success brought significant profits in an industry often characterised by chronic losses. The strength of the Manchester United brand was bolstered by intense off-the-field media attention to individual players, most notably David Beckham (who quickly developed his own global brand). This attention often generates greater interest in on-the-field activities, and hence generates sponsorship opportunities – the value of which is driven by television exposure. During his time with the club, Beckham's popularity across Asia was integral to the club's commercial success in that part of the world.

Because higher league placement results in a greater share of television rights, success on the field generates greater income for the club. Since the inception of the Premier League, Manchester United has received the largest share of the revenue generated from the BSkyB broadcasting deal. A key sponsorship relationship is with sportswear company Nike, who manage the club's merchandising operation as part of a £303 million 13-year partnership established in 2002.

Through Manchester United Finance and the club's membership scheme, One United, those with an affinity for the club can purchase a range of branded goods and services. Additionally, Manchester United-branded media services – such as the club's dedicated television channel, MUTV – have allowed the club to expand its fan base to those beyond the reach of its Old Trafford stadium and provides an example of brand extension and brand stretching.

(Adapted from several sources: Brand Finance (2010), Hamill (2007), Schwartz (2010) and www.wikipedia.org)

Reflection Point 5.3

Think of examples of sport organisations that have utilised a similar strategy to Manchester United to develop their brand. Do you always view the brand in a positive way and purchase the additional products/services on offer or do you seek alternatives (and if so why)?

Licensing the sport brand

Licensing is an increasingly common practice in the sport industry. It is an agreement between two parties to utilise an existing sport brand in exchange for a fee. In particular, sport merchandising follows this path with DVDs, magazines, toys, computer games etc., e.g. EA Sports' use of the FIFA brand on its FIFA Manager 11 video game series. This sport product strategy is beneficial to both parties as the sport brand owner (licensor) does not have the resources to manufacture and bring to market these items, and the user of the sport brand (licensee) has the expertise in production to exploit the awareness and equity of the sport brand. This strategy can result in healthy sales and be a very lucrative venture for both parties. The World Rally Championship (WRC) used this approach as one strand of their brand revitalisation of the sport. It helped to create a more mainstream extreme sport that could reach out to a new audience and attempt to become as popular as F1.

The sport service

As noted earlier in this chapter, I make no differentiation between a sport product and a sport service. To re-emphasise, as sport consumers our consumption actions are facilitated by a service component.

The key element of sport brand equity was identified as perceived quality, and the concept of quality lies at the heart of presenting an effective sport service. Remember the characteristics of a sport service and contemplate the heterogenous difficulties with presenting a sport service. The sport service component was first conceptualised when human interaction between the sport consumer and the sport organisation was foremost. Today we have become familiar with electronic transactions that have squeezed out the need to deal directly with a person during a sport consumption experience. Needless to say, such processes have been instigated for service enhancement reasons (24-hour access etc.). However, the assessment of the quality of the sport service can be performed from two perspectives: 1) sport product quality; and 2) sport service quality.

Sport product quality

Sport product quality is an assessment of the tangible product for purchase. There are two dimensions: 1) sport product design issues, and 2) sport customer satisfaction. *Sport product design* can create competitive advantage and has had a major impact upon the sport marketplace in recent times. As mentioned in Chapter 2, the impact of technology within the sport industry has resulted in a vibrant, diverse and economically valuable sector. Developments in materials (e.g. use of carbon fibre in golf clubs, tennis racquets and bikes) and processes (e.g. computer-aided design) have given rise to lighter and stronger sport products that have immediate and tangible performance benefits. The portrayal of these benefits in sport marketing communications stimulates consumption needs in the sport market; sport product performance, feel and aesthetic beauty drive this desire in sport consumers. Sport product customisation is the latest strategy to be incorporated into consumption behaviour, making each sport consumer an individual in his or her own right and stimulating sales at premium prices (e.g. the NikeiD collection).

Sport customer satisfaction usually dominates the focus of the sport marketer. This is a subjective measure of sport product quality that can be used as feedback to influence the design and manufacture of sport products. Several dimensions have been used to assess perception of quality including:

- performance – how well the sport product achieves its core function;
- features – quality of the key sport product elements;
- reliability – consistency of sport product performance;
- durability – lifespan of the sport product;
- aesthetics – quality design of the sport product.

Essentially, consistent improvements in sport customer satisfaction with sport products influences sport consumer loyalty, willingness to pay a premium price, and the potential to target new sport market segments.

Sport service quality

Sport service quality is wholly subjective but relates directly to the satisfaction of sport customer expectations. Whilst intangible, the savvy sport marketer will promise only that which can be delivered and will carefully manage the augmentation of the sport product through the service offering. Service quality is pertinent to many business sectors, not just sport, and great debate has ensued about the most suitable means of measuring service quality. At the most basic level, sport service quality assesses the extent to which a sport service meets the needs and expectations of the sport consumer. The need to manage sport consumer expectations is crucial because each sport consumer could identify a different key sport service element as their primary satisfaction component. This could result in variable satisfaction scores and the potential for low satisfaction.

The principal dimensions of sport service quality are:

- reliability – consistency and dependability of the sport service;
- assurance – confidence and trust in the sport service;
- empathy – delivery of a personalised sport service;
- responsiveness – willingness to assist the sport consumer and to provide the sport service on-time;
- tangibles – the physical features of the sport service, e.g. equipment, information etc. (Parasuraman et al., 1988).

The TEAMQUAL instrument (McDonald et al., 1995) – an adaptation of the widely used SERVQUAL survey instrument originally developed by Parasuraman, Zeithaml and Berry (1988) – measures sport spectators' perceptions of service quality against their expectations of the sport service. The purpose of identifying a gap between expectations and actual service delivery enables practical solutions to be implemented to ensure better customer satisfaction levels. The difficulty with such a tool is that the sport marketer could misinterpret and misrepresent the sport service quality 'gaps' identified and so incorrectly apply the practical solutions. The key to successfully satisfying the sport consumer is for the sport marketer to think like a sport consumer. Sadly, not all sport organisations uphold this principle.

Sport product/service development

The competitive nature of the sport marketplace signifies a viable and buoyant sport industry. To maintain the desire for sport consumption constant development of the sport product/service is a key feature. The purpose of the Sport Product/Service Lifecycle Model (see later section) and the product/market strategy and the sport PLC Model from Chapter 4 is to improve existing sport products/services or create new ones. Not too long ago who would have thought that you could wear a watch on your wrist that informed you how far you had run and your average time per mile/km, or a fabric that breathes, quite ridiculous! These developments replace previous versions or render earlier sport products/services obsolete.

New sport products/services

New sport products/services improve the offer to the sport consumer and account for changing sport consumer trends and tastes. They also maintain business growth for sport organisations despite my protestations that many new sport products/services are unnecessary. Nevertheless, new sport products/services fall into several categories from two perspectives:

1   The sport organisation's perspective of new:

- new-to-the-world sport products/services – new sports innovations such as Wii fit;
- new sport products/services category entries – new to the sport organisation, but not the world, e.g. the acquisition of Reebok's 'fitness' line by adidas;
- sport product line extensions – new sport products/services added to an existing line, e.g. Nike Golf equipment for women;
- sport product/service improvements, e.g. the 11-speed Campagnolo groupset;
- repositionings, e.g. Twenty20 cricket, Power Snooker etc.

2   The sport consumer's perspective of new:

- discontinuous innovations – similar to new-to-the-world sport products/services as they initially require learning by the sport consumer, e.g. BASE jumping, scootering or sports arbitrage betting;
- dynamically continuous innovations, e.g. compression sport clothing;
- continuous innovations – on-going improvements, e.g. the Burner 2.0 golf iron from TaylorMade.

The new sport product/service development process

Sport product/service innovation is moving at a rapid pace, but it is important for sport organisations to manage properly the delivery of new sport products/services to the sport marketplace. Sport brands can lose their equity with sport consumers if an ill-conceived and sub-standard new sport product/service is developed, therefore, a systematic process for new sport products/services is a necessity for the sport marketer to appreciate and uphold. Essentially there are five stages to this process, as identified in Figure 5.4 (adapted from Smith, 2008).

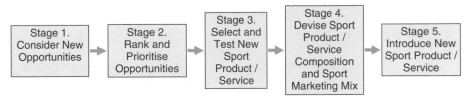

Figure 5.4 Stages of new sport product/service development (adapted from Smith, 2008)

1   Consider new opportunities – this is idea generation territory. All possibilities are considered from current sport consumers, employees, competitors, and even formal market research.
2   Rank and prioritise opportunities – ideas are screened against the specific product-related objectives of the sport organisation. 'Fit' can be ranked in relation to: a) relative advantage, that is, cost or features; b) compatibility, that is, within the external environment or with the current sport product mix; and c) perceived risk, that is, economic, physical, technological or social (Shank, 2009).
3   Select and test new sport product/service – highest ranked ideas are tested in the sport marketplace to gauge target market reaction. Purchase intention is measured to provide forecast sales estimates.
4   Devise the sport product/service composition and sport marketing mix – the final decision on the three levels of the sport product/service are made and the strategic composition of sport marketing objectives is determined.

5   Introduce the new sport product/service – often an initial trial or geographically limited rollout is enacted to test the response of the sport marketplace, that is, sales patterns, distribution channels, pilot scheme and competitor reaction. Confidence with these elements results in wholesale sport market entry.

As with many facets of sport marketing, the success of this process needs evaluation. The critical success factors for new sport products/services can include:

- trialability – in advance of the purchase, e.g. Decathlon have a product loan scheme available on some lines;
- relative advantage – better than existing alternatives;
- pricing – perception of quality versus price;
- distribution – available in enough places;
- competition – number of competitors and the effect of their reactions (Bovee and Thill, 1992).

The cycle of evaluation necessitates corrective action if any element is viewed as unsuccessful. A tweak to the tactical implementation programme of the sport marketing mix can have multiple benefits across the critical success factors and result in the achievement of the sport marketing objectives.

The Sport Product/Service Life Cycle

The Sport Product/Service Life Cycle (PLC, see Figure 5.5) is one of the fundamental concepts applied within sport marketing and is based upon the biological life cycle. After a period of development the sport product/service is launched into the market (introduction); it gains more and more sport consumers (growth); eventually the sport market stabilises (maturity); then after a period of time the sport product/service is overtaken by development and the introduction of superior competitors (decline), and is eventually withdrawn. However, most sport products/services fail in the introduction phase. Others have very cyclical maturity phases where declines see the sport product/service promoted heavily to regain sport consumers (see later section).

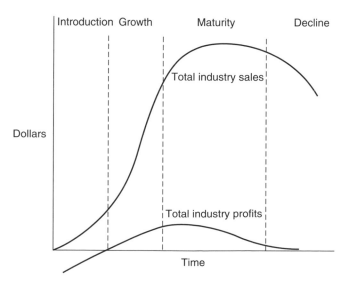

Figure 5.5 The Sport Product/Service Life Cycle

Strategies for the differing stages of the sport PLC

Introduction. There is no immediate pressure for profit as the sport product/service is promoted to create awareness. If the sport product/service has no, or few, competitors, a skimming price strategy can be employed (see Chapter 6). Often limited numbers of the sport product/service are available in a few channels of distribution.

Growth. Competitors are attracted into the sport market with very similar offerings. The sport product/service becomes more profitable and companies form alliances, joint ventures and take each other over. Advertising spend is high and focuses upon building the sport brand. Market share begins to stabilise.

Maturity. Those sport products/services that survive the earlier stages tend to spend longest in this phase. Sales grow at a decreasing rate and then stabilise. Sport producers attempt to differentiate sport products/services and so the power of the sport brand is key. Price wars and intense competition occur and it is at this point when the sport market reaches saturation. Sport producers begin to leave the market as poor margins mean little profit. Promotion often becomes more widespread and there is a greater variety of media used for this purpose.

Decline. At this point there is a downturn in the sport market. For example more innovative sport products/services are introduced or sport consumer tastes have changed. There is intense price-cutting and many more sport products/services are withdrawn from the sport market. Profits can be improved by reducing sport marketing spend and cost cutting.

It is the case that very few sport products/services follow such a prescriptive cycle. The length of each stage varies enormously. The decisions of sport marketers can change the stage, such as from maturity to decline by price-cutting. Not all sport products/services go through each stage, as some go from introduction to decline extremely rapidly (e.g. HFL Europe that disbanded in 2007). It is not easy to tell which stage the sport product/service is in, but remember that sport PLC is like all other tools, use it to inform your gut feeling.

As suggested, in addition to the standard Sport Product/Service Lifecycle Model, there are a number of variants (see Figure 5.6) that indicate the idiosyncrasies of a particular sport product/service in a sport market.

1   The fad – extremely rapid acceptance into the sport market mirrored by an equally rapid decline. Many of you will not be aware of the boom and bust of BMX and skateboarding as sports in the late 1970s/ early 1980s, as they have been re-born as an Olympic sport (BMX) and a 'street' sport (skateboarding). Similarly, those white nosebands to aid breathing during exercise seem to have disappeared. All good examples of the fad.
2   Classic – a usual speed of ascension followed by a continuous stage of maturity. 'Classic' ranges of sportswear have emerged of late, but some sport product/services never really went away, e.g. adidas Samba trainers and Puma King football boots.
3   Seasonal – sports not too long ago operated within a defined season, that is, football in winter and cricket in summer. Some sports now appear to be in full swing almost all year round (e.g. F1 and football). Nevertheless, ebb and flow of interest in many sports revolves around a sport event – try getting a table at your local snooker club during the World Snooker Championships in Sheffield in April or a tennis court during the Wimbledon fortnight. Nonetheless, indoor ski slopes have probably encouraged sports shops to stock ski gear all year round.

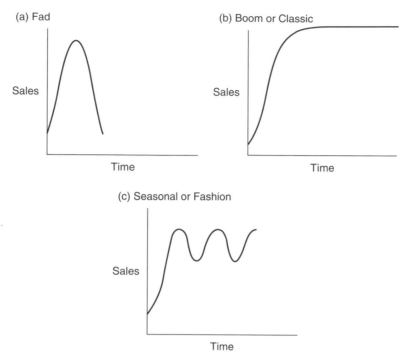

Figure 5.6 Variant Sport Product/Service Lifecycle Models

The savvy sport marketer will foresee such spikes and dips, peaks and troughs and manipulate a sport marketing strategy to cater for such requirements. Ensuring sufficient sport product/service is available is one key approach, and mitigating excess demand through structured activity in and around major sport events can diffuse demand.

Talking of diffusion, an important concept for the targeting of key sport consumers within a market is the Diffusion of Innovation (Rogers, 1962).

Diffusion of Innovation

As a new sport product/service is brought to the sport marketplace, its diffusion across the market segment is governed by three elements: 1) the characteristics of the sport product/service; 2) perceived newness; and 3) the nature of communication. Adoption of the sport product/service tends to occur in waves as risk-tolerant sport consumers purchase first, followed by increasingly less risk-tolerant individuals. New sport product/service adopters fill five categories (see Figure 5.7).

1   Innovators – the first individuals to adopt a new sport product/service. Innovators are willing to take sport consumption risks, especially when adopting technologies and are often youngest in age.
2   Early adopters – these individuals have the highest degree of opinion leadership of sport products/ services among the other adopter categories.

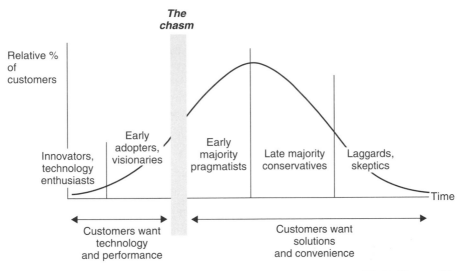

Figure 5.7 The Diffusion of Innovation

3 Early majority – individuals in this category adopt a new sport product/service after a varying degree of time and seldom have any influence on other categories.
4 Late majority – these individuals approach a new sport product/service with a high degree of scepticism and after the majority of society has adopted the innovation.
5 Laggards – individuals in this category are the last to adopt a new sport product/service. These individuals typically have an aversion to change-agents and tend to be advanced in age. Laggards typically tend to be focused on 'traditions', and are in contact with only family and close friends.

Sport consumption behaviour of this type necessitates that the sport marketer employs a differential sport marketing mix to reach each adopter type in the sport target market.

Reflection Point 5.4

Are you a member of Facebook? If so, think about all your friends and their postings on your wall over the last three months. Did anyone suggest a new band, product, TV show, shop, drink, venue, computer game?

If so, do you think your friend is an early adopter? Did this influence you to try it for yourself? Do you think you are ever a laggard? Or do you lead and others follow?

This same process may apply to the sport decisions and purchases of you and your friends.

Learning Activity 5.2
Controversy over London 2012 Olympic and Paralympic Games logo

The official logo for the London 2012 Olympic and Paralympic Games was launched on 4 June 2007 with Seb Coe saying 'This is the vision at the very heart of our brand.'

'It will define the venues we build and the Games we hold and act as a reminder of our promise to use the Olympic spirit to inspire everyone and reach out to young people around the world.'

'It is an invitation to take part and be involved.'

However, the logo proved controversial as the people of Britain provided it with some terrible feedback. The animated version had to be pulled as it caused epileptic seizures!

Go to the following link for further information: http://news.bbc.co.uk/sport1/hi/other_sports/olympics_2012/6718243.stm and click on 'alternative London logos' to see other possibilities.

- Why do you think the logo received poor reviews?
- Which of the alternative logos would better serve London 2012, and why?

Chapter Review

Sport products and services are the items that sport consumer's purchase. These are the focus of the sport marketing planning process in ensuring the sport products/services made available to the sport market match the purchase desires of sport consumers. The features of the sport product/service are fundamental to presenting a differentiated offering into a very competitive sport marketplace; branding is at the heart of this process. It is also imperative that acceptance of the sport product/service by sport consumers is understood by the sport marketer, so that the most likely prospects can be targeted. The remaining components of the sport marketing mix combine to ensure the success of the sport product/service.

Further Reading

Mason, D. S. (1999) 'What is the sports product and who buys it? The marketing of professional sports leagues', *European Journal of Marketing*, 33, 3/4: 402–419.

Professional sports have emerged as a lucrative business, with many opportunities for sport marketers. As a result, professional sports leagues provide a unique environment for marketing decisions and processes to occur, in a number of markets and at a number of levels, and should continue to be a growing segment within the broader, global, entertainment industry.

Manivet, B. and Richelieu, A. (2008) 'Dangerous liaisons: how can sports brands capitalise on the Hip Hop movement', *International Journal of Sport Management and Marketing*, 3, 1–2: 140–161.

This article examines the literature on diffusion and adoption processes, which stresses the ongoing adjustment of Hip Hop culture, the challenges, opportunities and constraint factors a professional sports team or an equipment maker should consider when approaching Hip Hop.

Chapter 6
Sport pricing

Learning Objectives

This chapter is designed to help you:

- consider the importance of sport pricing;
- explain concepts that underpin sport pricing;
- outline sport pricing strategies and tactics.

Introduction

Sport pricing is a key element of the sport marketing mix as it expresses the amount to be paid for a sport product/service and is the key source of revenue generation for most sport organisations. Sport pricing is shrouded in features that help determine the price to be paid, including sport consumer demand, the competitive nature of the sport marketplace, and the sport organisation's objectives. As with many elements of sport marketing, sport pricing has a psychological basis with the concept of value at its heart. Sport pricing is a sensitive issue for the sport consumer and can singularly determine the level of sport consumption activity. The subject, therefore, is a little more complex than simply plucking a figure out of thin air for a sport product/service as a price that is perceived as too high or too low can affect sport consumption levels.

Sport price

Sport price reflects the value placed on a sport product/service by sport consumers. It is an exchange process that includes a monetary (cash exchange), time (travel and venue time), and opportunity (consider alternatives) cost to the sport consumer. To add complexity into the exchange equation (see below), each component that makes up the total sport product/service – at a sport event for example – has an individual price, such as a price for parking/travel, entry to the stadium, a programme, refreshments, merchandise, or a bet. The total cost to the sport consumer, therefore, must satisfy the value perceived by the total price paid. The sport pricing exchange equation is stated as:

$$Perceived\ Value\ =\ \frac{Perceived\ Benefits\ of\ sport\ product/service}{Total\ Price\ of\ sport\ product/service}$$

Perceived value is an intangible measure in the mind of the sport consumer who reflects upon the sport consumption experience to create that value. Remembering the post-participation evaluation stage of the Sport Consumer Decision-Making Process, as part of the Model of Sport Consumer Consumption Behaviour in Chapter 3, allied to the three levels of the Sport Product/Service that bring an augmented sport product/service to the sport consumer to satisfy their basic needs and desires, we can begin to appreciate, from a conceptual perspective, how the sport marketer must carefully piece together a pricing strategy with the overall total price perspective in mind. As identified in Chapters 4 and 5, the sub-groups within a sport target market will each present a different pattern of sport consumption behaviour that the sport marketer must consider when presenting the total sport price. For example, season ticket holders of a sport team are offered additional services that create a greater level of perceived value for their involvement when compared with lower involvement fans. The announcement of ticket prices for the London 2012 Olympic Games made the media headlines in October 2010. Creative thought has been applied to the prices to be charged for children and senior citizens, that is, children being required to pay the equivalent of their age. Price bands have been structured to hit a revenue target with many tickets priced at £20. This example highlights the sensitivities surrounding sport pricing.

Determining sport pricing

Where decisions are made within the Strategic Sport Marketing Process, consideration of the sport organisation itself and its surrounding environment – internal and external factors – is always necessary. The determinants of sport pricing are no different (see Figure 6.1).

Figure 6.1 Internal and external influences on sport pricing (adapted from Armstrong and Kotler, 2005)

The sport price gives an expectation of the quality of the sport product/service available. It is communicated to the target sport segment through the sport promotion mix (see Chapter 7) and made available to those sport consumers via a number of sport distribution channels. Clearly, all costs (production, advertising, staffing) associated with bringing the sport product/service to the sport market need to be covered by the sport price, along with a profit differential that is determined in line with the objectives of the sport organisation. Each of these elements is mitigated by factors outside the control of the sport organisation (see Chapter 2) that reflect sport consumer demand as a result of economic conditions, the level of competition in the sport marketplace, legal constraints on sport pricing, and technological developments. Or to put it simply, higher costs need to be reflected by higher sport prices.

Concepts for sport pricing

Two fundamental concepts that underpin decisions about sport pricing relate to costs and sport consumer demand, and the relationship between the two. This is the point at which sport marketing and sport economics collide and you may see some mathematical equations. Never fear, as they are never as difficult to understand as you first think.

Costs

Every sport organisation carries the costs of performing its business functions. A sport stadium for example must be maintained, cleaned and supplied with utilities all year round, yet will be utilised for its primary purpose infrequently – maybe only once per week. Additional costs are incurred through staff salaries and other general business costs such as advertising of sports events. These costs constitute the fixed costs for the sport organisation that owns the stadium. Costs are heightened further by the costs of 'game day', e.g. the supply of refreshments, stadium lighting and heating, additional staff, etc. These costs are variable costs incurred by the stadium owners. Added together, fixed costs and variable costs equal the total cost of the sport product/service. To assess these costs and to help make a decision on the price to be charged, a break-even analysis is performed. It is a simple process that determines how many sport product/service sales must be made to equal the costs of producing that sport product/service. If more 'units' are sold than the break-even point, a profit/surplus is achieved, and if insufficient 'units' are sold, a loss or operating deficit occurs. The following formula is used to calculate break even:

$$\textit{Break-even point} = \frac{\textit{Total fixed costs}}{\textit{Price per unit – variable costs per unit}}$$

So, for example, a sport organisation that produces kayak paddles has fixed costs of £20,000 per month, variable costs of £48, and sells the paddles at £95. Within the break-even formula this would be:

$$\textit{Break-even point} = \frac{£20,000}{£95 – £48 \textit{ per unit}}$$

This would result in the need to sell 425.53 paddles per month to break even. Of course this approach necessitates a selling price to be identified for the kayak paddle; this rather negates the use of this process to help determine the price. Sport marketers can alter the price element of the formula to gauge break-even requirements at different price points, and then consider the feasibility of selling sufficient 'units' at each price. This suggests the need to account for sport consumer demand, and its supply, in the setting of sport pricing.

Learning Activity 6.1

A bicycle shop has fixed costs of £15,000 per month. It buys in bicycles at an average cost of £150 and sells them for an average price of £300. How many bicycles will it need to sell annually to exactly break even?

Sport consumer demand and supply

Sport consumer demand is potentially the most important concept in sport marketing. Demand for sport products/services is the crucial element in the matching process between identifying what sport consumers want (demand) and satisfying those needs (supply). Supply and demand is the central tenet of the economic system in the business world; the sport industry is no different. Demand, specifically, is the quantity of a sport product/service that sport consumers are willing to pay at a specified price. Supply, specifically, is the quantity of a sport product/service available to sport consumers at a specified price. You may expect that a lower price would equate to greater demand for a sport product/service, but sport consumer demand is not that simple. Supply also has idiosyncratic tendencies that are difficult to predict. Nevertheless, the ultimate aim of a sport organisation is to satisfy sport consumer demand for a sport product/service, as this would indicate the sport pricing decision to be wholly correct. This situation never occurs, rendering the sport marketing matching process as simply idealistic. Sport pricing objectives (see next section) are met through a strategic use of pricing options targeted at sub-segments of the sport target market.

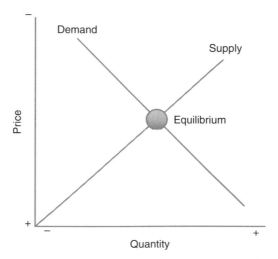

Figure 6.2 Sport Market Equilibrium (Smith, 2008)

A key dimension of sport consumer demand is the extent to which pricing of a sport product/service is price elastic. Sport price elasticity of demand determines sport consumer reaction to changes in sport price. Again, this is not a simple concept to judge, as different sport products/services will react differently at various price points. As Figure 6.3 identifies, elasticity of demand falls into three categories: 1) inelastic demand; 2) elastic demand; and 3) unitary demand.

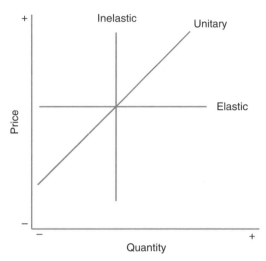

Figure 6.3 Sport price elasticity of demand (adapted from Shank, 2009)

Inelastic sport consumer demand dictates that an increase in the price of a sport product/service has no impact upon the quantity sold. Elastic sport consumer demand is the opposite, whereby an increase in the price of a sport product/service sharply reduces the quantity sold and a decrease in price creates a large increase in sales. Unitary sport consumer demand dictates that price increases for a sport product/service result in a very small decrease in the quantity sold, and vice versa, a price reduction creates a very small increase in sales. In both cases there is no net gain in revenue.

In the sport industry each of these three forms of sport consumer demand can occur, but for many sport products/services inelastic demand is observed rather than the more commonly expected feature of elastic demand. The reason is straightforward; the sport market is characterised by sport consumer segments that are less responsive to changes in price. For sport fans, sport brand loyalty and the lack of a genuine substitute sport product/service results in no change in demand despite prices increasing. Examples of this phenomenon include ticket prices in the English Premier Football League in recent years and the Revolution Cycling Series at the Manchester Velodrome. Research by Krautman and Berri (2007) has shown that this condition enables the sport marketer to concentrate efforts on selling refreshments (referred to as 'concessions' by US sport marketers) and other secondary spend items, as the guaranteed audience are encouraged to display consumption behaviour for such items. Where sport consumption behaviour becomes habitual, price is much less of a concern for the sport consumer as long as value is still being accrued from the purchase.

Nevertheless, inelastic sport consumer demand is mediated at sport events through variable seating/ entry prices, including some that cater for more price-sensitive sport consumers. The erection of temporary seating and standing areas at sport venues to increase capacity is an approach used to cater to this group of sport consumer. The ticket pricing policy of LOCOG for the London 2012 Olympic and Paralympic

Games to offer a 'significant' number of tickets for £20 or under meant the offer of 2.5 million tickets at this price point to stimulate elastic demand. It is evident that the economic conditions surrounding the sport market in 2010/11 are having an impact on sport consumer demand, as many sport events are struggling to maintain full capacity. This is also a signal that the lower boundary of inelastic demand is being drawn towards a greater level of elasticity.

One further effect upon live sport event attendance is the impact of live media coverage. The South Yorkshire derby between Doncaster Rovers and Sheffield United at the Keepmoat Stadium on 23 October 2010 was attended by 4,041 fewer spectators than the same game in the previous season; this despite the improved home team success throughout that time. Why? Live TV coverage. It is far easier to sit at home and watch for free on BBC2 than incur the costs of going to the game. Yes a media rights fee will have softened the blow, but loss of revenue on secondary spend items will have been significant, plus a loss of atmosphere. Even the most loyal of fans can be quite fickle at times! Manipulation of ticket prices would not have been possible as these are set well in advance, although innovative promotional practice in the local community could have ensured a greater audience turnout. This phenomenon is likely to increase as more live sport is made available through an increasing number of sport media channels; the impact will need an innovative approach to pricing of sport products/services in their pursuit of equilibrium in demand and supply.

Sport pricing strategy and tactics

Sport pricing strategy considers the conditions in the sport marketplace and the requirements of the sport organisation in offering its sport products/services to sport consumers. Specific sport pricing objectives govern the direction of sport pricing strategy and the likelihood of its manipulation through sport pricing tactics.

Pricing models

In effect there are five sport pricing models:

1 differential pricing;
2 new sport product/service pricing;
3 psychological pricing;
4 sport product/service mix pricing; and
5 cost-based pricing (Shank, 2009).

Differential sport pricing strategy

The sport product/service is offered to different sport market segments at different prices or at different times of the day, that is, peak and off-peak times. This is a common sport pricing strategy and often blends the elements of price and time to stimulate sport consumer demand when supply is available. Many sport facilities such as swimming pools, leisure centres and golf clubs encourage seniors, students and others to consume their sport activities during the day when demand is lower. Higher prices can be charged at peak times (evenings and weekends) to sport consumers unable to play during the day, but who are able to pay higher prices for the same sport product/service. Strabane Golf Club in County Tyrone, Northern Ireland prices full annual membership at £520, senior citizens at £405, students at £216, weekdays only at £290 and juniors at £43 (www.strabanegolfclub.co.uk). Interestingly, golf clubs have variable pricing approaches; some use gender as a basis for pricing strategy and dare to charge females less than males for the same membership package! Perhaps this decision was based on the (misguided?) idea that women will play less golf than men.

> ## Reflection Point 6.1
>
> Is it really appropriate to differentiate between sport target markets based upon price? Is the price differential between a full-time employed businessman and a student equitable? Take a look at the pricing structures of two golf clubs and identify the benefits assigned to each level of membership. Why might voting rights be based on an ability to pay? Go discuss.

New sport product/service pricing strategy

When a new sport product/service is introduced to the sport marketplace two main pricing strategy options are available: 1) penetration pricing; and 2) price skimming. Penetration pricing seeks to generate high sales or gain a significant market share especially where competition levels and sport brand loyalty are high. A low initial price can encourage trial of the sport product/service in price elastic or price sensitive sport consumer markets. The strategy is for the introductory price to increase steadily to the point of a sustainable level of sales. Price skimming targets less price-sensitive portions of the sport target market: those sport consumers most likely to pay the highest price possible. Technologically enhanced sport products/services, such as carbon fibre tennis racquets and bicycles, are priced high initially to recover the costs of bringing them to market. These prices reduce as sales increase and a wider range of target sport consumers (the early majority) are enticed to purchase. Of course when a new line is available and the price of the original line is reduced, it is a good day for the laggards: they may not look very fashionable but they get to keep a few pounds in their pocket!

Psychological sport pricing strategy

Who will pay £2,012 for a seat at the opening ceremony of the London 2012 Olympic Games? LOCOG hope demand will be high for this one-off occasion, and that the chance to claim exclusivity by saying 'I was there' will over-ride any rational purchase decision. Psychological sport pricing strategies also include:

- Prestige pricing – artificially high prices for premium packages aimed at a distinct yet small section of the sport target market. Ringside seats at world title boxing contests or courtside on Wimbledon finals day present such opportunities, e.g. ringside seats at the WBA Heavyweight fight between David 'The Hayemaker' Haye and Audley 'A-Force' Harrison at MEN Arena in Manchester were priced at £1,250 on www.gigsport.com. Increasingly, packages with special access to sports celebrities are available, and these provide a prestige sport pricing opportunity.
- Reference pricing – compares competing sport products/services directly, and is often a key factor in the 'evoked set' of alternatives considered during the sport consumer decision-making process.
- Traditional sport pricing – historically low-priced sport products/services, e.g. family enclosures at horse racing.

Sport product/service mix pricing strategy

A whole sport product/service range (e.g. NikeWomen) is considered together to maximise profit across the range. There are three approaches:

- Sport product/service line pricing – a related set of sport products/services with differing quality features that can be sold at different prices to different sub-groups in the sport target market. Sport events fall into this category with their range of ticket prices based upon seating position.
- Bundle sport pricing strategy – a frequently used pricing strategy that brings together a number of features under one price. Season ticket packages for sports teams include a face-value ticket discount, plus a range of benefits including merchandising discounts, access to open training sessions, and discounts with the products/services of corporate partners. Sport travel packages such as those available to the La Manga resort in Spain, present another example as they include transport, accommodation, food, and access to specialist training and coaching facilities on-site.
- Captive sport product/service pricing – separate items sell at individual prices, for example refreshments at sport event venues are priced high because sport consumers have no alternative outlet if they are hungry and thirsty whilst the game is on. This can be a controversial pricing approach especially if a sport consumer and their person and/or bag is searched and food and drink items are confiscated as I have witnessed at a number of sporting venues. The feeling of being forced to purchase refreshments in the stadium can mean sport consumers feel 'ripped off' – not a very positive occurrence. However, some events do need to remove glass bottles from fans before they become dangerous projectiles.

Cost-based sport pricing strategy

Simply combining all costs of producing the sport product/service and adding on the desired level of profitability required by the sport organisation; of course sport market conditions guide the setting of the price. A target profit sport pricing strategy or a break-even pricing strategy are variations on this theme.

Sport pricing tactics

Sport pricing strategies set the broad approach to price setting for sport products/services, but a structured, or merely reactive, manipulation of sport pricing based on sport market conditions and/or sport consumer demand can create the need for sport pricing tactical applications. These generally fall into two categories: 1) price reductions/increases; and 2) price discounts.

Sport pricing tactical reductions/increases

Price reduction is employed to stimulate demand and price increase is enacted to cover increasing costs or to moderate excess demand for a sport product/service. Both approaches can be implemented quickly as reactive measures, but both need to be considered actions. Price reductions seem to be never ending within the sports equipment and apparel retail sector. End of season sales or 'weekend price crash' are short-term sales tactics that aim to increase sport market share and to dispose of excess supply. The effect of price reduction needs to be considered carefully as sport consumers can associate reductions with a lower quality of sport product/service and competitors can react with their own decreases.

The effect of price increases can be justified by associating them with tax increases, inflation or other variables in the external environment imposed on the sport organisation. Sport consumers expect increases in the price of sport products/services from one year to the next, but it is good practice to inform them of the reason. The speed of technological change in the sport marketplace and the development of new sport products/services can mediate the negative perception associated with price increases as improved technologies are expected to be offered at premium prices. Relatively small increases/decreases in price may not be noticed, or at least not have any effect (up or down) on sport consumer demand.

Price discounts

This is a price reduction tactic that seeks to stimulate sport consumer demand or reward repeat purchase/loyalty via quantity (e.g. group ticket sales) or seasonal discounts (e.g. 'end of season sale'). More frequently 'early bird'/time-limited discounts stimulate early sales, e.g. Warrington Wolves RLFC offered an 'Early Bird' season ticket for non-season ticket holders at a discount of £80 (£60 instead of £140) before 4 January 2011. Of course for sport events, spectator levels are governed by capacity, therefore, discounting practice as the event approaches is not feasible in the same way as in other industry sectors, e.g. the travel industry where heavy discounting is possible for last minute bargain holidays. For a sport organisation, the relationship with each of the sub-groups in the fan base has to be considered carefully so that devoted fans do not perceive their ticket package compromised by other pricing activity.

Sport pricing objectives

The sector within which a sport organisation operates (public, private or not-for-profit) directs the setting of sport pricing objectives. Within two broad categories: 1) profit-based and 2) sales-based, several foci form the basis of the objectives to be achieved through the prices set for sport products/services. Sales-based sport pricing objectives include maximum sport participation opportunities and positive user attitudes; and profit-based sport pricing objectives include survival, profit maximisation, market share, and return on investment.

Case Study
Irish Rugby Football Union

A match against the world champions at the start of a Rugby World Cup year should have been the guarantee of a capacity crowd, especially as the match was Ireland's first at their Lansdowne Road home (now the Aviva Stadium) since the ground's stunning €410 million (£357 million) redevelopment. But only 35,517 spectators turned up for the showpiece occasion, leaving some 15,000 tickets unsold. Earlier in the week Irish Rugby Football Union (IRFU) officials admitted they had made a mistake by forcing fans to buy tickets for internationals against South Africa, Samoa, New Zealand and Argentina in bundles. Asked to pay €340 (£296, US$478), many fans stayed at home and that remained the case even when the IRFU changed tack to provide a combined two-match package costing either €191 or €151 (£166 or £131).

Learning Activity 6.2

The IRFU case study is a good example of the sport marketing strategy not being in-tune with the sport consumer. Are you aware of any other examples where large swathes of tickets for a sport event have gone unsold? If you became aware of a shortfall in ticket sales for a sport event for which you were responsible, what would you do to ensure all seats were filled?

Remember that sport events have multiple opportunities for generating income (e.g. sponsorship and media rights), but many sport products/services (e.g. sportswear) derive revenue directly from sales alone.

Case Study
Sport debentures

The selling of debentures in sport is an increasingly popular way for stadium owners to raise money, to allow fans to gain a financial stake in the sport organisation, and to foster a sense of community. A debenture is a certificate of agreement between two parties acknowledging a debt, usually an investment sum. The sum invested creates rights (e.g. the option to purchase tickets at a reduced price or gain free tickets), and is returned at a fixed point in the future. Debentures are used in tennis, rugby, cricket, football and motorsport, and with slightly different applications. For example, The All England Tennis Club issue a ticket each day for the Wimbledon Tennis Championships whereas the Welsh Rugby Union provide only the right to obtain a ticket at the Millennium Stadium for Wales rugby matches. The Rugby Football Union (RFU) permit debenture holders to ten years rights to the ticket issue at Twickenham, and the principal sum invested is returned 75 years from date of issue. Sport debentures can be traded on the open market and so can increase in value. Debenture issues in 2000 by the RFU for £3,950 were priced at £6,750 for a further issue in 2008. Individual tickets issued for Wimbledon are also now available for secondary sale.

Learning Activity 6.3

- Do you think the debenture approach in sport is a good idea?
- Can you think of any sport organisations that would be unable to instigate such a policy?

Chapter Review

Sport pricing is all in the mind! Actually it is the perception of value by the sport consumer that is key to the delivery of a positive sport experience and the price they are willing to pay for this privilege. Price is crucial to sport organisations as it is the principal means of revenue generation into the business, get it wrong and the sport organisation may be sunk. One very important point for sport marketers to remember is that pricing includes the wider costs of time and opportunity cost, not just the actual price paid for the sport product/service. Therefore, the total cost to the sport consumer is the key consideration in sport pricing.

Further Reading

Muller, P. and Arthur, D. (2007) 'Something for nothing: the free ticket myth', in Chadwick, S. and Arthur, D. (eds) *International Cases in the Business of Sport*, London: Butterworth Heinemann.

Despite a wealth of academic literature on sports marketing, scant regard appears to have been paid to an almost inevitable element of the event promotion mix – the distribution of free tickets. The few references tend to be dismissive of it as an old-fashioned, short-term solution to the problem of maximising stadium attendance for profit. Far greater attention is paid to more sophisticated and exotic promotional tools. Yet the practice of free ticket distribution stubbornly refuses to die out; which begs the question: if benefit remains, how can we maximise it?

Kyle, G.T., Kerstetter, D.L. and Guadagnolo, F.B. (2003) 'Manipulating consumer price expectations for a 10k road race', *Journal of Sport Management*, 17: 142–155.

Understanding consumers' response to price has become an important issue for managers of public sport and leisure services as they shift their dependence on revenue from government sources to user fees. Employing an experimental design, this study manipulated participants' price expectations for the race entry fee of a 10 k road race. One practical implication of these findings is that managers of public sport and leisure services considering price increases for their services should introduce them by outlining the purpose and the costs and benefits associated with the increase. Further, implementing effective communication strategies regarding price increases may significantly increase consumers' acceptance of an otherwise undesirable management decision.

Chapter 7
Integrated sport marketing communication

Learning Objectives

This chapter is designed to help you be able to:

- appreciate the need for a co-ordinated approach to the promotion of sport;
- explain the underlying components of a sport promotion campaign;
- consider the main components of the sport promotion mix.

Introduction

Integrated Sport Marketing Communication (ISMC), or Sport Integrated Marketing Communication (SIMC) as some authors (Beech and Chadwick, 2007) have referred to it, unifies the components of the sport promotion mix. Moreover, ISMC draws together the wider components of the sport marketing mix, in particular the sport product, sport price, and sport place. It transmits the key message(s) of the sport product/service, and lest we forget, non-sport products/services, to the sport target market. In a world of fast technological change, the mix of traditional and new communication mediums present the need for a clear and co-ordinated approach to the process of providing information to sport consumers. The ubiquitous use of sport sponsorship embodies the necessity for such an integrated approach to make best use of this 'investment' vehicle. Similarly, sport public relations activity has taken on an increasingly important remit within the sport promotion mix, resulting in sport PR and sport sponsorship necessitating a chapter each in this text. Reference to sport PR and sport sponsorship will be made here, but this chapter concentrates on the remaining sport promotion mix elements – sales promotion; direct marketing; personal selling; and advertising.

It is important to note from the beginning that sport promotion, and the sport promotion mix – used interchangeably – is an umbrella term comprising those elements already stated, and represented in Figure 7.1.

Figure 7.1 Components of the sport promotion mix

Stoolball integrated marketing communications plan January to July 2011

1. Increase the number of primary schools in West Midlands offering Stoolball from 2 to 10 schools by December 2011

Phase 1 Aims – West Midlands Schools Programme
- Deliver Schools Stoolball Initiative to 6 Primary Schools – Pilot to run in Summer Term April – July 11
- Develop opportunities for exit routes to local Stoolball club
- Increase number of Stoolball Leaders from 1 to 3.

Objective	Target Audience	Message	How – Communications Mix (Tools)	Anticipated Results	Resources Required	Responsibility	Timescales/Frequency
Create Awareness & Interest of Key Agencies in West Midlands	WM County Sports Partnership and PDMs	Build relationship and gain support for development work Opportunity for WM schools to be involved in free pilot	1. Phone call to CSP 2. Set up Meeting 3. Invite CSP Director and PDMs to Stoolball Championships 4. Programme of follow up 1 to 1 meetings/phone calls with CSP to keep informed	Support for Pilot Scheme from key decision-makers who can influence individual schools Identify resource available from CSP	Access to schools database	Stoolball Development Officer	January 2011 Diary monthly meeting/phone call/email
Create Awareness & Interest of Key Agencies in West Midlands	Primary School Heads & PE Co-ordinators	Safe activity, fun easy to organise, no specialist coaching skills	Direct mail – letter to Head/PE Co-ordinator	Appointment for meeting	Access to schools database and £50 postage	Stoolball Development Officer	February 2011

required – offer of starter kit		Staff time	
Follow-up phone call within 5 working days	Identify 4 primary schools for pilot		
Meeting with interested schools	Sign up schools		March 2011
Free in-service event for school staff	Build relationship with customers and develop staff skills	Facility, coach time, hospitality £500	April 2011
Press release – when scheme is fully developed		Support from National PR Team	
Information on CSP and Sports Partnership websites	Press article on Stoolball Schools Programme – Observer & News		
2nd press release during programme regarding visit of celebrity – photo opportunity		Support from National PR Team	May 2011
Sponsor Inter-Schools Tournament for the end of pilot scheme – to be run by staff in schools with support from SDO	Press article and photo opportunity – Observer & News	Sponsorship £1,000 for venue and trophies	July 2011

Objective	Target audience	Key messages	Actions	Desired outcomes	Resources	Responsibility	Timescale
Build parental awareness of Stoolball	Parents of children in pilot schools	Safe activity, fun and healthy – encourage your child to take up this trendy new sport	3rd press release relating to end of term event	Mass participation event – further press coverage	Support from National PR Team	Stoolball Development Officer	April 2011
			Develop Stoolball information leaflet for parents	Press coverage – Observer	Design & printing costs		
			Offer parents taster session	Parental support	Support required from National SBA Marketing Team		
			Sign up parents to Stoolball database	Develop interest in leadership courses			
			Develop a Facebook page	Build direct marketing relationship with interested children & their parents			
Increase demand for Stoolball out of school by children and exit routes to clubs	Children in pilot scheme	Stoolball is cool	Deliver pilot in school time	Create demand for summer holiday sessions	200 goody bags and T-shirts	Stoolball Development Officer	July 2011
			Stoolball goody bag				
			Visit of local sports star to school to try Stoolball				
	Parents of children	Well organised activities during school holiday	Direct mail – thank you letter to all parents & children				

Case study continued

Objective	Target audience	Benefit / message	Action	Purpose	Resources	Who	When
Increase local club involvement in schools Stoolball initiative & increase workforce capacity	Local Stoolball club and members	Potential to grow junior membership by running summer activity sessions Opportunity for free courses to develop Stoolball leaders	after programme including voucher for reduced price sessions during school holiday Set up meeting with secretary and qualified leaders Follow up monthly meetings	Inform club of schools programme Engage club's support & build relationship with club Get club information onto sports events website Involve in delivery of Mayfest Event	Equipment to support club deliver holiday activities	Stoolball Development Officer	February 2011 March–July 2011
Increase general public awareness in readiness for 2nd schools programme in autumn	Families in West Midlands	Safe activity, fun & healthy – encourage your child to take up this trendy new sport	Stoolball demo at Mayfest Event Facebook competition	Involve 1,000 young people in a 30 minute taster sessions Stoolball feature with local radio – present at event	£300 to rent stand Coaches from local club to staff event Promotional material & goody bags	Stoolball Development Officer and local club	May 2011

The objective of sport promotion is to communicate information about sport/non-sport products/ services to sport target markets. The sport promotion mix is sometimes, therefore, also referred to as sport communication or the sport communication mix. There is no need to confuse any of these terms, as they are simply indicating that the process of communication sits at their core. It is the co-ordination of this process to which ISMC refers.

So what is ISMC?

Integrated Sport Marketing Communication endeavours to affect the knowledge, attitude and behaviours of sport target markets through the synergistic action of sport communication techniques (synergy is often seen as $2 + 2 = 5$). It is sport consumer-focused and, therefore, takes full consideration of the channels, technologies and messages most appropriate for specific sport target markets. In a highly competitive sport marketplace, and within the broader societal environment that creates thousands of communication messages each day, the need to understand the preferences of the sport consumer is ever more important. The potential to use this insight to build an effective message that slices through the brain scrambling 'noise' that surrounds us all also enables the efficient use of resources for sport organisations. The complexity of the sport communication methods available is still emerging as the effects of new communication technologies are assessed. The boom in social networking, for example, is yet to be explored fully within the sport realm. The central question here is: whether, or how, sport consumers modify their behaviour due to the context of sport? Furthermore, are the Twitter and Facebook sites of leading sport organisations a happy intrusion into the lives of sport consumers? Only sport research evidence will tell us.

The 'public face' of the sport organisation

Nevertheless, the crucial importance of ISMC is its representation of the 'public face' of the sport organisation and the sport products/services it propagates for the target sport consumer. ISMC expresses the key features and benefits of the sport product/service, states the process of access, and features the price to the sport consumer. It creates sport brand image, develops its awareness, and motivates sport consumption behaviour. ISMC must be a carefully controlled process to create positive associations and perceptions, as it is also capable of transmitting damaging messages into the sport marketplace at the same time, as Sepp Blatter of FIFA found to his cost in December 2010. There is no blueprint to follow that can guarantee success here, as no two sport communication messages are ever the same. Often a sport organisation learns from its previous sport communication applications, and those of its competitors, and makes adaptations to its approaches to effect the desired response – even multi-million pound advertising campaigns are not foolproof – remember Nike's World Cup 'Write the Future' advert featuring footballers who underperformed at the 2010 World Cup or didn't even make their country's squad selection?

The case study above gives you an insight into the co-ordination required for each of the components of the sport marketing mix. The aim of the ISMC plan is outlined and more specific objectives are set. The sport target market is established and the actions for implementation are detailed with responsibilities and a timeframe attached. The plan is ready to be put into practice. It is based upon the concepts and ideas outlined in the remainder of this chapter.

To guide the planning and implementation of a sport communication campaign a number of fundamental concepts are applicable. The main concepts are: 1) the Sport Communication Process; 2) the Hierarchy of Effects; and 3) the AIDA principle.

The Sport Communication Process

So you as a sport marketer want to inform, persuade or remind your chosen sport target market about the opportunity to get involved as a 'Games Maker' at the London 2012 Olympic and Paralympic Games, or go watch the Henley Rowing Regatta, or participate in the Hyde Park Tri; you need to communicate through a simple process – the Sport Communication Process (see Figure 7.2).

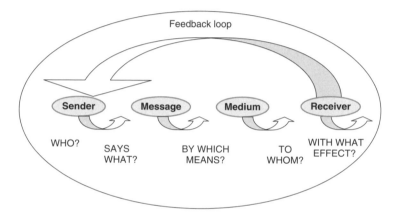

Figure 7.2 Schramm's communications process (adapted from Pickton and Broderick, 2005)

The sport marketer as the *sender* (source), and initiator, of the message *encodes* that message via words, expressions and symbols. The sender requires credibility to enact authority and trustworthiness in the message, often difficult in a scandal hit sport, e.g. betting irregularities in cricket, or the proliferation of 'dodgy' websites. The believability of the sport communication message can be lowered for future matches or endorsed products/services. Equity in sport brands is one way of providing credibility, e.g. *Nike*, but what of *Pro Touch*?

Encoding translates the thoughts and ideas of the sender into the message. Considering the essential information to portray and with the characteristics of the target market segment translation of meaning in mind, the message content is conceived. This is one of the most important points in sport communication, and sport marketing more generally, as this is the opportunity for innovative conceptualisation of the message. There are few boundaries to creative thought, and with only a rudimentary appreciation of publishing packages some impressive images can be created. The message should embody emotion (e.g. fear, rationality, functional information), or comparison (e.g. to the sport products/services of competitors). Transmission of the message necessitates choice of communication medium – the channel. Sport communication objectives guide the decision about the specific media to be used to carry the message, and are assisted by the following:

- the characteristics of the intended sport target market;
- the nature of the sport product/service being communicated;

- the cost to reach the sport target market;
- the flexibility of the media;
- the ability to reach a specialised sport target market;
- the lifespan of the media (Shank, 2009).

The sport communication message can be sent via a multitude of potential media options including: TV, radio, and billboards as traditional media formats, and web and mobile communication technologies as new media formats. *Decoding* is the interpretation of the message by the sport consumer – the receiver – from each conveyance medium. The process requires trial to assess the potential for successful receipt of the message because misunderstanding and misrepresentation of the message can occur. Sport consumer characteristics, be they age, gender, geographic region or personal values, can mean a different appreciation of the message. The need for a narrowly determined sport target market is required to ensure successful sport communication message receipt.

Feedback needs to be two-way: a response to the message by the sport consumer that is evident to the sender, and by the sender in response to the sport consumer. For example, the sport marketer notes a response through a sale or a request for further information or clarification. The seeking of additional information can move the sport consumer to the next stage of the *sport consumer decision-making process* and closer to the point of sport consumption. On the other hand, no/limited response by the sport consumer is a feedback message in its own right. Similarly, the nature of a further information or clarification request can highlight inadequacies in the original message thus requiring attention by the sender.

Noise surrounds all sport communication attempts. Noise interferes with the central message and can result from credibility issues with the sender, an inadequately encoded message, an inappropriate choice of medium or misinterpreted decoding. You might expect that mass communication approaches could suffer the effects of noise, but personalised direct marketing communication approaches can be affected in a similar way. We are all bombarded electronically by sport companies, and others, whom we have given authority to contact us, and those we have not. As a result, genuine messages may simply be deleted through noise fatigue.

The Hierarchy of Effects and the AIDA Principle

The *Hierarchy of Effects* (see Figure 7.3) guides the delivery of sport communication to the sport target market. Its premise is that sport consumers begin from a point of complete unawareness of sport product/ service existence. A series of sport communication messages can instigate awareness, develop a preference, and build a need that culminates in the action of sport consumption.

The sport communication objectives of informing, persuading and reminding sport consumers of the existence of a sport product/service link closely to the stages of the Hierarchy of Effects. Informing moves the sport consumer from the point of unawareness through awareness to develop knowledge about the benefits offered by the sport product/service compared to alternatives. Persuading continues the upward trajectory to encourage a positive feeling towards the sport product/service in preference to those presented by competitors. Additional persuasion is necessary to create a conviction to act. Where consumption of the sport product/service has occurred, reinforcement through reminding the sport consumer of the benefits accrued and future availability encourages continued sport consumption.

In effect the *AIDA Principle* (awareness, interest, desire, action) condenses the seven-step Hierarchy of Effects into just four, and is a more useful conceptual tool.

Figure 7.3 The Hierarchy of Effects

- Awareness – increase, e.g. through sport celebrity endorsement;
- Interest – attract, e.g. in the features and benefits of the sport product/service;
- Desire – arouse, e.g. by identifying the value and differential advantage;
- Action – initiate, e.g. sport consumption.

Together the Hierarchy of Effects and AIDA Principle identify the direction of movement that a sport communication campaign can have in the mind of the target sport consumer. The sport marketer would seek to enact the sport communication objectives through the manipulation of the sport communication mix. With the broader sport marketing objectives of the sport organisation as constant reference, and with the guidance of conceptual models such as the Ansoff matrix and sport PLC in mind, the sport communication objectives have two main foci: 1) expanding the sport market; and 2) penetrating the sport market. This presents the basis of a strategic sport communication plan, as co-ordination of activity in multiple sport target markets is necessary. Table 7.1 identifies the key strategic sport communication plan components.

Sport Communication Objective	Conceptual Relevance	Sport Target Market	Strategy
Sport market expansion	Ansoff matrix – market extension Sport PLC – Intro stage	Non-users	Increase awareness Present trial opportunities Remind lapsed users
	Ansoff matrix – product/service development	New segments	Brand stretching Inform benefits of use
Sport market penetration	Ansoff matrix – market penetration	Current users	Increase repeat consumption Identify new uses
	Sport PLC – growth stage	Competing product/service users	Encourage brand switching Build brand image Brand repositioning

Table 7.1 Strategic sport communication plan components

Sport market expansion targets non-users of the sport products/services on offer in the sport marketplace. It has conceptual relevance to the market extension objective of the Ansoff matrix and to the introductory stage of the sport PLC for new sport products/services offered to sport consumers. Strategy would focus upon increasing awareness of the sport product/service, generating trial opportunities, and reminding lapsed users of the benefits they are missing. New sport target market segments could also be identified through sport brand stretching – use of the sport brand name on new brands in un-related markets (see Chapter 5), and informing of the benefits available – a clear product/service development objective of the Ansoff matrix.

To penetrate the sport market further, current users can be encouraged to increase their consumption rate or identify new uses for the sport product/service. To drive users from competing sport products/services, brand switching through the development of the sport brand image or its complete repositioning, both growth stage activities of the sport PLC, will aid market penetration objectives of the Ansoff matrix.

To help you to visualise the process and determine the goal of an integrated strategy, the Sport Purchase Frequency Escalator (Mullin et al., 2007) illustrates the desired direction of movement in purchase frequency from non-aware consumer (unawareness) to heavy user (see Figure 7.4). The premise here is of sport market penetration, as moving existing sport consumers along the escalator is more cost effective for a sport organisation than 'fishing' for unaware or disinterested non-consumers. All sport communication mix efforts are designed to develop frequency of sport consumption, and its retention. Season ticket or membership sales are the obvious target, whether linked to football, rugby, golf, hockey or skiing, and applicable to spectator and participant purposes.

Learning Activity 7.1

- Where do you stand on the Sport Purchase Frequency Escalator for two different sport products/services?
- How have you been encouraged in each case to increase your frequency of purchase?
- How did you respond to these 'pull' factors?

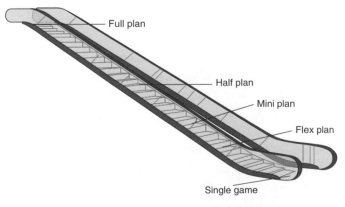

Figure 7.4 The Sport Purchase Frequency Escalator (adapted from Mullin et al., 2007)

The ISMC approach seeks to develop a co-ordinated implementation of the tactical components of the sport communication mix. To develop the sport communication campaign, each sport target market necessitates an individual strategic and tactical implementation in its own right. Figure 7.5 develops and adapts the IMC process outlined by Masterman (2004) by stating that the approach has concurrent ISMC programmes running at the same time. Furthermore, sport product/service, sport price and sport place communication decisions are all channelled through the sport communication mix.

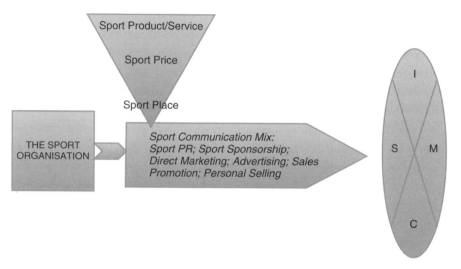

Figure 7.5 The ISMC process

Sport sponsorship and sport public relations will be the subject of Chapters 8 and 9 respectively, leaving the remaining sport communication mix components – sales promotion, direct marketing, personal selling and advertising – to be concentrated upon here. These components are presented through the media forms of personal media (e.g. direct marketing and personal selling), and mass media (e.g. advertising and sales promotion), both now presented increasingly via interactive methods (e.g. web and mobile).

Sport direct marketing

Direct marketing necessitates a database of information upon which to build a measurable response from the sport target market. The Marketing Information System (see Chapter 2) of the sport organisation stores the information about past, current and potential sport consumers collected from a variety of sources (e.g. membership records, previous purchases, surveys). Each point of contact with a sport organisation can be recorded electronically, even a simple enquiry phone call, and followed up to test responsiveness towards sport product/service consumption. Web-based technology can track your every movement on-line and use it to encourage sport consumption behaviour. The main forms of direct marketing are: 1) direct and email; and 2) telemarketing.

Direct and email

We all receive postal mail and email each day, much of it unsolicited, but do you read it and how do you react to it? Direct and email is targeted, personal, measurable, testable and flexible (Mullin et al., 2007). Increasingly email is the chosen route that sport organisations use to encourage consumption of their sport products/services. It is easy for sport consumers to unsubscribe, delete or bin direct and email marketing materials, and here lies one of its problems – a very low response rate. Nevertheless, it allows a variety of sport communication messages to be used including letters, leaflets, flyers, DVDs, podcasts etc. all sent direct to a named recipient – you! Direct and email marketing is personalised so that the sport consumer feels that their favourite sports star is contacting them. Receiving a message in your inbox from Andy Murray or Padraig Harrington enhances the possibility of that email being opened, considered and responded to positively.

Direct and e-mail approaches fit with broader advertising and sales promotion opportunities. They are also used to 'keep in touch' with valued sport consumers, maintaining the relationship between sport organisation and sport consumer. This drip-feed of information can develop the relationship and maintain loyalty covertly or be overt in its attempt to incite sport consumption through sales promotion offers. Clearly, email marketing is a lot more cost effective to distribute, but is dependent on the accuracy of that database.

Telemarketing

This is a two-system approach: a) the fielding of incoming enquiry calls; and b) prospecting out-going calls. Basic information about the sport products/services of sport organisations is now placed on the web to avoid the labour-intensive fielding of a multitude of calls. As a result, it is often difficult to speak with a representative of a sport organisation directly and so making an enquiry call can be frustrating for the sport consumer as they are often placed in a queue system and made to wait. Once connected though, the experience can be quick and satisfying as there is the opportunity to have specific questions answered. Prospect (cold) calling to generate sport consumption behaviour can be intrusive, but if a genuine and simple offer is proposed (e.g. 'We would like you to have free tickets for the game on Saturday'), then the recipient would be very interested no doubt. Prospect calling is an approach used in the offer of corporate hospitality packages, group sales and upselling.

Sport personal selling

Personal selling is proposed as a form of direct marketing as it is a face-to-face personal media approach. The sport communication message is transmitted from person-to-person and has an immediate response capability. Personal selling is a specialist sport promotion technique requiring specific personal skills such as listening, empathy and relationship generation. Its use in sport marketing is as a business-to-business technique concentrating on the serving of corporate sponsorship, corporate hospitality packages and group sales. Both sport market penetration and sport market expansion objectives can be set with each sport target market identified requiring an ISMC strategy and tactical implementation programme of its own. For many sport products/services personal selling is a necessity to secure valuable distribution channels. High street outlets are still key to sales for many sport brands despite the increase in web traffic. The high street develops new sport market opportunities and broadens exposure into the early and late majority mass market. Effective personal selling of the surf wear brand Protest into the high street meant that sales soared as the profile of the brand in the UK was seen by many more prospective consumers. Where sport and fashion collide in a product range its potential is exponential when a suitable distribution channel is negotiated. Personal selling can combine with sales promotion initiatives such as discounting or free samples to 'check out' the sport experience. As with all propositions made to sport consumers, satisfaction with the sport product/service must be achieved so it is important not to over-sell the deliverables during personal selling negotiations. Beware of making false promises!

Sport sales promotion

Sales promotion is a direct inducement to stimulate immediate action from the sport consumer. It constitutes short-term (time-limited) sport promotion activity that is either price-based (i.e. coupons and discounts) or non-price based (i.e. competitions and giveaways). In addition to boosting sales, sales promotion seeks to encourage trial, incite repeat purchase and gain more effective distribution, the latter aided by a co-ordinated and consistent sport communication message across multiple platforms. Sales promotion occurs direct to the sport consumer or via third party intermediaries (see Chapter 11) who receive heavy discounts for taking large numbers of the sport product/service (e.g. sport equipment and apparel retailers or sport event ticket and hospitality suppliers such as Ticketmaster).

It is important to consider the specific sport promotion objective to be achieved and then to construct a strategic and tactical use of sales promotion to achieve it. As identified in Table 7.1, increasing repeat sport consumption – a sport market penetration strategy – can be facilitated through non-price-based incentivisation such as giveaways and competitions. Presenting the opportunity to trial – a sport market expansion strategy – can be offered through price-based incentives such as coupons or other discount forms. The short-term imperative of sales promotion is extremely important, as it does not allow the sport consumer to become dependent upon the incentive. It is used alongside other sport communication forms to encourage 'sign up' to a bigger bundle (e.g. series of matches or physio sessions). These may have a price-inducement attached, but develop sport consumption behaviour patterns that are encouraged further towards establishing heavy user status. But remember what went wrong for the Irish Rugby Football Union (see Chapter 6).

The main incentives used in sales promotion include coupons, discounts, premiums, free samples and competitions.

Coupons – offer a price incentive on the basic offer, or on refreshments or a mixture of the two. They are in printed format, most frequently appearing in newspapers or magazines and, increasingly, in downloadable form on the web. Coupons are used to target specific sport segments even when offered through mass market communication media (e.g. national newspapers), as the offer is applicable to a national sport audience. Equally newspaper couponing may have a regional or local sport audience and the reach of the media channel will determine its choice and success. Manipulation of the basic ticket price is common (e.g. two-for-one or a child free with an adult), but free or discounted refreshments can boost spectator numbers. This sales promotion initiative can encourage consumption of associated refreshment items and aims to be cost neutral (e.g. a free small soft drink with the purchase of every packet of Walker's crisps). Ticket price and concession incentives can be offered to larger group sizes, thus increasing 'butts on seats' and the potential of increased secondary spend on other items (e.g. merchandise). Coupons can be utilised for less attractive games at less popular times of the week (e.g. Monday or Thursday). Consideration of the effect of couponing is necessary, however, as sport consumption dependence can emerge or the sport consumer perceives desperation for sales resulting in a negation of the image of the sport product/service.

Discounts – follow the price incentive theme of coupons by offering time-limited reductions (e.g. on season ticket renewal, as demonstrated in the previous chapter by the example of the 'Early Bird' season ticket offer until 4 January at Warrington Wolves RFLC), and price discounts on larger sales volumes. Group travel for sport events benefits in this way with the purchase of ten or twenty tickets often the trigger for a free ticket.

Premiums – or 'giveaways' is a non-price-based incentive. Less frequently used in the UK than the United States by elite level sporting organisations, free goodies are now part of the expected sport product/service at the finish line of mass participation running events or at all manner of kids sport contests. Premiums can take many forms (e.g. hats, fridge magnets, posters, water bottles), but need residual value so that they re-appear frequently to act as a sport promotional item in their own right. Premiums are designed to encourage sport consumption from new sport consumers and increase consumption frequency from existing sport consumers. Targeted use of premiums can reward frequent/loyal sport consumers (e.g. multiple ticket stub collection to receive a souvenir item) or the development of a seasonal theme (e.g. 100th anniversary) with intermittent, but planned, celebrations. Some giveaways are restricted to the first 100, 500 or 1,000 spectators to avoid promising a free scarf to 52,000 spectators when there are simply not that many available, as one English Premier League football club found to their cost a couple of seasons ago. Sending away dissatisfied fans is never a good strategy!

Free samples – a non-price-based incentive that can result in an immediate spike of sport consumption. Free samples of sports nutrition bars attached to sport magazines is a good idea, though a free edition of a sport magazine that you have to sign a direct debit mandate to receive and then cancel if you do not want to continue the subscription perhaps is not such a good offer. A free 'taster' of golf, tennis or a spinning class with a member can also induce sport market expansion or sport market penetration possibilities. Season ticket holders can be encouraged to upgrade to a higher priced offering by the sport organisation allowing the sampling of a premium view seat and its hospitality options. My kids now only eat Haribo sweets as a result of the free samples I have bagged on my visits to the Tour de France, thrown to spectators from sponsor vehicles as they pass!

Competitions – non-price based again; often used as half-time entertainment (somewhat underwhelmingly) (e.g. penalty shoot-outs, 'beat the keeper', lay-up competition) with a prize for the winner. A half-time draw necessitating a ticket purchase is also an example of a competition frequently used in UK sport stadia. Web-based competitions are also popular as they can reward more loyal sport consumers who seek information about their sport or team in this way (e.g. purchase tickets in advance and you will be entered into a prize draw for a trip for two to New York, including return flights, transfer to Saratoga Springs town, four nights bed and breakfast accommodation in the Hampton Inn and admission to the Premier enclosure at the Saratoga race track for three days, complete with lunch, as York racecourse did in 2010).

Several negative factors can emerge from the use of sales promotion techniques: cost implications are certainly to the fore. Costs attached to both price-based and non-price-based incentives increase as take-up of the offer increases. Nevertheless, where revenues are affected by lower ticket prices, secondary sales may off-set this reduction. The cost to the sport organisation proposing the sales promotion offer can be negated by the cost being carried by a sponsor (e.g. kit supplier or drinks provider). Where a high value prize is offered (e.g. a holiday), its cost can actually be minimal if the response (increased sales) to the sales promotion is positive. In the United States, NFL and MLB franchises view giveaways as merchandising opportunities (e.g. the offer of a baseball cap can be the start of a whole new range of 'historical' merchandise items).

There is often a drop in sport consumption subsequent to a sales promotion initiative. This is one reason for careful planning when using this technique and the reason for targeting specific sport segments with the offer. Season ticket holders can be undermined by price-based incentives for less involved spectators. However, an up-front explanation of the reasons such incentives are to be implemented can create harmony in the loyal spectator contingent. Doncaster Rovers FC instigated this policy by explaining that a price discount for specific games was designed to increase spectator levels to create noisier support for the team and to increase revenue to re-invest in the team to help their push for promotion into the Premier League. This approach could also encourage lapsed and new spectators to repeat purchase at the standard price for future games. The club chairman has also guaranteed that if Doncaster Rovers FC are promoted to the Premier League for the season 2011/12 all season ticket holders will receive a free season ticket. This offer does seem to go against the need for income generation from supporters, but is a genuinely, heartfelt initiative as the chairman will personally fund the guarantee.

Learning Activity 7.2

- How have you been touched by price or non-price-based sport sales promotion?
- What was the incentive and what was your reaction to it?
- Did it have the desired effect for the sport organisation making the offer?

Sport advertising

Sport advertising is the most readily available and visible form of sport promotion through which to deliver the sport communication message. When we consider the Sport Communication Process, the Hierarchy of Effects and AIDA Principle, and the Sport Purchase Frequency Escalator, it is with advertising as a medium to the fore. Advertising creates the noise and clutter that can stop a clear and consistent message being received by the sport consumer, but advertising also effects the 'buzz' that creates anticipation of an upcoming sport event or new to market sport product/service. The basis of advertising is as a non-personal, one-way, paid-for communication that can be carried across a number of media platforms, e.g. TV, radio, newspapers, magazines, billboards, buses, toilet cubicles and, of course, the web. More than for any other sport promotion mix component, the budget will determine the sport media strategy to be implemented. The sport advertising objectives establish the goal; the advertising budget determines the creative opportunities available; the sport media strategy emerges, and is implemented, ahead of an assessment of its impact (see Figure 7.6).

Figure 7.6 Designing a sport advertising campaign (adapted from Shank, 2009)

A sport promotion campaign can utilise multiple sport media channels directed towards a single sport target market. In effect, sport advertising necessitates an ISMC approach of its own, but must incorporate appropriate elements of each of the other primary sport promotion mix components for full effect. Sport advertising sets out to present sport communication messages that are understandable, believable and memorable. More specifically, advertising seeks to increase sport product/service consumption directly or via sales promotion advertising. These objectives can be achieved by targeting new sport segments or through the repeat purchases of current sport consumers. Furthermore, sport advertising seeks to increase awareness, enhance image or change attitudes. Each of these indirect objectives necessitates a behavioural response that can lead to additional sport consumption at a later point, perhaps in response to a follow-up direct approach.

TV commercials for sport products/services are rarely seen as the medium is too expensive to warrant the purchase of 'air time' for what is in effect a relatively small marketplace. TV channels will 'advertise' upcoming sport events on their own channels to encourage a media-based sport audience (the BBC also do this for sport events as it does not constitute commercial advertising), but alternative approaches are co-ordinated to maximise on the resource available. Advertising agencies are prevalent in this process to create the message and disseminate it. Agencies such as WPP and Sport Revolution have media buying power as they place numerous campaigns with the same media channel. Advertising agencies can be efficient with limited resources as a result of this factor, and can be more effective (if they are any good) with the co-ordination of the wider sport communication strategy. Allowing an agency to have creative input in sales promotion and sport PR can mean a more integrated message is conceived and implemented. Advertising agencies also have the ability to assess the impact of the advertising campaign or will contract a third party for this purpose.

The heart of the sport communication message is the creative appeal of the advertisement. This creative aspect aims to: 1) identify the benefits of the sport product/service, e.g. functional, fashion, social, entertainment; 2) design advertising appeals, e.g. health, emotional, fear, sex, pleasure/fun that form the basis of the message; and 3) the advertising execution, e.g. one-sided (positive stance only) or two-sided (positives and negatives); comparative to competitors; lifestyle (reflecting everyday scenes); scientific (technological superiority); and testimonials (endorsers) (Shank, 2009).

Learning Activity 7.3

Consider a sport advertisement (TV, radio, web, print) that is memorable for you. Against the criteria above, ask yourself why it appeals to you? Discuss your advert with a colleague.

A theme is developed for the sport communication message and is 'brought to life' thus creating appeal through pictures, sound and movement, depending upon which media platform is chosen. Remember that the greater the verbal, visual or auditory appeal, the more likely the message will cut through the noise of advertising clutter and create the desired response from the sport target segment. The sport media strategy is selected on the basis of the sport communication message to be transmitted, the target sport audience to be reached, the effect required, and as stated, the budget available. The sport marketer thereby considers several measures to guide the choice of sport media. These are:

- reach – the number of people exposed to the ad;
- rating – the percentage of households in the sport target market who tune to a particular TV or radio programme;
- frequency – the average number of times a person is exposed to an ad;
- gross rating points – reach as a percentage of the total sport target market multiplied by frequency;
- cost per thousand – cost of ads divided by the number of thousands of people exposed.

These measures provide information upon which the sport marketer can decide which media channel to use to most effectively convey the sport communication message. However, a further determinant is the basic nature of the message, e.g. visual and auditory = TV or web-based embedded formats; auditory = radio; text = newspaper, magazine or internet. Other media formats (e.g. billboards), offer complementary and reminder opportunities. A comparison of major media types was identified by Kotler and Armstrong (2005) and is reproduced in Table 7.2. This enables the sport marketer to decide which

Medium	Advantages	Limitations
Internet	Customised messages, interactive capabilities, reaches a specific sport market	Clutter, hard-to-measure effectiveness
Newspapers	Timeliness, good market coverage, high believability	Short life, poor reproduction quality, small pass-along audience
TV	Mass market coverage, low cost per exposure, appealing to the senses	High absolute costs, high clutter, fleeting exposure, low audience selectivity
Direct mail	High audience selectivity, allows personalisation, no ad competition within the same medium	Relatively high cost per exposure, 'junk mail' image
Radio	Good local acceptance, high geographic and demographic selectivity, low cost	Audio only, fleeting exposure, the 'half heard' medium
Magazines	High geographic and demographic selectivity, credibility and prestige, long life and pass-along readership	Long advertisement purchase lead time, high cost, no guarantee of position
Outdoor	Flexibility, high repeat exposure, low cost, low message competition, good positional selectivity	Little audience selectivity, creative limitations

Table 7.2 Profiles of major media types (adapted from Kotler and Armstrong, 2005)

sport media channel has the best chance of achieving the sport advertising objectives desired by the sport organisation.

The purchase of sport venue signage/advertising hoardings is one way to reach the target sport market directly at the venue, but more so through TV transmission – live or recorded. Sport sponsorship packages now have key advertising locations at the venue as part of the deal, e.g. the sponsors of the UEFA Champions League. However, the invention of revolving advertising boards enables a greater number of advertising possibilities. This also makes it easier to switch from UEFA sanctioned ads for UEFA games only, to English Premier League ads for EPL matches. Furthermore, virtual signage – computer-generated rather than actual – can be laid across the screen thereby offering one-off or short-term sport advertising options.

Chapter Review

ISMC is the public face of the sport organisation. It is a crucial, yet complex, manipulation of all of the components of the sport marketing mix. As with the whole approach to sport marketing, ISMC is a process that is built into a co-ordinated series of actions for implementation. This is the detailed 'battle' plan through which the sport marketing objectives are to be achieved, and is informed by the preceding stages of the sport marketing planning process. There is no blueprint, and external assistance from expert agencies may be required to utilise scarce resources most effectively.

Further Reading

Kliatchko, J. (2008) 'Re-visiting the IMC construct: a revised definition and four pillars', *International Journal of Advertising*, 27, 1: 133–160.

This paper re-examines a definition of integrated marketing communications (IMC) and introduces the four pillars of IMC as an offshoot of the proposed revised definition. The paper concludes by illustrating the interplay between the pillars and levels of IMC.

Masterman, G. and Wood, E.H. (2006) *Innovative Marketing Communications: Strategies for the Events Industry*, Oxford: Butterworth-Heinemann.

This text covers the events industry, but does include sport, and offers new aspects for practical and theoretical consideration.

Chapter 8
Sport sponsorship

Learning Objectives

This chapter is designed to help you:

- define sport sponsorship;
- explain the process of sport sponsorship management;
- be alert to the possibility of ambush marketing.

Introduction

Sport sponsorship is now a key form of sport marketing communications activity, and has assumed a dominant role in many sport, and non-sport, organisations' promotional mix. Historically, sport organisations, sports celebrities and, specifically, sports events have attracted the highest level of sponsorship investment across the arts, culture and music industries, as sport has become an integral part of an emerging global culture with widespread appeal across all ages and lifestyles (Verity, 2002). Sport consumers are inundated with sport promotional activity, and so have become immune to traditional forms of sport marketing communications. Sport sponsorship has become a way for brands to communicate with their sport target market(s) as it has the ability to cut through the noise of sport promotional clutter and is identified as a form of 'lifestyle' marketing as it appeals directly to the activities and attitudes enjoyed by sport consumers. This has resulted in considerable investment in sponsorship of sport evidenced by the annual spend attributed to some brands, e.g. adidas £243 million, Red Bull £183.5 million and Vodafone £57.6 million in 2009 (Sports Pro Media, 2010). To this end, corporate sponsorship of sporting events such as the Olympics, FIFA World Cup, Tour de France and Formula 1 have become a central focus of many organisations' global marketing communications strategy.

The amount spent each year on sport sponsorship programmes continues to increase –with North America, naturally, followed by Europe, spending the most. Germany is the biggest market for sport sponsorships in Europe, followed by the UK, and rapidly closing the spending gap are the less mature Asian sponsorship markets (Greaves, 2008). Furthermore, the key players in the UK sport sponsorship market are financial and insurance companies such as Standard Chartered and Aon. Football enjoys a dominant position in the sport sponsorship market due to its huge spectator base, media profile and its marketing appeal. Motorsport is the second most sponsored sport, followed by rugby union, athletics, cricket and horseracing.

This is a chapter of two halves, as it will consider both sides of the sport sponsorship sector – the sponsor and the 'sponsee' (the sport property). The sponsee is a sport organisation, club, league, venue or athlete who 'sells' the rights of association to the sponsor. The investment made by the sponsor aims, predominantly, to increase awareness of the brand. However, sport sponsorship is not a stand-alone sport marketing concept and requires leveraging support from other sport marketing communication mix tools for it to be effective, thus making it an expensive proposition. For example, Sony Ericsson invested £9 million (exclusive of sponsorship rights fees) in its integrated marketing campaign with the WTA (SportBusiness International, 2008). As a sport marketer, you need to appreciate the sport sponsorship process and, increasingly, the component that is sport sponsorship 'activation' as the most effective campaigns integrate sponsorship with advertising, direct marketing, PR and sales promotions. Sport sponsorship is also a sexy subject and one that you will be interested in investigating in all its capacities.

Sport sponsorship defined

There are a number of views on the definition of sport sponsorship in the literature. For example:

- Sponsorship as a commercial activity undertaken to achieve corporate, marketing and media-related objectives (Shank, 2009).
- Sponsorship as a two-dimensional business agreement involving mutual benefits to both sponsor and sponsored, wherein the sponsor provides money, goods or services in return for the commercial exploitation of the rights provided by the sponsored property (Masterman, 2007).
- Sponsorship as a communication tool used to disseminate corporate and marketing messages to its sport target audience in order to stimulate product sales, increase brand awareness and change or reinforce corporate image (Mullin et al., 2007; Masterman, 2007).

With these in mind, the following definition offered by Masterman (2007) provides a solid definition of sport sponsorship.

[Sport] sponsorship is a mutually beneficial arrangement that consists of the provision of resources of funds, goods and/or services by an individual or body (the sponsor) to an individual or body (rights owner) in return for a set of rights that can be used in communications activity, for the achievement of objectives for commercial gain.

(p. 30)

This definition explains the dynamics of sport sponsorship and provides greater insight about sport sponsorship agreements. It highlights a wide range of provisions the sponsored property can offer the sport/non-sport organisation in return for their investment to leverage into their sport marketing communication activities. The definition determines the kind of corporate involvement that can be classified as commercial sport sponsorship.

Sport sponsorship management

Sport rights owners have developed their sponsorship offerings into complete value propositions in recent years and so opportunities for sport sponsorship have multiplied. These developments have translated into the creation of specialised sport marketing departments in sport and non-sport organisations and a greater degree of management sophistication to assess the return on investment of these opportunities (Sports Business Group, 2007). As with many aspects of sport marketing, a process/framework is proposed to guide the strategic sport sponsorship management process (see Figure 8.1).

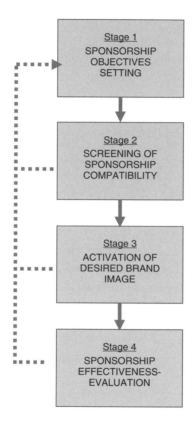

Figure 8.1 Sport Sponsorship Management Model (Blakey and Chavan, 2011)

The Sport Sponsorship Management Model (Blakey and Chavan, 2011) establishes four key stages to the process of sport sponsorship as a vehicle through which to engage the sport target market in order to achieve organisational goals:

- stage 1 – setting of clearly defined and quantifiable objectives that are in line with an organisation's overall strategic directions/goals;
- stage 2 – selection/screening to establish sponsorship feasibility, compatibility between the brand and the sporting property and integration with an organisation's existing marketing communication strategy;
- stage 3 – implementation of activation strategies to attain desired image and increase sport consumer's emotional involvement leading to brand advocacy;
- stage 4 – evaluation of sport sponsorship effectiveness in attaining overall objectives and its impact on key brand measures.

It is important to clarify that this model is appropriate for both parties (sponsor and sponsee) within the sport sponsorship relationship. However, the activation stage is designed with the associated leveraging activity of the sponsor in mind. The process of sport sponsorship management, from the perspective of the sport rights holder, is inadequately understood as little research has been undertaken to investigate the reasons, benefits and activities of the sponsee. Nevertheless, both perspectives will be noted as an explanation of the process of sport sponsorship management is outlined.

Stage 1: sport sponsorship objective setting

Traditionally, enhancing corporate or brand image and increasing brand awareness have been the two primary objectives for organisations to undertake through sport sponsorship. However, sport sponsorship objectives are diverse and may vary for different organisations, depending on their size, industry and market reach, but fall into three broad, but distinct, categories:

1   Media objectives – mostly related to cost effectiveness and reaching sport target markets.
2   Corporate objectives – mostly image related.
3   Marketing objectives – mostly brand, product or service and sales related.

Originally, attainment of media objectives in terms of gaining exposure was the driving factor for acquiring sport sponsorship rights especially when increased coverage of sporting events around the globe on TV delivered unprecedented exposure to sponsoring brands. The strengths of sport sponsorship were exploited by the tobacco and alcohol industry to overcome legal barriers and gain access to media coverage, e.g. Embassy sponsoring snooker and Camel in F1. However, sport sponsorship programmes have evolved and shifted to the achievement of a wider set of corporate and marketing objectives, which traditional advertising media has struggled to achieve as effectively. Well-implemented sport sponsorship programmes develop superior brand associations and favourable corporate image that influences sport consumers' purchase intentions.

The expansion of the range of objectives attainable has added new dimensions to the implementation of sport sponsorship strategies. Driving sales, for example, is a key objective due to a greater focus on a return on investment, and sales being one of the few sport sponsorship objectives that can be measured objectively. Sponsors are viewing sport sponsorship as a key facilitator of sales opportunities and using it to build business relationships using corporate hospitality opportunities. Sport sponsorship can also be utilised to pre-empt competition by providing exclusive rights that block rivals in the same business sector, e.g. Coca-Cola and Pepsi, Mastercard and Visa. The ability to increase productivity, efficiency and staff morale through employee involvement in a sponsorship programme is also a reason for agreeing a sport sponsorship contract.

Little has been written about the requirements of the sponsee. This does pose a number of research questions for investigation, e.g. sponsee objectives to be achieved and effective sponsee self-promotion techniques. Nevertheless, for athletes the desire to focus on training and competing sits at the heart of the search for a suitable sponsor. The agreement of cash or in-kind sponsorship will begin a relationship through which both parties will seek to benefit. In seeking this partnership the sponsee should focus upon their successes to date, potential, reach to the target audience through their sport, competitions in which they will

Broad Focus	Objective
Sponsor objectives:	
General public	To promote the public image of the organisation
	To form an overall brand perception
	To create a favourable community perception of the organisation
Sport target market	To increase sport consumer awareness of a product/service or brand
	To drive sales of a specific product/service
	To achieve competitive advantage
	To create 'image transfer' from sponsored property to sponsor
Internal stakeholders	To improve staff morale, relations and satisfaction
	To promote shareholder satisfaction
Sponsee objectives:	
Corporate objectives	To promote the public image of the sport property through a credible relationship
	To increase general public awareness of the property (directly or indirectly)
Marketing objectives	To increase sport consumer awareness of a sport product/service or brand (directly or indirectly)
	To increase credibility (through the sponsor) among sport consumers
	To create 'image transfer' through brand association
	To position or re-position the sport brand in the mind of the sport consumer
Operational objectives	To obtain funding, resources and/or services to support operational functions
	To increase staff satisfaction
	To promote credibility with stakeholders (politicians, shareholders, media. etc.)

Table 8.1   Sport sponsorship objectives (adapted from Smith, 2008)

feature, current and potential media exposure, personal appearances/coaching event availability, and event tickets/hospitality opportunities they can provide. The potential sponsee needs to enact a sales pitch!

Stage 2: selection/screening of sport sponsorship compatibility

The rapidly increasing costs of sport sponsorship rights fees and the sophisticated nature of implementing sport sponsorship programmes has led organisations to place more focus on the initial process of sport sponsorship selection. Media coverage potential, the geographical coverage of the defined sport target market, the importance of associated promotional opportunities, the importance of duration, exclusivity and commitment from both parties, and the budgetary requirement are important factors for consideration in the selection process. Cornwell, Weeks and Roy (2005) noted the need to associate a brand and sport that demonstrate similar values and image compatibility. By using this process, potential sponsors can identify relevant values and compare them with different sport properties to analyse a suitable 'fit' in order to select the most appropriate sport sponsorship platform.

Sport rights owners also pursue the concept of 'fit' through an understanding of the exploitable potential of their property. This is established from the characteristics of the key sport markets served by the sport property and by performing an audit of potential sponsors. The format of sport sponsorship options can be judged against this initial information, but packages have tended to be 'off-the-shelf' fixed bundles requiring limited negotiation between sponsor and sponsee or a bespoke approach that brings the objectives of the potential sponsor into consideration. Bespoke sport sponsorship packages can create greater value for both parties and this approach establishes the basis of a one-to-one relationship that seeks to secure a tailored package of benefits for the sponsor. Developing an understanding between the two parties enables the mutual benefits to form a longer-term commitment, e.g. the relationship between McDonald's and the IOC.

Sport events are a good example of the application of sport sponsorship. Multiple rights levels tend to exist, dependent of course on the size and scale of the sport event. Common rights levels include:

- *Title rights* – the name of the sponsor appears in the title of the sport event, e.g. The Gore Bike Wear TransWales enduro MTB race.
- *Presenter rights* – the sponsor is acknowledged alongside the name of the sport event, e.g. 'The FA Cup sponsored by Eon'.
- *Naming rights* – usually a sport venue incorporating the name of the sponsor, e.g. the Emirates Stadium.
- *Category rights* – frequently multiple categories, but with a sponsor with exclusive rights in their business sector, e.g. Epson as official office equipment partner of Manchester United.
- *Supplier rights* – acknowledgement of sport event service suppliers, each having exclusive status as above, e.g. PowerBar at the Tour de France.

Depending on the strategic necessities of the sport property, sport rights are structured into one of three types (see Figure 8.2):

- *Tiered structure* – each of the rights categories (title, supplier) present a hierarchical structure of benefits that accrue greater or lesser monetary value dependent upon their status, e.g. London 2012.
- *Solus structure* – one sponsor receives the benefits of all the rights offered, e.g. Brit Insurance for England cricket teams.
- *Flat structure* – all sponsors have equal status, but rights/benefits may be different, e.g. the Goodwood Revival motorsport meeting (Masterman, 2004).

The picture in Figure 8.3 shows two such structures in action at a ballooning event in Switzerland. The balloon in the centre of the shot has a solus structure sponsorship approach with Total, whilst the balloon on the right is using a tiered structure with De Ster as the title sponsor and several other lower level sponsors.

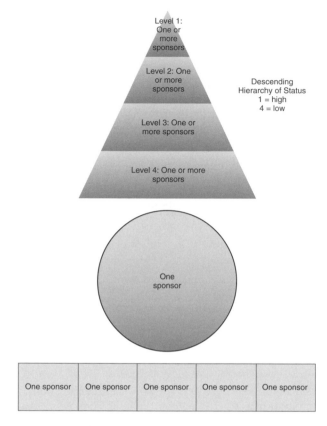

Figure 8.2 Tiered, solus and flat sponsorship structures (adapted from Masterman, 2004)

Figure 8.3 Example of solus and tiered sponsorship of a ballooning event

Learning Activity 8.1

For three sport events or sport organisations with which you are familiar, seek out the sponsorship structure(s) they have instigated. Which of the structures – solus, tiered or flat – exist and why do you think they have been used in each case?

Negotiations between sponsor and sport property revolve around a number of considerations before agreement of the sponsorship package is finalised. These include:

- *Specific rights and benefits* – relating to the placing of the sponsor's logo at and around the physical venue; the territory the rights extend, e.g. local, regional, national; and communications availed, e.g. web or print.
- *Identification of a mutual sport target market* – the 'fit' of brand attributes, market status, competitors etc.
- *The process of evaluation* – determining the satisfaction of objectives to feed the development of the relationship.
- *Pricing* – costs, profit level desired, value, return on investment.

It is common for a sport property to approach a potential sponsor with a written sponsorship proposal and presentation. This document outlines the key factors addressed above, namely 'fit' and the specific benefits of the package. When considering approaching an organisation with a sport sponsorship proposal, it is imperative that the proposal is targeted towards that particular sponsor. Undertaking research of the potential sponsor (e.g. background/history, business performance, target markets) indicates a professional approach to identifying mutual benefits in the relationship. As a general guide, the sport sponsorship proposal should present an overview of the sport property including its key sport market segments, the benefits of the sponsorship opportunity including alignment with the objectives of the potential sponsor, the investment required, and the methods available to provide feedback to the sponsor regarding the impact achieved through the implementation of the sport sponsorship package. The following list summarises the key elements of a sport sponsorship proposal guideline:

- *Introductory letter* that briefly outlines the sport organisation and what it has to offer.
- *Executive summary* that highlights the key elements of the partnership emphasising the benefits that the sponsor will realise.
- *Profile of the sports property* to give the sponsor a better understanding of the sport organisation. This should give reasons why the sponsor should be comfortable entering into the partnership (demonstrate sponsorship 'fit'). Identify the sponsors' objectives for this sponsorship.
- *Sponsorship benefits* determine all sponsor opportunities and benefits ensuring that the benefits meet the sponsors objectives.
- *Sponsorship investment* listing the menu of opportunities for sponsorship and their associated costs.
- *Impact measurement* detailing how the sponsor's benefits will be measured and evaluated.

One focal point for any potential sponsor is the degree to which leveraging activity can support the purchase of the sport rights. This has become the basis for determining the success of a sport sponsorship partnership as negotiations discuss the broader facilitation of the sponsor activation strategy. As suggested in Chapter 7, sponsorship is attributed to the sport promotion mix, but in reality it utilises the components of the mix in their entirety in its own right. Sport sponsorship activation also incorporates sport PR (the subject of Chapter 9) to achieve maximum benefit in the conveyance of the sport communication message.

Stage 3: activation of desired brand image

Sport sponsorship is supported by the synergistic execution of an array of elements of the sport marketing communication mix, which complement each other to achieve optimal communication effectiveness. Sport sponsorship is often described as an aspect of public relations due to its complex relationship with the other sport communication tools, but sport PR can play a significant role in activating the rights of a sport property. Sport sponsorship offers the opportunity to build brand relationships with a diverse set of sport target markets by engaging sport consumers on an emotional level. Organisations now integrate sport sponsorship into their overall marketing strategy to develop themes that run throughout their marketing communication, a mix which communicates and creates real interactivity with sport consumers (Pickton and Broderick, 2005). As a sport marketer it is important for you to understand the application of different activation strategies and the impact they have on sport sponsorship programmes. However, there are no 'golden rules' that identify which activation strategies are the most effective.

Research has consistently shown that sponsorship needs to be advertised, publicised, utilised in tie-ins such as sales promotions and other communication techniques such as direct marketing initiatives and online presence to achieve optimal communications effectiveness and greater consumer impact (Tripodi, 2001; Fahy et al., 2004). For instance, 2008 Beijing Olympic-themed Coke cans featured Coca-Cola script in different international languages for the first time in the United States along with a special 'six pack' featuring athletes such as swimmer Natalie Coughlin and basketball player LeBron James on the packaging. This form of sponsorship-leveraged packaging is a common and inexpensive activation strategy used by the fast moving consumer goods (FMCG) industry (Fullerton, 2007) to gain attention for brands and to increase consumers' product consideration (Woodside, 2005). Also, by integrating sport sponsorship investments with other promotional tools, sponsors are able to curtail the ever-growing threat of ambush marketing which aims to reduce the impact of sport sponsorship (see later section).

The level of activation investment has been an ongoing debate and there is no single universally accepted formula in the sport industry. For instance, according to the IEG/Performance Research Sport Sponsorship Survey (2006), 46 per cent of sponsors devoted an amount equal to the rights fees, nearly 23 per cent of sponsors spent at least three times their rights fees on activation, and overall on average sponsors spent $1.70 (£1.44) to leverage their deal for every $1 invested in rights fees. In terms of the minimum expenditure to consider, industry convention says that the activation budget should at least equal the cost of the original sponsorship rights fees (Fullerton, 2007). Table 8.2 highlights MasterCard's exploitation of their Euro 2008 sponsorship.

Sponsorship activation strategies
Sponsorship activation programmes include direct marketing, sales promotion, advertising, public relations, CSR and web-based marketing strategies. The strategies highlighted are by no means complete,

Sport Sponsorship Objectives	Activation Strategies
Business targeted marketing:	
To offer MasterCard's partner banks and merchants to develop and implement business building programmes for both its credit (MasterCard) and debit (Maestro) card brands	200 promotions in over 30 markets around the world driving card acquisition, issuance and usage (linked to 60 per cent card issuance and 40 per cent card usage)
	Theme for Euro 2008 'Winning Moments' linked to business building programmes consisting of packages such as 'VIP Stadium Tours', 'Follow your team', 'Road Trip' and 'Block Party'
	For the first time ever key Swiss issuing partners, acquirers, banks and merchants such as Aduno, Concards, Cornercard, GE Money Bank, Swisscard, Telekus and Viseca co-operated in a single marketing initiative
Consumer targeted marketing:	75 per cent of the promotions with the partner banks and merchants focused on end users
To work with partner banks to acquire new cards, increase card usage, and move MasterCard cards to top of wallet	'Spot the Ball' national TV campaign (i.e. competition), wherein MasterCard holders required to spot the ball on still images from previous Euro matches with a chance to win Euro 2008 tickets and prizes
	On-site event activation (at all UEFA Euro 2008 stadiums):
	Exclusive payment partner in fan shops and PayPass at the UBS-Viewing Arenas in 16 Swiss cities (i.e. cross promotion with co-sponsors)
	'Photo Bus' in fan zones allowing fans to take photos alongside Euro 2008 trophy and MasterCard Football Ambassador Pierluigi Collina
	On-line presence (official website):
	Contests and promotions: allow football fans and cardholders to win match tickets, learn more about Pierluigi Collina – MasterCard Football Ambassador and purchase merchandise directly from the site using MasterCards
	Classical advertising:
	Global print and electronic advertising with a common theme spreading the message of 'Winning Moments'

Table 8.2 Adapted from Sport Business International (2008)

as this section intends to give a brief overview of sport sponsorship activation strategies with reference to successful examples from the global sponsorship industry.

Co-branding: is a new and advanced concept of image transfer wherein the brand and sporting property come closer in terms of values and consumer perception and yet retain their brand identities. This pro-actively managed process is conducted gradually over time and was used to great effect by adidas and the New Zealand Rugby Team. High visibility public relations activities, logo inclusion in all marketing collaterals and branding experience creates a relationship and reinforces a desired brand image.

Cause related marketing (CRM): creates consumer gratitude, often through grassroots development of sports where the brand demonstrates itself as an authentic partner of the sport that improves both image-based and direct sales-related outcomes like the partnership between UK Athletics and Aviva (formerly Norwich Union).

Sponsorship theme-based advertising: creative advertisements that reflect the character of the sponsored property. Electronic, print media, sport event programmes as well as outdoor advertising channels are used to present a common theme in order to intensify the relationship between the sponsor and the property in such a way that the target audience recognises, and is inclined to purchase, the sponsors products. For instance, Nike as an official apparel sponsor of the Indian cricket team used cricket themed advertisements set in a traffic-jammed Indian street to connect with Indian sport consumers (Fawkes, 2007).

Sponsorship leveraged packaging (SLP): enhances the overall effectiveness of the sponsorship investment by depicting the sponsored property's image, trademarks or logos on product packaging. Pepsi's use of David Beckham was particularly successful in this way.

Point-of-sale (POS) communications: many consumer purchase decisions are made at the point-of-sale locations (Fullerton, 2007). Sponsorship-related POS communication is supported by posters, shelf liners and new high-tech interactive displays placed in high-traffic locations.

Internet communications and website tie-ins: support existing offline marketing communications and offer sponsoring brands penetration and interactivity. The development of official websites was instigated to pursue web-marketing strategies such as provision of information, ticketing and merchandising related to promotion and transaction, and interactivity through relationship marketing with supporters.

The extent to which a sponsor involves its consumers with the sponsored property through well-implemented activation strategies determines the consumer's attitude and purchase intention towards the sponsors' products. IEG suggests that sponsorship will deliver a return on investment only when it is a central platform around which consumer, trade, internal and media activities are developed. The concept is important for sponsors, and for rights owners as well, in order for them to deliver solutions and provide results-based sponsorship programmes for their clients (Fullerton, 2007).

Case Study
Twenty20 cricket sport sponsorship management strategies: a comparison between India and the UK
Introduction

Sports sponsorship offers an opportunity for brands to get an edge over its competitors by differentiating and owning a distinct place in the consumer's mind. Technological developments are further driving sports sponsorship towards being an optimal positioning tool and a prime vehicle for marketers to deliver brand messages, enhance brand experiences and establish relationships with a diverse range of audiences on a global scale. This international comparative study analysed the sponsorship management practices applied to the new and innovative concept of Twenty20 cricket in the UK and India and highlighted the capabilities of sponsorship as an aspect of the promotional section of the sport marketing mix. Specifically, the study was designed to investigate:

- *the sponsorship management processes in terms of selecting the most appropriate sponsorship platform;*
- *how the sponsors in the UK and India are exploiting the marketing potential of the Twenty20 cricket platform;*
- *the activation of the sponsorship rights through an integrated approach.*

Methodology

A quantitative, non-probability sampling strategy was adopted as the targeted sample were official sponsors of the Twenty20 cricket cup in the UK and the DLF Indian Premier League. It comprised mainly the financial services/banks, sports equipment/apparel manufacturers, plus liquor/brewing companies in the UK and real estate organisations in the Indian sample. Respondents were senior brand/marketing/sponsorship managers in each organisation. A 20-item questionnaire was developed including questions, predominantly from previous studies to off-set issues of reliability and validity. A 31.1 per cent response rate was observed from the 91 targeted.

Findings and discussion

The integration of sponsorships into the marketing function featured in the planning processes of both countries. Surprisingly, the Indian sample appeared to be more target audience oriented and planned programmes that are more synergistic with the existing marketing communications and corporate plan. Organisations in both countries prioritise critical success factors and implement a rigorous selection procedure in acquiring sponsorship rights; however, the Indian sample appeared to be more strategic in nature.

Twenty20 cricket sponsorships have been integrated with an extensive range of marketing communications tools despite, in some instances, a limited activation budget, particularly in the UK. Public relations and sponsorship-theme-based TV, print and outdoor advertising emerged as the most effective sponsorship activation strategies, whereas traditional tools such as direct marketing and sales promotion were not considered very effective, along with new and emerging tools such as internet communications and CRM. Differences existed between activation strategies implemented and their respective reported effectiveness, in both the sample groups, suggesting a lack of understanding in the application of effectiveness of these techniques.

The study concluded by discussing the sponsorship management framework, along with the changing dynamics of the global sponsorship industry and the factors that are propelling the development of sports sponsorship management practice through the most effective means of deriving greater returns on investments for sponsoring organisations.

(Blakey and Chavan, 2011)

Learning Activity 8.2

Go to www.ecb.co.uk/ecb/partners/ to identify the corporate sponsors of Twenty20 cricket in England.

Go to three sponsor websites and identify how they utilise their sponsorship of Twenty20 cricket towards the achievement of their corporate objectives.

Stage 4: sponsorship effectiveness – evaluation

The integrated nature of sport sponsorship through the associated activation strategy makes its evaluation as an isolated function extremely difficult. Nevertheless, this does not negate the need to perform a process of evaluation to assess the effectiveness of the sport sponsorship programme. The setting of sport sponsorship objectives establishes a benchmark against which to gauge success and, as with any process of evaluation (see Chapter 12), this assessment can identify the need for corrective action where necessary. Both parties in the sport sponsorship agreement have input into the process and it can help to determine the future direction of the sponsorship relationship.

Sales objectives have become very important to organisations entering into sport sponsorship agreements, and so these are a straightforward means of assessing sponsorship performance, e.g. pre- and post-sport sponsorship activation sales figures tracked over time. A range of measures can be implemented, however, to assess broader performance along media-related or customer-related lines. Media exposure documents the type, frequency and duration a sport sponsor's name or logo appearing in TV, radio, print, or web sources. These 'metrics' apply a monetary value to them to give a greater sense of comparison to advertising value equivalents. Unfortunately, the direct comparison is not wholly reliable as there is no evidence of comparative validity between advertising and sponsorship. The deeper and broader capacity of sport sponsorship necessitates sport consumer evaluation to assess awareness and attitude effects. These require surveys and focus group interviews to determine the higher order recall, recognition and perception effects. Brand image and brand association angles can provide insight into brand equity and brand loyalty likelihood. Table 8.3 identifies the type and nature of evaluation questions that are asked of sport consumers and sponsors of sport. See Chapter 12 for further examples.

Learning Activity 8.3
Sport sponsorship proposal

In groups of three or four, construct a sponsorship proposal for a potential investor for one of the sport entities below:

- an elite snow-sport athlete;
- a semi-professional football team;
- a children's rugby 7s tournament;
- a women's netball team;
- a promising teenage tennis player.

Utilise the sport sponsorship proposal guidelines on page 117 to form the structure and content of your proposal.

Question	Response Categories
Sponsor	
How did your overall spending on sport sponsorship differ from the previous year?	Stayed the same Increased Decreased
What percentage of your organisation's total marketing budget was spent on sport sponsorship?	1–10 31–40 11–20 41–50 21–30 51+
Which of the following actions do you take before buying sport rights?	Objective setting Assessment of 'fit' Identify the interest of your target audience Planning of potential activation strategy Establish evaluation measures
Which of the following marketing communication channels have you used to activate your rights?	Advertising (TV, radio, print, web) Outdoor advertising PR Sales promotion Direct marketing Point-of-sale Product packaging Other
Sport consumer	
Which of the following do you identify with the Polo Masters Cup?	Rolex, Mercedes-Benz, Porsche, Ralph Lauren
In what order of importance for the event would you place the sponsors you named above?	Rolex 1 2 3 4 5 Porsche 1 2 3 4 5 Mercedes-Benz 1 2 3 4 5 Ralph Lauren 1 2 3 4 5

Table 8.3 Evaluation of sport sponsorship programme

Ambush marketing

It is pertinent to mention ambush marketing at this point, as the activity tends to raise its 'ugly head' in connection with sport sponsorship programmes. Ambush marketing refers to the practice of a company associating itself with a sport property when actually it has none. The most overt examples of this practice revolve around large-scale sport events such as the Olympic Games and Football World Cup between multinational companies in the same business sector such as Coca-Cola and Pepsi, Nike and adidas, and MasterCard and Visa. The association is created through TV and other media advertising, broadcast sponsorship, the purchase and leverage of subcategory rights, athlete sponsorship, and non-sport promotion (Smith, 2008).

You will no doubt remember the alleged ambush marketing attempt at the 2010 football World Cup in South Africa when 20 beautiful Dutch girls were 'advertising' an unofficial beer brand at the Netherlands v Denmark game. The attempt to prosecute the girls did seem a little extreme as I perceived the wearing of orange T-shirts simply to be a symbol of their support for the Dutch team, as no brand logos or names were on display. Nevertheless, this example indicates the sensitivities surrounding the practice of ambush marketing. It is right that companies who have invested heavily in the rights to a sport property should be able to activate those rights to best effect and, to this end, legislation is now in force across the world to aid this process. Legislation restrains ambush marketing activity, but cannot eradicate it. Perhaps the best method to manage ambush marketing is to plan for its existence by thinking like an ambusher. Sport sponsorship programmes now consider ambush marketing prevention, and these are defined within the rights packages on offer. For example, the sport venue is kept 'clean' from competitor names and logos; partners (sponsors and broadcasters) have clear boundaries for with whom they can sign further agreements (e.g. advertisers), and leveraging activity is encouraged to exploit the rights so that competitor communication messages are not heard.

Whilst rules are required for life in general, it is a pity that innovative sport promotion activity is discouraged when the sport sector could derive benefit from this additional revenue stream. It appears that 'anything does not go' in the business of sport, and that the lawyers have spied a lucrative income avenue!

Chapter Review

Sponsorship is a component of the ISMC mix, but it can create a communications plan all of its own through the activation of sports rights. Sponsorship is omni-present and big business in an increasingly competitive sport marketplace. Companies entering into sponsorship agreements are seeking more innovative solutions to the leveraging of the rights they have acquired. Activation strategies are now fundamental to bringing closer liaison between the sponsoring property and the sport target market. Their competent evaluation is also a key focus for establishing long-term relationships with partners.

Further Reading

Lagae, W. (2005) *Sports Sponsorship and Marketing Communications: A European Perspective*, London: Prentice Hall.
   This is the first book to describe the leverage of sports sponsorship with sport marketing communication.

Masterman, G. (2007) *Sponsorship for a Return on Investment*, Oxford: Butterworth-Heinemann.
   This text provides a unique insight on the use of sponsorship for a return on investment, building a conceptual framework for the development, planning, implementation and evaluation of strategies.

Chapter 9
Sport public relations

Learning Objectives

This chapter is designed to help you:

- appreciate the role of sport public relations in the sport communications mix;
- explain the role and importance of public relations in the sports industry;
- consider underlying theoretical components of sport PR;
- introduce a range of sport PR tools and techniques.

Introduction

Sport public relations (PR) is the final piece of the ISMC jigsaw. Sport PR adds a human dimension to the sport communication messages that sport organisations seek to project to each of their key publics. Sport organisations as social entities present an image into the sport marketplace derived from many factors including the personalities of famous sports people and the general perceptions of a given sport. Sport PR attempts to control this image, through portrayal of the sport, sport team, or sport player in the most favourable light.

In recent years, new challenges have arisen for each of these sport entities. In particular, developments in media technologies have changed the speed with which information is communicated around the globe. The increased power of the sport media has also meant that sport entities in all sections of the sport industry operate under a much more intense microscope. Every move that sport entities make, especially the star athletes, in their sporting and private lives is recorded and reported. The pressure this creates to perform well and conduct themselves with dignity in their everyday lives creates constant newsworthiness. Sport PR seeks to address these issues from a proactive and reactive standpoint, and is therefore, increasingly, a strategic sport promotion mix component that all sport entities should consider.

This chapter will focus on the importance of image as a sport communication tool for sport entities and develop an understanding of the techniques used to create an image of an athlete/sport/sport league. The management of sport PR will be considered, including one very important component, sport crisis communication, something the 'handlers' of Wayne Rooney will know a great deal about.

Sport public relations

There are many definitions of public relations with most defining it as maintaining a relationship with a public, be they investors, the media, employees, customers, the general public or government. The many definitions of public relations contain words such as 'mutual' and 'reciprocal' to describe the relationship a sport organisation has with its various publics. In line with the concept of ISMC, sport PR is fundamentally a communication medium that is used to tell the 'story' of the sport entity. Figure 9.1 identifies the variety of publics that a sport entity must 'speak' to through the activities of sport PR.

Figure 9.1 The publics of a sport organisation (adapted from Black, 1993)

Sport PR deals in an environment that has developed celebrity status in many quarters and, therefore is scrutinised very closely by the media. The proliferation of 24-hour media outlets, both sport and non-sport specific (see more in Chapter 10), seeking stories to fill their airtime, column inches, or web-space suggests that sport PR is more important to sport entities than to those in any other business sector. To date, the study of sport PR in academic circles has received only a cursory glance. Nevertheless, Hopwood and her associates (2010) have done some good work to develop the application of general public relations practice into the sport arena.

Sport PR is defined as

the management of information flow between a sport entity and its key publics, both internal and external, to present the sport organisation in the most favourable manner possible and to establish mutually beneficial relationships.

(Pederssen et al., 2007, p. 261)

At its core, sport PR seeks to promote a favourable image of the sport entity. In a competitive sport marketplace, sport brand image is one means of differentiation from competitors – just ask Tiger Woods or David Beckham. Image, and its management, enables professional athletes to make more money from endorsements than from pro contracts. Sport PR consultancies are, therefore, contracted to control public perception of sport entities to ensure the correct image is promoted. Sport PR is vital for constructing Intellectual Property (IP) – a term used to describe the individualism of a person/team/league (name, logo, likeness, photo, etc.) and is protected in law. It is the IP that is the brand value of the sport entity's image. It is the role of sport PR to protect the value of these sport brands.

The functions of PR

Sport PR has many functions as the remainder of the chapter will detail. These are the main functions according to Mullin et al. (2007):

- *Informing and communicating* – sport PR serves to maintain contact with the core support of a sport organisation. This is the most frequently utilised form of sport PR and it uses the full range of dissemination methods appropriate to each sport public.
- *Shaping and enhancing image* – a complex function through which the sport organisation attempts to show to its publics that its sport products/services are high quality and vital to the sport industry, and that the sport organisation is a responsible citizen in the local community. Consider the underlying reason for increased charitable activity in sport organisations today.
- *Promoting employee relations* – an open flow of information for morale purposes but, more importantly, so that employees can present the sport organisation honestly, and favourably, within their employed capacity and beyond it.
- *Gaining political or popular support* – an education function so that sport publics can appreciate the needs and requirements of sport organisations in the performance of all aspects of their business.
- *Recruiting and developing business* – to create an awareness of all opportunities the sport organisation is capable of providing; stadia require seven day per week revenue generation through entertainment and business-related activity.
- *Launching new products or innovations* – presenting new sport products/services so that target sport publics can make them a part of their lifestyle.
- *Generating and collecting feedback* – public attitudes, economic indicators, sport consumer preferences, societal events and their impact on the sport organisation.
- *Coping with crisis* – affecting the way sport publics interpret the actions and words of the principals involved in the crisis.

In all sports, there are always a few select athletes who could be described as iconic representatives for their sport. For example, in swimming we think of Michael Phelps, in tennis Roger Federer, Raphael Nadal, or Venus and Serena Williams, in rally driving Sebastian Loeb, in athletics Usain Bolt, and in downhill skiing Lyndsey Vonn. In order for sport PR professionals to create positive images of sports, they first need to build the IP of these athletes, creating 'heroes' (or figureheads) out of them. It is through these images that the objectives of sport PR can be implemented, as the athletes become the 'story'. Adopting a strategic sport PR philosophy is important so that a sport entity can attract media and supporter attention in the global sport market.

The strategic dimension to sport PR has dual foci: 1) a communications/media relations strategy; and 2) a relationship marketing/community relations strategy. Each of these will be outlined in greater detail shortly, but first the underlying conceptual components of sport PR need to be addressed. These are: persuasion and perception; sport reputation management; sport relationship management; and sport issues management.

Persuasion and perception

Seital (2001) suggested that individuals do not have strong opinions on most aspects of life, but attitudes can become settled once formed. These are influenced by 'opinion formers' based on evidence, such as facts and figures (e.g. about team/individual/sport organisation business performance), through personalisation of information (e.g. e-newsletters), and focused on sport consumer individual needs (e.g. the desire for one-on-one player interviews). The nature of the message can influence perception of the sport entity for different publics. For example, the enhancement of affiliation with the sport entity (e.g. loyalty) can be facilitated through frequent sport media exposure for high -involvement publics. Exclusive interviews with star players on team-owned media outlets such as MUTV or Chelsea TV speaks directly to loyal publics through the sport PR mix. This sport media channel will be perceived as having credibility, and can control the sport communication message. Understanding the perceptions of each public and presenting them with persuasive messages is a fundamental component of a sport PR strategy.

Sport reputation management

Reputation management is used to enhance or maintain the brand image of the sport entity. A positive reputation is extremely valuable and needs nurturing and protecting because once tarnished, it is incredibly difficult to recover. A sport entity with a good reputation is given more freedom to operate as it sees fit. Interdependence is created when the sport entity's publics form trust with the sport organisation. Another benefit of a good reputation is when the sport entity experiences a crisis; it will be less severe, as trust equity is traded. Sport PR professionals refer to this is as credibility on deposit (COD) (Young, 1995). A sport entity that wants a good reputation must build it based on mutual relationships, therefore, the sport organisation must listen to its publics. This is an on-going action within any sport PR strategy. Hopwood (2005) suggested that the development of a reputation occurs with strangers and that a relationship occurs with friends and associates. The development of a relationship marketing strategy is therefore necessary for many of the publics with whom a sport entity has contact (e.g. sponsors).

Sport relationship management

Developing relationships takes time and is probably the most important sport PR practice. Everyone in the sport organisation needs to be involved in relationship building, whereby a loyalty to the sport organisation by its publics is created. The concept of relationship marketing is at the centre of relationship management. Smith (2008) identified seven components of relationship marketing:

1   The creation of a relationship, or the initial attraction.
2   The development or enhancement of that relationship.
3   The maintenance or preservation of that relationship.
4   The interaction between two parties who co-operate and exchange things.
5   The potential for lasting long-term relationships.
6   The emotional elements of these relationships such as commitment and trust.
7   The potential for these relationships to be profitable and rewarding for both parties.

Relationship marketing recognises the long-term value of customer relationships and extends sport communication beyond intrusive advertising and sales promotional messages. The growth of the internet and mobile platforms has meant that relationship marketing has continued to evolve as technology opens more collaborative and social communication channels.

One concept that underpins relationship marketing is the 'ladder of customer loyalty' (customer in its widest sense, that is, each public; see Figure 9.2). The aim of the sport PR plan (see later section) is to move a sport public from being unaware of the sport organisation through to happy and returning 'partners'. Social media marketing (see Chapter 10) has the potential to reach out at each rung of the ladder. For example, 'suspects' read blogs, watch peer-generated video and listen to podcasts; 'prospects' use social networking sites such as Facebook; 'customers' use RSS feeds and tag web pages; 'clients' comment on blogs and post ratings and reviews; and 'advocates' publish web pages, maintain a blog and upload video to YouTube (Golvin, 2007). Of course not all publics will respond in these ways, but a multiple strategy approach pertinent to each public will enable the development of a closer relationship that is more profitable and rewarding for all parties.

Figure 9.2 The relationship marketing ladder

Actions speak louder than words; publics believe and trust action more than insincere words.

Sport issues management

A sport entity that practices issues management can prevent the need to withdraw from its credibility on deposit. Issues management 'is the proactive process of anticipating, identifying, evaluating and responding to public policy issues that affect [sport] organisations' relationships with their publics' (Cutlip et al., 2000, p. 17). In addition, issues management is the searching of trends or issues that might affect the sport organisation in the future, and steps are taken to position the sport organisation in a more favourable situation. An example of issues management was the death of Khazak cyclist Andrei Kivilev in the Paris–Nice race in 2004 which led directly to the compulsory wearing of helmets in the professional peleton. The UCI scanned the environment for relevant information and then applied the findings to prevent future crises. The policy has been successful, as no further tragedies of this kind have occurred since. Furthermore, the responsiveness of the UCI probably created a positive image in the perception of its publics.

If issues management is performed correctly a potential crisis may be averted, thereby negating the need for crisis management (see later section). This makes issues management a preventative technique within the realm of a sport PR strategy. The sport PR department identifies a possible issue and takes steps to mitigate the issue before it escalates. Early identification and early intervention are crucial to successful issues management.

Environmental scanning gathers pertinent information regarding the sport organisation and the sport organisation's publics. Monitoring the sport industry environment, trends and issues and aligning the sport organisation with this information is the basis of a sport PR strategy. However, sometimes information gathered during environmental scanning is not truthful; sport organisations should not ignore this information. Rumours can be just as disastrous as real events and strategies to overcome rumours can be devised (DiFonzo and Bordia, 2000).

Models of sport PR

The most frequent, and pertinent, theoretical interpretation of the approaches to sport PR is outlined by Grunig and Hunt's (1984) Four Models of PR.

Press Agentry/Publicity Model. Model 1 is referred to as the press agentry–publicity model. It suggests that any publicity is good, whether the information is negative, positive, true or false. The main purpose is to get the name of the sport entity out to the publics. Information is transferred one-way (from the sport entity to the audience), and does not allow for feedback from the audience. The process of research is not used in this approach. The selling of sport event tickets is an example of this method.

Public Information Model. Model 2 involves the one-way transfer of information as in Model 1, however, it allows for limited research and some evaluation of the programme. It is used by government organisations, including UK Sport and Sport England, to supply objective and accurate information (e.g. regulatory material). Model 2 requires truth in its reporting of information and primarily produces media guides, press releases and the staging of press conferences.

Two-Way Asymmetrical Model. Model 3 (also called the scientific persuasion model) tries to persuade audiences to accept the sport organisation's point of view. The feedback involved in this model is usually done through surveys and polls in which the sport entity finds out audience thoughts and feelings about the sport organisation and then uses that information to push its agenda. The model is sport organisation centric.

Two-Way Symmetrical Model. Model 4 (also called the mutual understanding model) is the basis of an excellent sport PR strategy. This model seeks dialogue with the audience. The sport entity uses feedback from the audience in its decision-making, ultimately giving the audience power within the sport organisation. Website forums and blogs are good examples of methods that can be used to integrate feedback from one key public – fans.

Public relations practitioners that primarily practice models one or two are called practitioners of craft public relations, as they simply put information out to the appropriate sport media. This is merely a sport communications role. Those who practice models three and four are called public relations professionals as they have 'strategic purpose for an organisation: to manage conflict and build relationships with strategic publics that limit the autonomy of the [sport] organisation' (Spicer, 1997, p. 65), that is, a responsive approach that considers other publics and not simply the sport organisation's own agenda.

Summary

To recap, sport PR is:

- more than just dealing with the press or media;
- a corporate, financial, marketing, community, and internal activity;
- not optional;
- concerned with reputation and credibility;
- proactive and/or reactive;
- uncontrollable but can be planned for;
- not how the sport organisation/entity sees itself, but how it is perceived;
- a two-way process.

The role of sport PR

The corporate sport climate means that sport entities, especially the athletes, have to be socially presentable, astute and a little humble. Some have to work just as hard off the field as on it to be a good role model who presents a favourable image to each of their publics. An athlete's PR success is proportional to their ability to deal with the media and public expectations.

The popularity of many sports ebbs and flows over time. For example, sports such as cricket and snooker have had times of low interest; however, sport PR has worked hard to rebuild the popularity of these sports through the development of new sport brands, e.g. Twenty20 cricket and Power Snooker that present a new TV-friendly 'face' of the sport and showcases the talents of the athletes.

Training for the demands of corporate and media appearances is becoming more common, so that a professional presentation style emerges. The skills developed by sport PR training programmes, as implemented by the British Olympic Association (BOA), focus upon interview technique. The summary points to remember for TV, radio or written media interviews are:

- Be yourself.
- Show emotion – show how you feel.
- Think before you speak. Before you have the interview, think what possible issues could arise. Think what you want to say and have a clear view as to how to tackle difficult issues. Prior to interview ask the interviewer what the questions will be. If there is a difficult issue, don't avoid it. If you're not willing to give your views then someone may make up your views for you.
- Be natural. Do not be over prepared, you will come across false.
- Have a conversation with the person giving the interview. Forget about the millions of people listening and watching! Listen carefully and answer each question.

- Speak clearly – not too fast (even if excited).
- Look the interviewer in the eye – you will come across as a sincere, believable person.
- For TV and radio, answers should not be too short, that is, one word, but don't ramble. They may only have a small time slot and you can cover several points.
- Sponsor coverage should be subtle. Any blatant logos may be edited.
- Don't alienate the media. Be open and available for interview and they will report favourably. Build relationships with sports journalists.
- Enjoy it. People want to know about you. Sell your sport. Especially minor sport (adapted from the BOA Athletes' Guide to Dealing with the Media, undated).

Nevertheless, some athletes who have benefitted from such media training are not always able to follow the protocol. It can be very difficult not to reveal your true feelings after a race defeat (or win) when a microphone is pushed into your face for an immediate view. The 'Manx Missile' Mark Cavendish, the most successful British Tour de France rider of all time is one good example. Cav is natural, speaks clearly, enjoys talking, but sometimes tells it a bit too much as it is and leaves the expletives in his comments. Refreshing yes, but his team HTC-Columbia often have to issue apologies on Mark's behalf. Go to www. markcavendish.co.uk to see Cav in action.

This example, and there are many others, indicates that sport organisations construct a PR strategy that evaluates the potential damage to its image, reputation and relationships by taking steps to limit it. This is an example of sport crisis management.

Sport crisis management

A crisis is a turning point for better or for worse brought on by an issue or event that has the potential for widespread, long lasting impact. Athletes, coaches, or sport organisations can suddenly find themselves in the middle of controversy – think of betting scandals in cricket or horseracing; doping in athletics; and as for football (play acting, refereeing errors, attempted rape claims, extra marital affairs, attacking fellow citizens, drink-driving), the PR people are busier off the pitch than the midfield players are on it! Sport, on and off the field, can be a dirty business with the threat of a crisis ever-present. Therefore, sport organisations are constantly in crisis management mode.

Sport crisis management practice prepares a sport organisation strategically and logistically for a crisis. This removes some of the risk, and so allows the sport organisation to implement damage limitation when necessary. Sport crisis communication sets those activities into action; it is the actual verbal and written communication between the sport organisation and the various publics prior, during and after management of a crisis.

A sport crisis manual is a tool that enables a sport organisation to respond quicker, better and with confidence to sensitive issues in the media. It is crucial in order to maintain, or in some cases repair, the image of a sport entity. Swift and honest dialogue with the various publics indicates that a crisis is being managed and corrections are being made. Having pertinent materials and documents on-hand, and in particular having a knowledgeable spokesperson to address the sport media will enhance the image left with fans and the media. Nevertheless, during a crisis it does not always matter what the facts are, but what the public thinks the facts are. The public may give a sport organisation the benefit of the doubt, if a strong relationship has been fostered.

> ## Reflection Point 9.1
>
> The issue of honesty is a point worth considering for a moment. Many sport entities, especially those with the biggest sport media profiles, would do well to simply be honest about the crises they face. When was the last time you heard a star athlete tell the truth when faced with the option of doing so after being involved in a controversy? Did snooker champion John Higgins really 'throw' frames for money; Alberto Contador really eat contaminated beef; or Wayne Rooney really sleep with ...?

Some crisis situations are personal issues that the sport media feed off for weeks or months. Where an honest denial or acceptance can be issued it really should be forthcoming to move on past the claims and counter claims – lawyers again! A more serious question that could be asked is 'When did Wayne Rooney last visit a local school in Salford to give a coaching clinic or for a Q & A session?' It is all well and good interacting with young footballers for a high profile (and potentially lucrative) Sky TV show, but if the logic of sport PR is to be followed, greater good (for self, team and sponsors) could be effected by generating a favourable relationship with local kids. I have a phrase for the philosophy that should underpin sport PR, and that is 'professional athletes as community assets'. Who buys the tickets, the merchandise, the sponsors' products and services, Sky Sports? Yes, the fans do. Professional sport clubs would not exist without the patronage of the local (and wider) community. Perhaps a little recompense, as is the case in Rugby League where players often visit schools, could be a wider sport PR strategy in a very competitive sport marketplace. The fostering of goodwill does, however, have an effect on the golf handicap of a very well paid sports person!

Sport crisis management models

To conceptualise sport crisis management for a moment, Gonzalez-Herrero and Pratt (1995) proposed a four-phase crisis life cycle similar to the sport PLC. The crisis life cycle passes through birth, growth, maturity and death and a sport marketing intervention can occur at any point. Phase One scans the environment for public trends or for crises affecting competitors that may in turn affect the sport organisation. Sport PR activity aims to deter its onset. Phase Two recognises that a crisis is about to occur and a proactive policy needs to be set into motion. Phase Three is the sport organisation's response to the crisis, and Phase Four monitors the various publics until the crisis has subsided completely. The model draws upon reputation management approaches to consider preventative measures to minimise sport crisis issues. It does, however, need to more fully consider sport entities' developing relationships with their publics so that closer on-going liaison can in itself off-set the potential for crisis.

As with all elements of ISMC, planning is central to sport PR and so the need for a strategic sport PR plan is a necessity. Here is an overview structure of a sport PR plan to help you place the many facets mentioned in this chapter into a coherent whole.

The sport PR plan

(See further reading for more information.)

1 Corporate mission and objectives

These must be in evidence at all stages of the sport PR plan to guide activities. The mission and objectives guide the philosophy and values that underpin the sport PR message.

2 Situational analysis

Undertaken as part of the broader on-going audit of the internal and external environments for the sport organisation as a whole. Particular focus is provided by the sport communications audit that identifies the effectiveness of current activity; consistency across the sport organisation; and uses benchmarks to measure current awareness levels.

3 Sport PR objectives

As with all objectives, those for sport PR are SMART, consistent and shared throughout the sport organisation. For example, a community-relations plan would likely seek to:

- cultivate greater personal and emotional involvement between the players and the fans;
- secure positive publicity through involvement in charitable events;
- develop goodwill within the community by showing commitment to local events.

4 Sport PR strategy

Target the various publics (internal and external) through a variety of sport PR tools and techniques. Research during the situational analysis feeds the tone and style of the editorial policy; publishing details, e.g. frequency/copy deadlines; circulation/audience, e.g. size, area, coverage and reader profile. This ensures that there is consistency between the messages and objectives for each target public.

A community-relations plan revolves around personal appearances, and these would include: schools, sponsors, charities, and outreach programmes.

5 Implementation plan

Sport PR activities are outlined with times, target results, and responsibilities stated (see example of sport communications plan in Chapter 7).

6 Set budget

Costings for each sport PR function, with an overall summary.

7 ISMC

Co-ordination with all sport promotion mix components is crucial in the provision of effective and efficient sport PR solutions.

8 Evaluation

Evaluation activity can occur in the following ways:

- sport event – attendance/sponsorship/participant numbers;
- equivalent advertising costs;
- shift and/or quality in awareness/reputation;
- impact value in overcoming crisis;
- enquiries/complaints received;
- frequency of reports/sightings;
- sport market share improvement.

Evaluation is an on-going process across all sport PR activity. Sport PR adds nothing to the bottom-line of a sport organisation; in fact it is a cost. However, with a fully operational strategic approach, sport PR can reward the sport organisation immeasurably with its ability to develop and maintain relationships.

To complete this chapter we need to consider the two strategic foci of sport PR mentioned earlier – media relations-based strategy and community relations-based strategy.

Media relations-based strategy

A media relations-based strategy aims to enhance the relationship between the sport entity and the media to facilitate maximisation of positive media coverage. It is essential when creating the IP of a sport entity that the most appropriate media is utilised. Public opinion is very powerful and can 'make or break' the relationship between a sport entity and its various publics. The issue of honesty is pertinent again here, as the media do not always report the facts and are seeking an 'angle' to report. Mistrust of the media can lead to less openness in the relationship and so contravene the central tenet of sport PR. Nevertheless, the main sport PR tools and techniques are identified in Table 9.1.

With reference again to the BOA Athletes' Guide to Dealing with the Media (undated), it is possible to draw upon the features of the main forms of media contact that a sport entity (in this case an athlete) would have with the media.

Why deal with the media?

- To build a personal profile.
- To build the profile of the sport.
- To promote a sponsor.

Understanding the media

There are two basic types of media:

1 Broadcast – radio and television.
2 Written.

Sport PR Media	What it does . . .
Advertorials	An advertisement written in the form of an objective article, and presented in a printed publication. It is designed to look like a legitimate news story but the tone of an advertorial is usually closer to that of a press release.
Feature articles	Feature stories are becoming more common as they can be more engaging to read. At many newspapers, news stories are sometimes written in 'feature style,' adopting some of the conventions of feature writing while still covering breaking events.
Spokespeople	Many sport organisations are employing professionals who have received formal training in journalism, communications, and PR in order to ensure that public announcements are made in the most appropriate fashion and through the most appropriate channels to maximise the impact of favourable messages, and to minimise the impact of unfavourable messages. Popular local and national sports stars are often chosen as spokespeople for commercial advertising purposes.
Direct mail (letters/email)	A common form of direct marketing. Advertisers refine direct mail practices into targeted mailing, in which mail is sent out following database analysis to select recipients considered most likely to respond positively.
Newsletters	A regularly distributed publication about one main topic of interest to subscribers. Newsletters delivered electronically (e-newsletters) have gained rapid acceptance for the same reasons email in general has gained popularity over printed correspondence.
Face-to-face (WOM/Urban tactics)	Encompasses a variety of subcategories, including buzz, blog, viral, grassroots, cause influencers and social media marketing, as well as ambassador programmes; can be highly valued by sport marketers. A layer of credibility is added to the sport product/service through this advocacy.

Table 9.1 Sport PR media tools and techniques (from various sources including Goodman (1998), Grewal et al. (2003), Merriam-Webster (2010) and www.wikipedia.org)

Broadcast

Radio

This is a very flexible medium that operates pretty much 24 hours a day. It is an immediate medium because of its ability to turn around interviews and features quickly.

Radio covers sport in three basic forms:

1   Live coverage of events.

2   News – sports bulletins and radio programmes.
3   Magazines and documentary programmes which look behind the scenes.

As a result of its nature, radio gives minor sports a great opportunity to gain coverage especially through local and regional radio. There is also the possibility of gaining coverage at the Olympic Games through BBC Radio 5, which collates both national and regional coverage for broadcast.

So what makes a good interview:

- trying to answer succinctly;
- trying not to 'um' and 'er';
- always turning up on time;
- preparation.

Television

Television interviews will either be done in the studio/outside broadcast unit or at a venue. They will either be live or pre-recorded depending on deadlines and the accessibility of technical equipment.

Television covers sport across the same basic areas as radio and will operate across the following formats:

- live coverage;
- recorded coverage;
- studio-based items;
- outside broadcast items;
- news;
- documentary feature programmes.

There are two main areas of TV:

- terrestrial TV, e.g. BBC and ITV;
- satellite/cable, e.g. Sky, Eurosport.

Television offers the strongest opportunity to get a message across because sound combined with vision creates the most powerful method of delivering a point of view. Like radio, TV can be a very immediate outlet and relies on many of the same techniques to deliver its messages.

Techniques for TV interviews:

- Before the interview, ask:
  - TV company and programme name;
  - Type of programme and the expected audience;
  - What the interview will be about.
- Always assume that you are being recorded.
- Eye contact with the interviewer – very important.
- Don't fidget!
- Listen to the question and answer it straight on.

- Speak clearly.
- Plan ahead. There are only five questions – how, what, why, where and when.
- Never be condescending.
- Take three deep breaths before the interview starts.
- Smile and enjoy it (www.olympics.org.uk).

Written media

The written media covers everything from local/regional papers through to national papers and magazines. There are an increasing number of magazines coming into the market place these days offering athletes the chance to gain coverage in sports specific magazines or more general lifestyle publications. The written media representatives can be grouped into four main areas:

1 News reporters – looking for a story, often linked to scandal.
2 Sports reporters – supportive to athletes and sport.
3 Columnist – looking for an overview. Opinion based.
4 Feature writer – covers sport/athlete in depth.

Press conferences

The reason for having a press conference is to brief the media on major issues whether they be proactive, such as highlighting aims of forthcoming competition or reactive to events that have already taken place. A press conference could take place prior to, during or after a competition depending on the circumstances.

Preparation:

- Make sure you are aware of its purpose and the message you want to get across.
- Issue a press release to coincide with the press conference. This should also include an explanation as to why you wish to hold the press conference.
- Talk through potential question and answer situations that might arise in advance.
- Prepare a press pack for the media attending. This folder should include a press release, and other relevant background information.

Press release

A means of getting your message/information across to the media. It should be short and to the point. Basic guidelines for writing a release are:

- Who, What, When, Where and Why.
- Try to put a quote into the release that the media can use in their stories.
- Put contact details on the bottom of the release so that the media can contact someone for further information or to arrange interviews.

Example Press Release

The Queen to visit Wimbledon
17 May 2010
*STATEMENT FROM TIM PHILLIPS, CHAIRMAN OF THE ALL ENGLAND LAWN TENNIS
CLUB, CONCERNING THE PROPOSED VISIT TO WIMBLEDON BY HM THE QUEEN, PATRON
OF THE ALL ENGLAND LAWN TENNIS CLUB, ON THURSDAY 24 JUNE 2010*

*'We are delighted and honoured that the Queen has indicated that she will be attending The
Championships this year and we very much look forward to welcoming Her Majesty back to
Wimbledon.'*

*'Wimbledon has changed considerably since the Queen's previous visit in 1977, most
notably with a transformation of the infrastructure bringing new and much improved
facilities, including the Centre Court roof which was unveiled last year.'*

*'What has not changed, though, is the essential character of Wimbledon, created
by the passion of players and spectators alike who want to be part of one the world's
most exhilarating sporting events. It will certainly be an exciting occasion for everyone
here.'*

(www.wimbledon.org, 2010)

Learning Activity 9.1

All sport occasions create interest so write a press release for the next sports match you are to
participate in. In addition to the basic content, consider likely interested parties and utilise language
that they will understand.

Community relations-based strategy

A community relations-based strategy has emerged to deliver out-reach programmes aimed at enhancing
understanding and gaining public approval and acceptance of the sport entity. A successful strategy
will promote goodwill and lead to public support for the sport entity (Irwin and Sutton, 1996). Such a
strategy is player, team or league initiated, but player involvement is central to all. This element is lost in
many community relations PR strategies as my earlier point about athletes as community assets noted.
Contractual obligation to undertake regular community activities, as is performed in rugby league, should
be considered across all sports to foster good relations with all publics. The following guidelines are set in
relation to requests for player appearances at St Helens Rugby League Club:

As part of the club's policy of serving the local community, St Helens RLFC is aware that its players are perceived as role models within our community. Players will be available to make appearances on behalf of schools, not-for-profit organisations and community events.

CRITERIA:
In order for appearances to be beneficial for all involved and to assist in the selection of possible appearances the club has put together the following criteria:

- *There needs to be a clear role for players at each of the appearances.*
- *All appearances must ensure that the maximum number of people are influenced by the visit (an entire school assembly rather than classroom).*
- *Each organisation is limited to one appearance per calendar year (unless otherwise agreed).*
- *The requests must be non-activity based.*
- *The requests must last up to a maximum of one hour.*
- *All appearances are subject to club approval and are not guaranteed.*

PLAYER AVAILABILITY:
Players are available on a rota basis and at the discretion of the club. Requests for particular players cannot be guaranteed. Players are also unable to attend events 24 hours before a match day.

(www.saintsrlfc.com)

Appearances such as this are particularly pertinent for the objectives of a community relations strategy as they tend to be longer term, e.g. fan development. Nevertheless, it is possible to measure its impact through structured activity that results in ticket sales, merchandise sales, sponsor interest and value.

One strand of a community relations-based PR strategy that has developed recently is corporate philanthropy. This is corporate giving and indicates that sport entities have a social conscience and want to be seen as a 'good neighbour'. However, this role model status necessitates socially responsible behaviour, something some sport entities find difficult. Linked to this approach has been the creation of 'foundations' that take on the charitable focus of the sport entity. For example, the Chelsea FC Foundation supports a local 'Help a London Child' charity and an international charity 'Right to Play' (www.chelseafc. com). Similarly, the Manchester United FC Foundation has charity partnerships with two local charities – Francis House Children's Hospice and The Christie Charity, and continues its long-standing partnership with UNICEF (www.manutd.com).

Along this vein, the Tennis Foundation of the Lawn Tennis Association (LTA) is developing fun tennis opportunities for all through their *One Game All* theme. However, this initiative requires funding, rather than being monetarily philanthropic, and so the Foundation seeks more resources for community tennis through EU and government sport funding schemes (www.lta.org.uk).

Case Study
Lance Armstrong

Seven times Tour de France winner, cancer survivor, cancer campaigner, father of five children and resident of Texas, Lance Armstrong was to ride his last international professional cycle race at the Santos Tour Down Under in Adelaide, Australia in January 2011 and then go on to complete the Rotorua Triathlon in New Zealand (No – 'hold the home page', it's off as he has a sore knee! Actually, it is all over, Lance has retired – again!).

Lance was reviled by many cycling fans, especially in France, at the height of his successes due to being perceived as brash and outspoken. Lance is currently under federal investigation for doping offences after allegations were made against him by an ex-teammate. With an extremely busy daily schedule of meetings, training and family life, Lance used Twitter as a PR tool to communicate his message to interested parties. This approach informs fans, the cycling press and broader media outlets sufficiently for them not to request more of Lance and for him to have to say no.

Lance's tweets (and picture and video posts) suggest an agenda related to his good works e.g.

Holy ....!@movember raises more than 63 million bucks! All of us @LIVESTRONG are so psyched to be your partners. http://tinyurl.com/2by7qyr

   Re. the Livestrong Foundation;

@LIVESTRONG & @AmericanCancer just had gr8 meeting w/ @AmbassadorRice's team @ the US Mission to UN re: global health & cancer. Excellent!

RT @LIVESTRONG Help us reach our goal of 10,000 surveys taken-We need 658 more. http://bit.ly/bEGyl1 Don't have to have had cancer-Please RT

   Re. his LIVESTRONG Cancer Foundation

Made it to Al Asad, Iraq, hung w/ the troops, had some bkfst, and now off to the next base. True honor to be here.

   Rocking crowd last night here in Bagram, Afghanistan. We're all so humbled and honoured to be here! http://post.ly/1LGFz;

   Admiral Mullen talking to the troops. Great man. http://post.ly/1KXep

   Re. his visit to Iraq and Afghanistan to meet US troops in December 2010

Family dinner @UchiAustin. Cool when your kids finally start digging sushi and want to eat it. Lucky us;

   6 mi run w/ @maxarmstrong1 in the baby jogger. Little man loves that.

   Hanging poolside w/ a beautiful lady. A certain @cincoarmstrong. http://post.ly/1GqDn

Re. his family

Interestingly, Lance tweeted his sporting activities as his alias Juan Pelota (Spanish for one ball – go figure!), the name of the café at his bike shop Mellow Johnny's (sounds like Maillot Jaune – French for yellow jersey). Cycling aficionados like me love this kind of thing ...

   Go to http://twitter.com/lancearmstrong to see more.

Opportunities for sport PR practitioners

Sport marketing offers a myriad of opportunities to utilise the public interest to promote sport products and services, and there is a huge opportunity for sport PR practitioners in this field. Below is an actual advertisement for the post of a Sport Marketing and PR Intern, a position you may like to apply for before the end of your studies:

Sport marketing and PR intern

The individual must possess the following knowledge, skills and abilities and be able to explain and demonstrate that he or she can perform the essential functions of the job:

- Execute Consumer Promotions;
- Execute Targeted Marketing Initiatives;
- Perform Competitive Analysis and Research;
- Instigate Internet/Web Marketing;
- Research and recommend new social media tactics to build our sport brand;
- Develop and execute tactics with social media tools to help us drive our sport marketing priorities (building awareness, collecting insight about guests, increasing guest loyalty, etc.);
- Implement Public Relations such as writing press releases;
- Possess strong written and oral communications skills;
- Possess strong organisational and research skills.

Once experience has been gained you may be able to move to a more senior role and would therefore require the attributes detailed here:

Sport PR manager

Description: An international marketing agency based in central London seeks an experienced Public Relations manager to take on a new client in the Sports Equipment sector and manage all their PR both online (social media) and through trade and national press. Applicants will need over 4 yrs commercial PR experience and experience in the sports industry. This role will initially be for 12 months and has the potential to turn into a full-time post.

Salary: £30–40 k depending on experience + bonus + health benefits.

Chapter Review

Sport PR is an important and versatile sport marketing communications tool and forms an intrinsic part of the integrated sport marketing communications (ISMC) mix. Sport PR creates and maintains mutually beneficial long-term relationships with key groups of people – sport consumers, sponsors, the media etc. In this respect, sport PR has seen a dramatic increase in prominence as a strategic internal and external sport marketing communications tool. Sport PR builds an understanding a sport entity has with its 'publics', which augments the credibility of sport communication messages by improving image and reputation. Sport PR can lead to competitive advantage in the sport marketplace. It is not optional and it can either be proactive or reactive, but it must be planned. As the sport industry grows, opportunities for sport PR practitioners are developing in areas including: image protection; contract negotiations; sport crisis management planning; and media training. Sports bodies are moving beyond the basics of sport PR as they have realised it is important in competing for corporate patronage.

Further Reading

Hopwood, M.K. (2005) 'Public relations practice in English county cricket', *Corporate Communications: An International Journal* 10, 3: 201–212.

The main reason for conducting this research was to conduct an analysis of the extent of public relations activity in domestic first-class cricket in an attempt to offer a strategy for effective, proactive public relations. Durham CCC has already implemented some of the proposals and the author's continuing work with other sports organisations has been founded on this research.

Hopwood, M., Skinner, J., Kitchin, P. and Chadwick, S. (2010) *Sport Public Relations and Communication*, London: Butterworth-Heinemann.

This is the first book to explore PR and communications in the sports industry in a global context. It brings together applicable strategies for the sport marketing student, and provides a concise guide to how public relations and communications strategies and principles can be applied to sport marketing issues.

Chapter 10
Sport media

This chapter is designed to help you:

- consider technological developments in traditional and new sport media formats;
- investigate the implications for sport marketing of new sport media formats;
- identify social media sport marketing practice.

Introduction

The traditional sport media formats of TV, radio and print continue to dominate sport consumption for sport audiences away from the live sport venue. Nevertheless, new media technologies are affecting the way sport consumers are demanding sport, and the sport industry is responding. The digital revolution has arrived and sport media technology has jumped on board. The traditional platforms now bring exciting new viewing and listening opportunities, and these are enhanced by web and mobile communication channels. For sport marketers, social media and the opportunities to engage with sport consumers via social networking is the new frontier. This chapter considers the advancement of technologies for traditional and new sport media formats and considers some of the implications of these developments for an increasingly 'tech savvy' sport consumer in a very competitive sport marketplace.

The state of play

You may be familiar with many of the facets of sport media technology as they exist today. However, this really is a fast-moving, sport consumer-driven subject. There is a significant effect upon sport marketing practice, as sport organisations seek to understand the implications of the technological developments and utilise its potential to create competitive advantage in the sport marketplace. The sport media sector is accepting of the technological advancements presented and is bringing forward sport products/services that provide enhanced quality of sport experience in a convergent digital landscape. Critically, this landscape is able to deliver an interactive and responsive sport product/service that is targeted at the changing lifestyle and expectations of the sport consumer.

The fundamental component of sport media for sport marketing purposes is its ability to convey a message – the sport communication message. Previous chapters have considered approaches to the generation and communication of the sport product/service, however, the key here is for an appreciation and understanding of the mediums through which those communication messages are conveyed. To add context to the discussion, many of the key issues surrounding the ability of sport media to create, and enhance, the consumption of sport will be considered.

The two distinctive components of sport media are: 1) traditional sport media; and 2) new sport media. Each form is digesting the technological advances available, but it is important to remember that whilst the technology undoubtedly improves the quality of the consumption experience of the sport product/service for the sport consumer, the sport product/service effectively stays the same. A tennis match at Wimbledon is a tennis match at Wimbledon, is a tennis match at Wimbledon (yes thrice), but the enjoyment of the match is facilitated by armchair gadgets that help to engage our senses in new ways. Before considering traditional and new sport formats in more detail, it is pertinent to outline the broader sport media context.

How it works

The fundamental business plan for all sport media platforms is the same – a combination of advertising and/or subscription. Sport consumers subscribe to Sky Sports to receive English Barclays Premier League football, Aviva Premiership rugby union, golf, darts etc. and purchase the products and services advertised on the hoardings that surround the sport venue or the banners that pop-up across web-based sport content. Fortunately, for sport rights holders and broadcasters, consumers of sport love watching live sports on TV and like watching highlights programmes. This demand for sport, therefore, will drive revenues and interest in the consumption of sport via the digital platforms now available. However, there is tension between sports rights holders and broadcasters regarding the awarding of rights. The Court of the European Union in 2007 ruled that the practice of awarding sole live rights for English Premier League football to Sky TV was uncompetitive. This ruling necessitated six rights packages be created and sold separately. The packages consisted of live rights for a period of three years that featured games occurring at a particular time on a particular day; the 'premier' package being kick-off at 4 pm on Sunday afternoon. A process of sealed bidding took place to establish the highest bidder, and therefore winner, of each package. Across two such bidding cycles since the end of season 2006/7, Sky TV has won five of the six packages, only succumbing to a bid from a competitor for Saturday evening games kicking-off at 5.30 pm. Unfortunately, the Irish broadcaster, Setanta Sports, who won the live rights could not generate sufficient subscriber numbers to be sustainable and ceased broadcasting in Britain in 2009. The US, Disney-owned giant ESPN picked up the rights and is establishing a foothold in sports broadcasting in the UK.

The multinational broadcaster BSkyB, owners of Sky TV and the Sky Sports brand, is an excellent example of the evolution of the sport PLC. From its inception in 1990, growth in subscribers began with the securing of live English football rights for the 1992/93 season, and the establishing of the English Premier League. The popularity of the league has grown significantly, and symbiotically, as subscriber numbers have increased alongside demand to watch matches live at the grounds. This is evidence that pay-TV is no barrier to the level of interest shown by sport consumers in a given sport. The pay-TV model has been applied in a similar way in rugby league, rugby union, cricket, boxing and golf in the UK, although the same effect on live spectatorship is still to fully emerge.

Audience size

One other fundamental aspect to the function of sport media is the size of the sport audience. All media formats monitor audience size, be that subscriber numbers or audience share for a sport event, actual sales numbers of a sport publication, or hits on a website. It really is all about the size (not my assessment!) in this industry, as broadcasters and advertisers calculate the cost and value of their investments by size of audience. Clearly, decisions are made about which sports to 'buy into' and how advertising revenues can be stimulated on a size of audience basis. The changes in the sport media industry with the advent of web and mobile communications has meant the management of sports rights has become more difficult as broadcasters seek to understand which sport media platform will operate best for a particular sport property. This process is compounded by the speed of roll out of new technologies, as it is occurring at different rates in countries across the world.

The size issue is particularly pertinent as the emergent sport media formats create an increasingly fragmented sport market. The increased number of viewing options for sport and the increased airtime available from 24-hour sport channels does mean that less popular/minority sports have an opportunity to capture some of that space. This development brings new sport audiences into the marketplace, but can mean that some audience share is lost for existing programmes. Programming is becoming more targeted, e.g. the Extreme Sports Channel targets the youth audience – a notoriously difficult sport target segment to reach. This segment is deemed pro-active in attracting discerning viewers who seek out sport programmes. These viewers will multi-task (Generation M) by watching TV and surfing online at the same time (Curran, 2008). Habits such as this necessitate content that reflects the consumption behaviour patterns established, thus opportunities for greater exposure of minority sports is being enabled by web technology, and web streaming specifically.

Clearly, new sport media formats have begun to make in-roads into the viewing habits of receptive sport consumers with the aim of generating revenue through web and mobile communications. TV revenues (advertising and subscription) still dominate in the sport media world, but the ability to advertise one-to-one on the web and mobile, and to measure its impact, means that this form of advertising becomes a highly targeted media spend. Having made a purchase on www.wiggle.com recently, I returned to my browser home page to see a quarter page-revolving advert from Wiggle for associated items. Here the web scraping and indexing technology, along with paid advertising had been enacted to draw me back to the site. This was their second attempt after a 'You might also like to consider these items' message on several pages of the website whilst I was there initially.

The broadcasters are also considering their digital convergence approach. Brand strength is being leveraged to extend the brand across multiple platforms. In the UK, Sky TV is at the forefront of convergence having entered the broadband and telephone markets. Sky Sports content can now be accessed across TV, online and mobile platforms. Similarly, BT – originally the national telephone company – has established Internet Protocol TV (IPTV) through BT Vision. This is the ability to connect the internet and TV via a home-hub; Virgin Media has a similar cable-based system. Their impact on the sport marketplace is taking effect, as the power-base of English sport – live Premier League football – is now available via these companies after legal wrangling as Sky TV responded to the competition by extending their online sports content on Sky Player free-of-charge to all Sky Sports TV subscribers. This is a good example of cross-promotion of medium to encourage new sport consumption behaviour activity and to defend their current position in the market by adding value to the current sport product/service.

Two further observations about the development of digital media platforms is the ability of high-definition (HD) TV to transform the viewing experience of the sport consumer. HDTV will very soon be the norm. Finally, the craze that appears to be social media and, in particular, social networking. There are commercial opportunities here, something that major sport organisations such as Nike are seeking to exploit. Currently, this form of new sport media is causing a major buzz in the sport marketing world.

We now return to the two distinctive components of sport media to investigate some of their inherent technological advancements and the impact on the sport consumer.

Traditional sport media

Traditional sport media relates specifically to TV, radio and print (newspapers and magazines) formats. These formats still dominate in terms of the sport audience and revenue streams from subscription and advertising. Radio emerged as the first mass communication medium in the 1920s, bringing the sounds of live sport and the names of sports people to the airwaves that the sport audience could recognise. The format of live commentary, phone-ins, debates etc. has emerged recently to engage listeners on sport-only radio such as talkSPORT as competing mediums have continued to evolve. Radio is used as a complementary medium to TV, since TV emerged as the dominant force in the late 1940s. However, the current boom was enabled in the 1980s with the advent of cable and satellite pay-TV broadcasters such as Sky TV. The traditionally dominant channels, BBC, ITV and Channel 4, have been squeezed of sport content as the dedicated sport channels of Sky Sports, Eurosport and ESPN have arrived.

The print media includes newspapers, magazines, books, and the internet. Originally in printed format, the advance of technology has moved the sport consumer increasingly towards e-formats. As with all sections of the sport industry, sports publishing is extremely competitive. Newspapers are losing circulation figures in the UK, but remain a strong medium for sports news. Sport sections/inserts have increased the depth of coverage of sport, however, the UK has not been able to sustain a daily sports newspaper unlike France with *L'Equipe* and Italy with the *Gazzetta Dello Sport*. Sport magazines may be weekly, monthly or quarterly and categorised as specialist interest. They are subscription only, available through local outlets, posted direct to the subscriber or available electronically through publishing services such as Zinio. Sports books still feature strongly in sales figures, but again, e-books are a preferred choice increasingly (about 10 per cent of sales). It isn't that sporty consumers are reading less, it is that they are reading differently. The business model for printed media is changing to account for the habits and behaviours of sport consumers.

The key technological advances adopted by the traditional sport media centre on TV as a medium. The BBC 'red button' is a great example of enabling sport consumer choice by offering additional viewing options such as live tennis matches at Wimbledon which are additional to those catered on the two main channels of BB1 and BBC2, and enhancing delivery quality by allowing further viewing angle options and the provision of on-screen statistical information to inform and engage the sport consumer. Digital video recorders (DVRs) have also added the dimension of real-time viewing by enabling the pausing of live sport. As suggested in the previous section, HDTV is already with us and is gently diffusing into the marketplace as new TVs are HD compatible. Also available in increasing quantities is 3DTV, which will further improve the viewing of live sport and the viewer's experience of being ever-closer to pitch-side. It is expected that these advances in technology will drive in-home plasma screen HDTV sales so that the improved product can be appreciated fully. This will negate, somewhat, the impact of new sport media options (Stuart, 2008).

The emergence of technologies such as these provides augmentation to the basic sport product/service, in line with Kotler's (1997) Three Levels of Product. However, new features today become expected tomorrow and so will be superseded by technology that has yet to be created. Nevertheless, the enhanced sport consumption experience felt by consumers enables revenue streams to be lucrative as subscription numbers increase and advertising is seen by more and more of the target sport segment.

The power of TV over sport is best evidenced by two sports – football and rugby league. The sports rights that Sky TV have acquired in each of these sports have been leveraged, controversially in some quarters, by the influence exerted to breakaway from the Football League, and to establish the Premier League. The influence of Sky TV on match kick-off times has benefitted the TV audience to the detriment of the live sport event spectator. Saturday lunchtime kick-offs are not always appreciated by the players and can make it more difficult for the travel plans of the fans. Judging from web forum comments by West Bromwich Albion fans regarding the switching of their away game at Blackpool to a Monday evening, such changes are not always welcome – some football fans do have day jobs! More controversially, rugby league changed its traditional playing season from winter to summer in 1996 to accommodate live rights awarded to Sky TV. However, the switch appears to have given a new lease of life to the sport and it currently seems to be in a healthy place.

New sport media

New sport media relates to devices capable of sending and receiving digital content (images, spoken and written word) in real time. The predominant formats are web-based and mobile communication vehicles that enable innovative, personalised sport communication messages to be provided to sport consumers. New opportunities have been created for web and mobile sports rights exploitation on platforms that are less expensive for sport consumers than traditional sport media formats. There do appear to be mixed messages about the suitability of the mobile TV market, in line with the comment made earlier about the positive influence of sport on HD plasma screens. Mobile phones (smartphones in particular) offer such great features that more use of them is being made in the home as well as on the move (Loos, 2008), and there are fast-growing mobile markets in India and China, both of which also like European sports (Stuart, 2008). The global growth in new sport media is a key opportunity for sport rights holders to seek to gain access, and one that cannot be ignored by the sport marketer. Live sport broadcast rights in overseas markets is a key growth factor for several sports, e.g. IPL, NFL, English Premier League.

New sport media enables any sport organisation, big or small, to access their sport target market(s) directly. Geographic distance is no barrier to the increased volume of sport communication by these means, and speed of communication is enhanced also. Interconnectedness between platforms is enacted (e.g. PC to smartphone) and interactive communication is growing sharply via forums, blogs, etc. This interactivity has helped to establish 'virtual communities' of like-minded individuals worldwide and has replaced the 'one-to-many' model of traditional mass communication with the 'many-to-many' web of communication (Croteau and Hoynes, 2003). The attempt to infiltrate such communities in order to target each potential sport consumer separately is now a major focus for sport marketers, e.g. Nike advertising in the virtual world of *Second Life*.

Sport websites

Sport websites are ubiquitous, but as a sport organisation if you do not have a website, then for many sport consumers you do not exist. A website is constantly available and carries all the information that the sport organisation deems important for its key publics. However, to be effective for a sport target audience a sport website must ensure the following:

- awareness – knowledge of its existence;
- findability – easily, when it is required;
- availability – when access is required;
- popularity – it can attract visitors;
- accessibility – of the pages desired;
- usability – to navigate and perform tasks;
- trust – confidence in the information and security of the site;
- fulfilment – to complete the tasks required, e.g. ticket purchase;
- reputation – enhance the reputation of the sport organisation through the smoothness and satisfaction of all the previous features.

Fundamentally, a website for any sport organisation should tell the story of the organisation, answer questions for sport consumers, add to the list of contacts, provide clear contact information, make a good first impression, and bring in sport consumers who would not normally be reached. There is no reason why any of these criteria cannot be met by any website today. The level of assistance in their construction is well founded, but still I find annoying issues of usability and fulfilment on many sites. As a sport marketer, you are paid to think like a sport consumer; there are no excuses for errors with sport website development.

Learning Activity 10.1

Go to three different sport websites of your choice and consider each of the nine elements of an effective website. Identify the ease and difficulty of your surfing experience; do any similar issues arise across each site, and how would you improve the experience for other sport consumers?

The technological developments behind each of the new sport media platforms have occurred at an amazing pace, and will continue to do so. Mobile communication technology advances are spellbinding, enabling SMS, MMS, email, internet access, video streaming, video calling and even serving as a wireless modem, and soon to be fourth generation (4G) broadband capability. The Nokia Nseries, HTC Dream and Apple iPhone provide the hardware that addresses the needs of the mobile sport communication target segment. Sport marketers are working on how best to use mobile to engage fans at the arena, and beyond, and in building mobile platforms for sport sponsorship (see IPL case study on p. 151).

But it is the platforms that have transformed the capabilities of new sport media, and social media is at the forefront. Sport marketers are focusing on adding social features to websites to leverage Facebook and

Twitter, and to manage fan communities. Sport marketers have realised that individual passion for teams, players and leagues will create millions of social actions acting as megaphones to build awareness on the backs of the most passionate fans in a cost-effective manner.

There are several key platforms in use that are pertinent to sport consumers and, by extension, sport marketers. Social networks such as Facebook, MySpace and LinkedIn are most frequently identified as having the greatest reach to potential sport consumers; blogs and forums are heavy with use from sport fans; and the micro-blogging site Twitter has numerous sports stars with their growing list of followers. Team Sky Pro Cycling collates the tweets of their athletes and team personnel, thereby establishing an internal community of their own, which is shared externally and so gives fans an insight into the team.

Twitter was born in 2006, enabling messages of 140 characters to be communicated to a user profile page and made accessible to 'followers'. There are 190 million visitors monthly (Costolo, 2010) and 750 tweets posted per second (www.blog.twitter.com, 2010). A tweet record of 2,940 per second was set in the 30-second period after Japan scored against Cameroon on 14 June at the 2010 football World Cup in South Africa (Miller, 2010). Enhancements to the site have enabled picture and video connectivity to multi-media sites such as YouTube. The philosophy behind the use of Twitter does pose questions about narcissism and banality in everyday life, but sport entities (athletes and sport organisations) are using the service as a sport PR tool. Twitter gives 'followers' the opportunity to see into the everyday lives of top sports stars and for the sports stars to promote themselves and their sponsors. When tweets form the basis of sports news through the reporting of tweet posts in sport magazines and on sport websites, clearly, micro-blogging is a key sport communication medium.

Reflection Point 10.1

But are social networking and micro-blogging sites dangerous tools? There have been occurrences when a little too much information has been provided on such sites, e.g. the Australian cricketer Phillip Hughes, whose tweet about his dropping from the team scooped the official announcement by hours and the case of the mother of the Liverpool footballer Paul Konchesky who let her fingers do a little too much talking after her son was criticised for his on-field performance. Are you aware of any other cases – an Aldershot or Liverpool footballer perhaps? To what extent do you think that social networking is a dangerous tool in the hands of some sports people?

The technology stretches to other multi-media platforms such as video sharing via YouTube and livecasting through websites such as Justin.tv and Ustream. Livecasting enables the production and consumption of live video streaming, including sport events. There appear to be some issues with the quality of content with this medium, but despite flouting the principle of sport media rights broadcasting, it does allow the circumvention of subscription charges made by multinational companies. By extension, lifecasting goes one stage further with wearable technology enabling broadcast of a person's life activities. This is 'permissive Big Brother' along the lines of 'fly-on-the-wall' TV. Actually it could provide a good sport PR opportunity for a professional sport team to provide insight into its everyday existence by revolving the technology between players, coaches and other employees – would any sport team be brave enough to try this out?

Case Study

Indian Premier League (IPL) on YouTube

- *The Google IPL deal is worth USD$ 250 million for a period of two years.*
- *The Google-owned video-sharing website will stream every game of the next two IPL tournaments (60 matches) online with a five-minute delay to an international audience.*
- *YouTube has scored 54 million channel views and over 90,000 subscribers – a global record – with viewers from over 200 countries led by India and followed by the United States.*

Broadcast sponsorship of IPL on YouTube

- *Live streaming of IPL matches on YouTube evoked a very positive response amongst advertisers in India.*
- *Google brought on-board sponsors who contributed an approximate value of US$750,000 to 1.2 million, including HSBC, Hewlett Packard, Airtel, Coca-Cola, Samsung; and specifically in the UK, Brylcreem and Lebara Mobile.*

Advertisement formats for online stream

- *Ads appear across several formats, including: pre-roll advertisements, mid-roll advertisements, YouTube homepage advertisements, banner adverts next to the live player and on video watch pages.*
- *Only the UK did not accept ads from sponsors on YouTube.*

Integration with Orkut (a social media site very similar to Facebook)

- *Sponsors adverts featured on the IPL-branded Orkut community page, which hosts player interviews, contests and match polls to engage fans.*

Off-line Promotion of the live stream on YouTube

- *A complete ISMC approach was enacted including an entire train painted with the YouTube live streaming ad.*

(Courtesy of Ravi Chavan)

Learning Activity 10.2

- Did you access the IPL on YouTube?

What are your YouTube habits? Discuss your behaviour profile with a colleague, e.g. what, when, for how long do you watch, and what is the quality of your viewing experience?

Finally, Facebook and YouTube. Facebook with its 500 million active users (Zuckerberg, 2010) is the epitome of social networking. The philosophy of joining common interest groups means that Facebook users are increasingly being targeted by sport organisations through advertising and engagement in social chat that is seeking conversion to commercial activity. Sport organisations are trying to occupy the same space in which sport consumers spend a great deal of their time. They are creating official Facebook pages that provide a good combination of interactive features and official pictures, videos, polls and RSS feeds, in-page applications and rich graphics. Sport consumers appear to want high-quality content online and don't want to leave Facebook to find it. Best practice also utilises sport event/games, interviews and exclusive content releases such as team photos and HD-branded video that fans can share with their friends. Sport consumers are shouting 'Engage me, Entertain me. Make me feel cool and want to share' (www.directmarketingobservations, 2008).

Learning Activity 10.3

Go towww.facebook.com/nikefootball (along with 4.3 million others) to identify the points of attachment for football fans. Explore how you are able to connect directly with Nike products, and how your favourite team is showcased. There are activation tools available such as kitbuilder – have you used it?

Does this site engage and entertain you? Discuss the elements that do this for you with your friends.

YouTube, the video sharing website, created a first in 2010 by broadcasting free, live streaming of the IPL (see case study). The concept of user-generated video content has created an internet culture in its own right, and an addition to the lexicon of life.

The use of social media as a sport marketing vehicle through the ISMC mix centres upon the creation of content that encourages sharing through social networks. The principle of the viral that spreads worm-like from user to user is pertinent here; often produced with the support of a commercial sponsor. The following link to a short video on YouTube of street trials rider Danny MacAskill is the perfect example of the use of a viral video by Red Bull: www.redbull.co.uk/waybackhome.

Smith (2008) conceptualised the six key elements of new media sport marketing as:

- Customisation – of the sport marketing message and the sport products/services offered to a targeted sport market, e.g. Bont cycling shoes that you place in the oven and which subsequently mould to your feet.
- Modularity – a flexible and responsive approach to sport marketing that enables smooth information flow, e.g. effective sport e-ticketing systems.
- Sticky branding – innovative sport brand promotional ideas that 'stick' in the mind of the sport consumer, e.g. Pepsi, David Beckham and the Sumo wrestlers.
- Networked communication – encouraging virtual communities, e.g. Facebook, fans forums, blogs etc.

to develop the more powerful and credible communication channel of sport consumers talking directly to each other and advocating sport products/services virally.

- Inclusivity – virtual communities generating a sense of belonging, e.g. the Fulham FC fans forum www. friendsoffulham.com.
- Permission – sport consumers are more responsive to sport marketing approaches having given their permission to receive sport communication messages.

The application of these six elements is proposed through the new media sport marketing process (see Figure 10.1). The process appears most relevant for social media by first establishing contact with the sport communication message via traditional or new sport media formats. These direct the sport consumer towards other users with whom a conversation can be had that connects them together through their mutual interest. A stronger sense of community emerges through that social connection for the sport consumer to then become a convert to the consumption of the sport product/service. The convert can advocate the benefits of the sport product/service to develop additional contacts for whom the virtuous circle continues. The social belonging and tribal attributes of sport are certainly to the fore in new media sport marketing and this has some (virtual) resonance with the 'fandom affiliation and tribal behaviour' in the work of Dionisio et al. (2008).

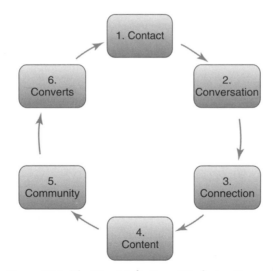

Figure 10.1 The New Media Sport Marketing Process (adapted from Smith, 2008)

Case Study
Beer sponsor grabs social media by the Vuvuzelas at World Cup

Sport marketing has been around for a long time, but the mediums used to target consumers have evolved as much as the strategies. For example, the 2010 World Cup was one of the first major sporting events since the boom of social media – Facebook, Twitter, LinkedIn, Flickr, among others – that was used to reach sport consumers.

Take Facebook, for example. During the 2006 World Cup, it had more than 12 million active users. Today, Facebook has more than 400 million active users. Yes, traditional advertising still exists and is frequently used, but unique, interactive tactics have become the 'norm' for brands to break through the clutter. Budweiser is a great example of brands adopting innovative marketing strategies during the World Cup.

Budweiser, the official 2006 and 2010 World Cup Beer Sponsor, has strongly embraced social media in 2010 by launching their unique global marketing campaign, 'Bud United', an online reality TV series that started at the beginning of the World Cup. The campaign follows 32 'football' fanatics, one representative from each country with a team in the World Cup, living in one house, the 'Bud House'. As teams get eliminated, the representative from that country is forced to pack his/her bags and head home.

This entirely web-based campaign includes:

- Episodes of Bud House on YouTube.
- Interactive online polls that offer a platform for viewers to influence events in the house.
- Facebook and Twitter accounts where fans can follow the representatives who will be posting their experiences throughout the process.

So far, Budweiser's campaign appears to be gaining momentum:

- Its Facebook page has been 'liked' by more than 850,000 users.
- Its YouTube channel has been viewed more than 1.4 million times.
- Within the first 30 hours, 60,000 users took advantage of the Facebook app, changing their profile picture to one painted in their team's colors.

(Adapted from www.griffinyorkkrause.com, 2010)

Learning Activity 10.4

Consider the social media use in sport of four of your classmates and present this to the remainder of your colleagues. How often and for how much time do you interact with others on Facebook etc. What type of 'discussion' are you having? Do you 'follow' a particular thread? What benefits does it have for you? etc.

Do you consider social media in sport to be a phenomenon that will mean some traditional forms of sport media will no longer be required, and if so which ones?

Chapter Review

Sports and social media are at the crossroads of fan participation. Social sport media will continue to escalate with even more user-generated content and platforms created to showcase that content. It is also very likely that the voice of the fan will become more and more prominent in the sport industry.

Traditional formats of presenting sport will continue, but they will need to continue their development as the lifecycle of new sport media formats becomes ever shorter.

Further Reading

Dionisio, P., Leal, C. and Moutinho, L. (2008) 'Fandom affiliation and tribal behaviour: a sports marketing application', *Qualitative Market Research: An International Journal*, 11, 1: 17–39.
The aim of this paper is to identify the existence of tribal behaviour in football fans and the impact of this tribalism on the consumption of brands associated with the club. Managerial implications are related to the club needing to maintain an open channel with supporters. Sponsor brands should also develop a long-term strategy and support another sport besides football.

Hutchins, B. (2008) 'Signs of meta-change in second modernity: the growth of e-sport and the World Cyber Games', *New Media Society*, 10, 6: 851–869.
Media, communication and information flows now define the logic and structure of social relations, a situation that affects almost every dimension of cultural life and activity. This article analyses the transformation of the relationship between computer gaming, media and sport in the global age of 'second modernity'. This analysis is undertaken through a critical case study of the World Cyber Games (WCG). This popular event and the 'cyber-athletes' that compete in it cannot be explained fully by reference to existing studies of computer and video gaming, media and sport, media events or organised sporting competition. It is not possible to think in terms of sport and the media when considering the WCG and organised competitive gaming. This is sport as media or e-sport, a term that signifies the seamless interpenetration of media content, sport and networked information and communications technologies.

Chapter 11
Place in sport

Learning Objectives

This chapter is designed to help you:

- understand sport distribution as an important function of sport marketing;
- consider the basic concepts of sport distribution;
- identify the variety and key features of the sporting arena as 'place'.

Introduction

Sport place generates the least interest of all the sport marketing mix elements, but is no less important. It is frequently uppermost in the mind of the sport consumer – ever thought or said out loud to yourself or someone else, 'how do I get hold of one?' or 'when can I get hold of one?' referring to a ticket for the 2012 Olympic Games 100 metre final or your team's unexpected day trip to Wembley for the final of the Johnstone's Paint Trophy. There is no point producing innovative new sport products/services and creating demand in the sport target market without being able to supply the items to the sport consumer when they want it and where they want it. Sport place, therefore, refers to how a sport organisation distributes the sport products/services it offers to the sport consumer. Sport place and sport distribution are used interchangeably in this context, although sport place refers also to the broader environment within which sport is consumed.

Sport place/distribution

The principles of distribution apply across many industry sectors, but sport has place issues for sport spectators and participants based upon the location where the activity occurs. For consumers of sport products (e.g. a table tennis bat or pair of cricket pads) e-distribution is possible. The use of new forms of technology has necessitated changes to sport distribution practice, as you will see in this chapter.

To decide which sport distribution channel to use for the delivery of sport products/services to sport consumers, sport organisations must address the requirements of the sport customer segment (e.g. familiarity with the use of new technologies); the stage of the sport PLC because channel changes may be required to cater to the wider sport market as sales grow (e.g. supply via high street sport retailers); the fit of image between the sport brand and the distributor (e.g. a specialist sport retailer or general retailer such as a supermarket). This latter decision is likely to be dependent upon the sales strategy being followed (e.g.

niche or undifferentiated), and the level and quality of service to be attached to the sport purchase. For example, the purchase of ski footwear and binding equipment is best facilitated by a knowledgeable service encounter in a specialist store, whilst this is not so necessary for the purchase of the associated ski wear such as gloves, hat and goggles. Therefore, the level of training and on-going support to aid the sport purchase encounter is a key decision in a sport organisation determining its distribution approach. Not all retailers are the same, and as noted in Chapter 5, the level of sport product knowledge between sports outlets is variable and points to the importance of the sport service element in many sport consumption decisions.

Conflicting advice

With winter conditions prevailing and the mountains beckoning, I had a recent experience of looking at crampons in two different outdoor sport retailers. In the first the sales assistant said crampons can be fitted to any boot. In the second I was told that, because crampons are classified as personal protective equipment, staff are not allowed to give advice other than in relation to the specialist boots that are specifically designed to take a crampon. It's a safety issue.

But isn't there an equally worrying, but more universal example? How many 'runners' go to a large high street store and buy, with no informed advice, a pair of trainers which provide little shock absorption and, over time, could lead to one of a number of over-use injuries and perhaps long-term damage to the athlete?

So clearly, the sport organisation must distribute the sport product/service to the sport consumer in the right place at the right time. Efficient and effective sport distribution is important if the sport organisation is to meet its overall sport marketing and broader business objectives. If a sport organisation underestimates a demand and customers cannot purchase sport products/services because of it, organisational profitability is affected.

There are four main sport distribution channels:

1 Sport wholesalers.
2 Sport distributors/sales agents.
3 Sport retailers.
4 Direct.

Sport wholesalers 'break bulk' – buy in large quantities from sport manufacturers and then break them into smaller quantities to sell to sport retailers. This reduces transport costs to the sport manufacturer (fewer journeys to the sport wholesaler rather than many journeys to sport retailers) and sport retailers can order in smaller amounts from sport wholesalers. Sport wholesalers provide storage facilities and, increasingly, co-ordinate the logistical process of ensuring demand meets supply at the point of purchase.

Sport distributors/agents provide a link between sellers and buyers. Agents are not always employed by the sport company, but sell the sport products/services for a commission. Agents are mainly used in international markets.

Sport retailers may miss out the sport wholesaler, instead ordering directly from the sport producer and then using their own system of distribution. The advantage for a sport producer is the greater level of control over the marketing of the sport product/service. Alternatively, a sport wholesaler acts as the intermediary through which the sport retailer sources their stock of sport products/services. Sport retailers hold several sport brands and sport products/services are promoted and merchandised by the retailer. The sport retailer also determines the final selling price of the items for sale.

Direct approaches are used by other sport businesses as their key distribution channel to sell sport products/services directly to the sport consumer. The most common channels for direct distribution are:

- direct mail;
- mail-order catalogues;
- telephone sales;
- internet.

Internet sales across all sectors are at record levels and show no likelihood of slowing down. Most sport consumers are now familiar with the process of online purchase and are happy to engage in the practice. The internet caters to a geographically dispersed sport market, and niche sport products/services are capable of reaching that wider audience. There are low barriers to entry into the sport market as set-up costs are low. E-commerce technology (for payment, shopping software etc.) is commonplace and so there has been a paradigm shift in sport commerce and sport consumption behaviour that benefits distribution via the internet.

With these four sport distribution channels in mind, there are six sport 'channel' decisions that determine the sport distribution strategy:

1 Direct or an indirect channel, e.g. 'direct' to a sport consumer, 'indirect' via a wholesaler (see Figure 11.1).
2 Single or multiple channels, e.g. e-retailer, high street, catologue.
3 Degrees of market coverage, e.g. intensive, exclusive or selective distribution.
4 Cumulative length of the multiple channels, e.g. long or short.
5 Types of intermediary, e.g. importer/distributor, retailer.
6 Number of intermediaries at each level, e.g. the number of different sport retailers.

The decision centres upon the direct versus indirect sport distribution approach, that is, whether it is necessary to use an intermediary. An intermediary simply mediates between sport manufacturer and sport consumer. Indirect sport distribution involves distributing the sport product/service through an intermediary, e.g. a sport manufacturer selling to a wholesaler and then on to the sport retailer. Direct sport distribution involves distributing direct from a sport manufacturer to the sport consumer. The advantage of direct sport distribution is that it gives a sport manufacturer complete control over their sport product/ service throughout the whole process.

The process from sport manufacture to sport consumption is a complex one, and one you might not have thought about too much. In actual fact, the process of sport manufacture also includes supply of the raw materials such as fabric for wetsuits, running shorts etc. by a third party. You may be aware that a great deal of manufacturing of sports equipment and apparel takes place around the world in Asia (Korea, Vietnam, Thailand, China) and South America (Brazil, Mexico), and across Europe. This is so that manufacturing can occur close to the production or source of the raw materials and/or where labour

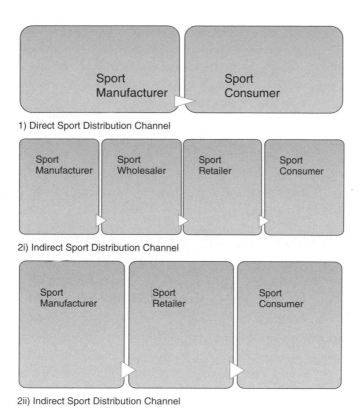

1) Direct Sport Distribution Channel

2i) Indirect Sport Distribution Channel

2ii) Indirect Sport Distribution Channel

Figure 11.1 Types of sport distribution channel

costs are low. Many of the multinational sport brands in the marketplace manufacture their sport products via a network of suppliers. For example, adidas–Salomon work with over 800 independent suppliers in over 65 countries (www.adidas-group.com). The role of the commissioning sport organisation becomes one of control, ensuring quality of the final sport product. As sport consumption does not often occur close to sport product manufacture, a decision is required as to how best to bring the two together. The advent of the internet, in particular, has expanded the opportunities for direct sport distribution (sport manufacture to sport consumer). However, where sport consumption occurs in a sport retail environment, an intermediary is now involved and the sport distribution approach becomes indirect.

From the perspective of the sport consumer, the choice of sport distribution channel is relatively straightforward. 'Should I go to Nike.com or JD Sports in town for my Air Max 90?' Using the website means that the sport consumer is engaging in a direct sport distribution channel, whilst visiting a sport store is an indirect sport distribution channel. Clearly, Nike operates a multiple channel approach to the supply of its sport products, e.g. internet, sport retailers, department stores and own brand stores. This is an example of a 'click and mortar' retailer, that is, online and high street, as opposed to a 'pure-play' e-tailer, that is, online only (e.g. wiggle.com).

Technological developments now enable the convergence of the manufacturing and wholesale (assists in the distribution of sport products) roles to shorten the length of the supply chain. The delivery of sport products/services from raw material supplier to sport consumer is now one continuous process of inventory management. It is computer controlled by bar code to ensure every piece of fabric is tracked and delivered safely to the end user. Picking and packing (order processing) can be performed at the point of manufacture and shipped via a third party, that is, local and international carrier and then Royal Mail, and others, to your door. The process aims to be seamless for the sport consumer, and is being managed and controlled to ensure that no sport product is ever out of stock.

Reflection Point 11.1

Does it really matter to the sport consumer where manufacturing of sports equipment and apparel takes place, just as long as the items arrive by next day delivery?

The direct/indirect sport distribution approach, as with all elements of the sport marketing process, should be considered from the perspective of the sport consumer. You can now purchase tickets for sport events at any time of the day or night with a few clicks of your mouse or by touch-tone phone. You may think that during this process you are dealing directly with the sport organisation whose sport products/ services you are purchasing, but this is unlikely. Outsourcing (the handing over of the task to a third party) is rife, so when you are purchasing sports tickets online you will probably be being 'hosted' by the technical expertise of a company overseas. If you do speak directly to a sales advisor, they are likely to be in another part of the UK or further afield – not that it matters to you.

If you are watching live sport on TV, the internet or listening on the radio, the process is effectively the same, that is, the teams/athletes supply the raw materials that sport media production companies manufacture into the sport product/service content, which is then brought to the sport consumer via a cable, satellite or terrestrial broadcaster (see Figure 11.2).

Figure 11.2 The sport broadcasting value chain (adapted from Gratton and Solberg, 2007)

Another important decision in the choice of sport distribution channel is the extent of market coverage desired for the sport product/service. A multiple channel approach to sport distribution is an example of *intensive distribution* to the mass market, not just the sport market. *Selective distribution* occurs when a limited number of outlets distribute the sport product/service. Credibility of the sport brand is frequently an important consideration in this decision and so the selection of an outlet that can provide a specialist service or one that brings the sport product/service directly to the target sport segment or to the widest possible market is foremost. This is now the position of Sky TV with its live rights to the EPL. *Exclusive distribution* of the 2012 London Olympic Games will fall to the BBC, but it could be for the last time. Another example is Sky Box Office that has exclusive UK TV distribution rights for big fight boxing coverage – for an additional fee!

Furthermore, the collective length of the sport distribution channels utilised by a sport organisation decreases the level of control throughout the process. The length of the supply chain is greatest for the sport retail option and that is the reason for sport multinationals wanting to concentrate their efforts on limiting the number of stages in the process. Intermediaries can play more than one function (e.g. as importer, distributor and retailer), particularly of niche or specialist sport products/services (e.g. yellow.co.uk with high-spec Pinarello bikes). Finally, the greater the number of intermediaries at each level, the less control a sport organisation will have over the ultimate sport consumption decision. For example, the use of multiple high street retailers such as JD Sports, Sports Direct, Soccerworld, FootLocker, Intersport means that the retailer can control price rather than the sport brand, as The North Face found to its cost in December 2010.

Sports electronic retailing (sport e-tailing), as highlighted, has become a major player in bringing sport products/services to sport consumers. Transactions at all levels of the supply chain are now electronic as the world has digitised, and so e-commerce exists not just between a sport business and a sport consumer (B2C), but also between sport businesses (B2B), sport consumers (C2C), and through mobile commerce (m-commerce). Ebay is a good example of what initially was a C2C e-transaction channel, but one that has morphed into a B2C e-tailing channel. Viagogo (and others) now perform an electronic (and legal) function that ticket touts outside sports stadia have been doing for years.

If you think about some of the e-transactions you have undertaken, they were probably inexpensive items that are frequently purchased, with a standard specification and from a reliable/well-known vendor or sport brand. These factors suggest that sport e-tailing is useful for sport purchases that are packaged and which can become rather more habitual purchase activity. If you are ever unsure about an e-tail purchase, I would suggest you speak to an advisor to clarify the issue, or 'try before you buy'. Sport e-tailers are increasingly providing the option of returning higher priced, more involved or complex sport product/service items to increase confidence for the sport consumer in the purchase process.

Returning items

Nevertheless, having had need to return items purchased through a sport e-tailer on several occasions it does become tiresome. I once had to phone the US to access a return number that then needed to be entered into the sport company's website to download a return label to be stuck onto the re-packaged item. This was then collected from my house at a pre-arranged time with UPS for the item to go to the

Netherlands. One half size difference in the footwear I ordered was required, but none were available online or in any of the several outlets I visited to find a pair. I ended up with a very nice replacement pair, but not the ones I really wanted.

The use of the internet for sport e-tailing has forced sport organisations to focus their distribution options (see adidas case study on p. 163). The process of removing the layers of intermediaries from a sport organisation in the supply chain is known as disintermediation. The impact of software (intelligent agents) to facilitate the process of inventory management is known as cybermediation (or electronic intermediation). A mix of human and electronic intermediation that provides assistance, where necessary, throughout all phases of the e-commerce process is known as hypermediation. The complexity of the sport product/service on offer determines which approach is necessary. For example, the purchase of a corporate hospitality package can be performed electronically, but if additional requirements were required (e.g. special occasion celebrations or a price negotiation), then human interaction would be necessary.

It is interesting to think for a moment about entry into a new sport market. Increasingly, sport consumption takes a global focus as new sport technologies (including new sport media technologies) have created the boundary-less sport marketplace. In taking a new sport product/service to a new international territory, key decisions on distribution must be made. For example, the mode of entry into an international sport market is the channel(s) that a sport organisation employs to gain entry. The alternatives are many and diverse such as:

- internet – used as either a sole channel or part of a multi-channel approach;
- exporting – either direct to the sport consumer or indirectly via a handler in the destination sport market;
- licensing – e.g. franchising which provides the sport brand, business expertise etc. but is managed locally by the franchiser;
- international agents and international distributors – agents simply promote the business abroad; distributors additionally take ownership of the sport product/service;
- strategic alliances – regarding manufacturing, distribution and/or marketing, but the sport companies remain separate;
- joint ventures – as above, but both/all sport companies own a proportion of the sport business.

Nike shoes are carried by multi-brand stores, and the exclusive Nike stores across the globe. Nike sells its product to about 20,000 retail accounts in the US and in almost 200 countries around the world. In the international markets, Nike sells its products through independent distributors, licensees and subsidiaries. Wiggle, based in Hampshire, is a successful sports internet company that now exports directly (sells into) to over 70 overseas countries. Franchising is a common occurrence in US sports and has become an ownership mindset in the EPL at Aston Villa, Liverpool and Manchester United. Strategic alliances and joint ventures with Chinese manufacturers are now commonplace, e.g. China Rising Shoes Co. supplying adidas weightlifting and golf shoes.

The following case study of adidas incorporates many of the elements discussed throughout this chapter. It provides a great deal of insight into the strategic direction of the company and the means by which it seeks to achieve its overall business objectives. You should by this point have sufficient grasp of the key elements of sport distribution to appreciate and interpret the information presented to interested publics (predominantly shareholders) by the adidas Board. Focus on three things that are emphasised in the case study:

- sport distribution channels;
- the supply chain;
- the efficiency drive in sport retail management.

Case Study
adidas

The adidas Group 2015 strategic business plan aims at growing the business compared to the expected 2010 results by 45–50 per cent to €17 billion in 2015. The adidas Group aspires to outperform total market growth (both GDP and sporting goods market) and to continue growing its bottom line faster than its top line. In addition, the Group plans to lay the foundation for leadership in the sporting goods industry by outgrowing its major competitor in the next five years. Several growth initiatives within Global Sales (including Own Retail, eCommerce and Retail Space Management) and efficiency projects across the Group (including Planning, Virtualisation and Organisational Efficiency) will further support the adidas Group on its way towards qualitative growth and long-term success. In terms of geographical distribution, North America, Greater China, Russia/CIS, Latin America, Japan, UK and India have been identified as key growth markets.
The adidas Group strategy is discussed in the following sections.

Reorganisation of Group provides solid platform for growth

In 2009, the adidas Group moved from a vertically integrated brand structure into a functional multi-brand structure for the adidas and Reebok brands. This led to the creation of a global sales function responsible for the commercial activities and a global brands function responsible for the marketing activities of both brands. In addition, the global sales organisation was split into wholesale and retail, to cater more appropriately to the different needs of these two distinctive business models. This new structure follows two important principles: to foster further alignment and strengthen brand management to drive long-term sustainable growth

Investments focused on highest potential markets and channels

With almost 180 subsidiaries worldwide, the adidas Group has prioritised investments based on those markets which offer the best medium- to long-term growth and profitability opportunities, particularly China and Russia. The Group tailor the distribution strategy to present the brands to the consumer in the most impactful way. This is achieved by following a distinctive channel approach. The adidas Group strive to provide their customers with superior service to secure prime shelf space for the brands, while continuing a commitment to building a strategic competency in own retail and e-commerce.

Creating a flexible supply chain

Speed and agility are key to outpacing the competition. The adidas Group are committed to meeting the full range of customer and consumer needs by ensuring product availability in the correct size and colour, providing game-changing technical innovations and also the latest high-end fashion product to the highest quality standards. The Group strives to shorten creation and production lead times by continuously improving infrastructure, processes and systems. By sharing information from point of sale to source and vice versa, the adidas Group strives to connect, and more closely integrate, the various elements of the supply chain to enable quick reaction to changing consumer trends. To this end, the Group focus on building maximum flexibility. While leveraging the efficiency of common infrastructure and processes, the Group strives to provide tailored solutions for all business models, be it the wholesale or retail channels.

Wholesale: becoming the leading sales organisation

The main strategic objective of the wholesale segment is to deliver profitable market share growth by becoming the most effective and efficient sales organisation in the sporting goods industry. To realise this, the wholesale sales organisation takes the go-to-market strategies across various distribution channels. The most important distribution channels are sporting goods chains, department stores, independent sporting goods retailer buying groups, lifestyle retail chains and e-tailers. In this respect, wholesale strives to establish strong partnerships with the most dynamic retailers in their respective channel of distribution by offering best-in-class and tailored services.

Retail Space Management to drive efficiency

Retail Space Management (RSM) comprises all business models helping global sales to expand controlled space in retail. The wholesale function is cooperating with retailers along the entire supply chain to bring best-in-class service all the way through to the point of sale. By helping to improve the profitability per square metre for the Group's retail partners as well as improving product availability, the adidas Group can achieve higher customer satisfaction, thus driving share of retail shelf space. The three predominant models to drive the success of RSM for the adidas Group are Never-out-of-stock, FLASH collections and Franchising.

Never-out-of-stock (NOOS): the NOOS programme comprises a core range of basic articles, mostly on an 18 to 24 month lifecycle, that are selling across all channels and markets. Overall, the NOOS replenishment model secures high levels of product availability throughout the season, allowing for quick adaptation to demand patterns. Retailers have to provide dedicated retail space, co-invest in fixtures and fittings and commit to a 'first fill' representing about 25 per cent of total expected seasonal demand to participate in this programme. In return, customers can profit from significantly reduced inventory risk on these products. Most NOOS articles are on an end-to-end supply chain, thus limiting the adidas Group's inventory risk as product is re-produced following customer demand.

FLASH collections: the FLASH programme consists of pre-defined collection packages that are delivered every 4 to 6 weeks to retailers' doors, including basic point-of-sale promotional materials to promote dedicated retail space provided by the retailer. All articles of the FLASH packages are exclusively developed for this programme with the intention to bring freshness to the retail space. With a short development lead time, the Group are able to reflect recent product and colour trends in the FLASH range. As no samples are available during sell-in, the customers buy into a business proposition rather than traditionally selecting individual articles. In return for this commitment, the retailers have the right to selectively return articles of every FLASH collection that have not sold out during the defined retail window. Overall, the FLASH programme helps to

*improve brand image while limiting inventory risk for the customers. The FLASH programme was
started in 2010, with full-scale rollout planned from 2012 onwards.*

*Franchising: mono-branded store franchising is one of the Group's prime growth
opportunities, as it offers superior brand presentation. Franchise stores are financed and operated
by franchise partners. The adidas Group normally contributes to the costs for brand-specific
fixtures and fittings each store has to be equipped with. Further, the Group support franchise
partners with a comprehensive franchise concept, including range propositions, IT systems,
training concepts, and guidelines for store building and store operations. This ensures that the
quality of the brand presentation and the service offered to the consumer are at all times high and
comparable to own retail stores.*

Retail: becoming one of the top retailers in the world

*The strategic vision for retail is to become one of the top retailers in the world by delivering
healthy, sustainable growth with outstanding return on investment. Over the past five years,
the adidas Group has evolved into a significant retailer, operating more than 2,200 stores for
the adidas and Reebok brands worldwide. In light of the increase in importance of retail to
the Group's performance, a new retail leadership team was established in 2009. This team
is mandated to create global retail guidelines that enable higher efficiency and a common
framework to drive long-term profitability for the adidas and Reebok retail operations around
the globe.*

E-commerce: building a successful channel

*At the beginning of 2010, a new leadership team was put in place to define and outline the further
strategic direction of the Group's e-commerce business activities for the adidas and Reebok
brands. Although both brands have made advances with their respective e-commerce platforms in
recent years, it is believed there is considerable untapped potential for the Group in this channel of
distribution.*

(Adapted from adidas Group 2015 Strategic Business Plan)

Learning Activity 11.1

Identify three different high street sport retailers who stock adidas products. Go to each store and:

1   Note whether each store carries the same items.
2   If they do, are the prices exactly the same?
3   If not, ask for a stock item that is not available to determine the reason for its unavailability, and
    consider why this might be so.

Sport arena as 'place'

The stadium or sport facility is often referred to by sport marketers as 'place', but what exactly do they mean? It is a concept that has resonance with the work of the sport geographer John Bale and of John Urry's 'sense of place'. The idea expresses the sporting venue as the place where delivery of the sport product/service occurs, particularly sport events, and is therefore the most important channel of sport distribution. Based on the characteristics of the sport arena, the most important features of that arena can influence the sport consumer experience. Both Smith (2008) and Shank (2009) focus on the sport stadia, and in particular its location and accessibility (i.e. convenience, parking), design and layout (i.e. attractive design, weather protection), infrastructure (i.e. seating quality, scoreboards and screens), and customer service (i.e. queuing and waiting times, efficient and helpful staff). These have become some of the basic sport consumer expectations and requirements in sport stadia, but not all sport takes place in a stadium; the sporting arena, nevertheless, is the focal point of most sports activity.

The sporting arena is the place where the rules of everyday life are embellished by those of sport. The daily existence of sport consumers is suspended for a short time and the values and rituals of sport take precedence. The law of the jungle and the survival of the fittest are played out in the sporting arena against a foe (competitors) or against oneself. Sport has this effect for spectators and participants, and can occur in a sporting arena of any format, e.g. a mountain pass in the Tour de France, the hushed confines of the Crucible Theatre, the manicured expanses of St Andrews, or the pisted slopes of the Hahnenkamm. These are the sporting arenas that focus the attention of so many sport consumers. Not for them the highest possible level of access, comfort or customer service, but the equivalents of Wembley, Old Trafford and the Emirates create their own unique ambiance, attractive location, premium viewing spots, and food and drink options. Sporting arenas can eschew many of the features of sport stadia such as good signage and directions, accessibility by public transport, weather protection, toilet facilities, scoreboards and screens, and prominent information stands/booths. This is the reality of many sport arenas; it is not the micro-controlled, 'prawn sandwich, let's leave ten minutes before the end to beat the traffic' sport environment. These arenas grab hold of the consciousness of the sport consumer and transport him or her to their own 'Neverland'. Here they can play out their own fantasies by sprinting for the road sign signifying the finish line, or schuss in a tuck position down the ski slope like Bode Miller, or simply feel free and relaxed on the open water. These are the sporting arenas for the majority of sport consumers and lest we (as sport marketers) forget.

Despite these protestations the reality is that many of the features of sporting stadia are being installed in all sporting arenas – just look at the number of sporting venues that have big screens available with live footage of the action. Sport consumers now expect toilets, refreshment stands, merchandising options etc. and so every sporting arena has to consider how these can be provided. Figure 11.3 of the temporary (you could call it transient) cycling arena adjacent to the finish line of the British Cycling Road Race Championships 2010 in the village of Barley in Lancashire indicates this point. Neverthless, it was a case of 'ass on grass' rather than 'bums on seats'!

Sports tour companies such as Sports Tours International provide the services that sport consumers demand to ease their passage to the sporting arena (transport) and to provide the comfort (hotel), the view (sole use of the best vantage points), and information services (live TV of the action and internet facilities) in situ. Even standing in a Welsh forest watching rally cars passing at 100 mph is becoming less feral, as

Figure 11.3 Temporary cycling arena at 2010 British Cycling Championships

sport marketers seek to enhance the sport consumption experience. As more consumption opportunities are developed there will be fewer sporting arenas remaining free on entry. The constant creation of new ticket revenues by sport marketers prevails!

So how does a sport marketer utilise such a sporting arena? Here are some possibilities:

- Ensure the back drop is spectacular by passing iconic locations such as Buckingham Palace and Tower Bridge for the marathon races at London 2012. This is a key promotional opportunity for the TV viewer to be informed about the location and to be stimulated to want to visit the sporting event or the place itself in the future.
- Use the sporting arena for sponsor/advertising opportunities.
- Create merchandising opportunities.
- Enable sponsor leveraging activity.
- Provide the basic facilities expected of a sport stadium to enhance the sport consumer experience, e.g. parking, signage, spectator zones with screens and sound systems, toilets, catering provision, overt security and emergency assistance, points of contact for sport event information and general assistance.

Learning Activity 11.2

Think of a sporting arena (not a stadium) where you have witnessed live sport.

- Name the sport event and its location.
- Describe the main features of the sporting arena.
- List five features that led to your enjoyment of the sporting event.
- Identify any features that detracted from your enjoyment.

Chapter Review

Sport place/distribution is a key element of the sport product/service experience for sport consumers. Access to all sport products/services necessitates a process through which sport consumers must pass to satisfy their sport consumption desires. This process is now much easier and more complex, at the same time. Choice of channel is greater, but the sport service encounter has been lost where disintermediation in the sport distribution channel has occurred. Furthermore, the place that sport is consumed can determine future sport consumption behaviour patterns. To this end sporting arenas for many sports (be they in urban or rural sport environments) are becoming conformist in their offerings to sport consumers.

Further Reading

Bale, J. and Vertinsky, P. (eds) (2004) *Sites of Sport: Space, Place, Experience*, London: Routledge.

The sport place, like the theatre, shapes the play while also providing a context for experiences and social interactions within and beyond it. Having a greater appreciation of the place that sport occurs will enable you as a sport marketer to provide an augmented sport product/service.

Smith, K. A. (2007) 'Distribution channels for events: supply and demand-side perspectives', *Journal of Vacation Marketing*, 13, 4: 321–338.

Distribution involves the dissemination of information, the means of booking and purchase, and product bundling or packaging. This article systematically integrates data from interviews with events organisers and a survey of attendees at four events in Wellington, New Zealand. The complexity of event distribution channels is influenced by the event's target market, capacity, partnership relationships, and other factors. Free events have simple distribution channels focused on disseminating information; channels for ticketed events are more complex. There is limited bundling of event packages and a number of barriers exist to their further development in this destination.

Chapter 12
Sport marketing implementation and control

Learning Objectives

This chapter is designed to help you:

- explain the importance of implementation and control of sport marketing planning;
- identify approaches to assist sport marketing implementation;
- consider approaches to sport marketing control;
- provide insight into sport industry practice.

Introduction

So let's do it! The planning is done and the action is about to start. Sport marketing implementation does exactly that: the actual implementation of the sport marketing plan. More specifically it focuses upon the sport marketing mix, and predominantly, the ISMC mix. Sport marketing implementation is the tactical implementation of the plan with a sharper, time-limited focus usually up to 12 months hence. Each of the actions for implementation requires monitoring, so the process of sport marketing evaluation is enacted to control the implementation phase and to keep it on track towards the achievement of the sport marketing objectives. This is the final piece of the sport marketing planning process (1,000 piece) jigsaw. It is extremely important to ensure all previous phases have fed into the strategy appropriately to enable success for the sport organisation in achieving its sport marketing, and broader organisational, objectives. So this is a chapter of two halves: 1) sport marketing implementation; and 2) sport marketing control, that make up the final 90 minutes of the process.

Sport marketing implementation

Sport marketing implementation is a big deal – as indicated by Figure 12.1, it gets its own stage (or arena). Little is written in any sport marketing textbook about the implementation phase, possibly due to all sport marketing implementation activity being implemented differently, as no two plans are ever the same. The ISMC strategy that works for one sport organisation will not be successful for any other sport organisation because the preceding and prevailing factors in its strategic development cannot ever be exactly the same. There is no blueprint. The sport industry moves at lightning pace, changing old practices and developing

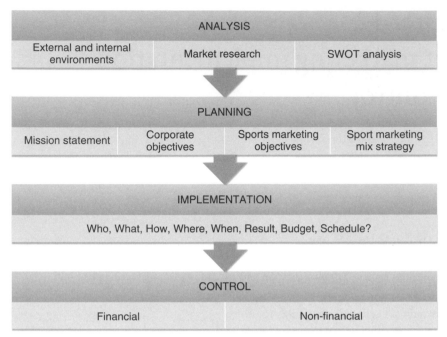

Figure 12.1 The sport marketing planning process

new methods, mentalities, technologies and sports products/services, all impacting upon the planning and implementation of the sport marketing plan.

The key elements of the final two phases of the strategic sport marketing planning process are encapsulated by Figure 12.2. The setting of sport marketing objectives, devised in line with the mission

Figure 12.2 The sport marketing implementation and control process

statement and corporate objectives of the sport organisation, state the desired aim of the sport marketing strategy. Specific lines of responsibility are assigned to different personnel who have the authority to create the strategic initiatives and to put these activities into action. The assigning of responsibility continues throughout the remainder of the process of monitoring, review and evaluation to determine the relative success of the plan. This is the human element of the sport marketing implementation phase. Someone in the sport organisation will either be praised and rewarded or asked to explain the performance of the sport marketing plan based upon its observed ability to satisfy the sport marketing objectives. There are more general sport organisation factors at play here that impact upon the success of the sport marketing plan and these include:

- the skills of the sport marketing team, including their creative abilities as sport marketers;
- the ability of the team to communicate with each other and co-ordinate their day-to-day activities;
- the reward system the team are subjected to;
- the budget available for completion of all planned activities.

Good sport marketing implementation needs 'buy-in' from all those individuals who are to carry out the plan. The best way to achieve this is to have the team, or a representative group of sport marketing employees, participate in the development of the sport marketing plan. A feeling of ownership will serve to create the level of 'buy-in' desired, and serve the implementation of the plan. However, these are the functions inherent within any sport organisation, so enough of that as this is a sport marketing text.

Strategy and its execution

So, the success of any strategy is only as good as its implementation. Bonoma (1984) emphasised this point through the strategy and execution matrix (see Figure 12.3) that indicates four outcomes of strategic implementation: 1) success; 2) chance; 3) problem; and 4) failure. Clearly, success is the preferred option, but even with an appropriate sport marketing strategy, poor implementation is likely to render it problematic, that is, not able to fully achieve the sport marketing objectives set for it. So, for example, if the sport marketing team is unable to utilise the budget allocation in an efficient and effective manner, that is, they overspend, then the strategy as devised cannot be actioned. Similarly, if the monitoring process of the sport marketing strategy during implementation is not performed well, then any difficulties arising will not be spotted. For example, poor sport sponsorship recruitment or distribution issues result in the

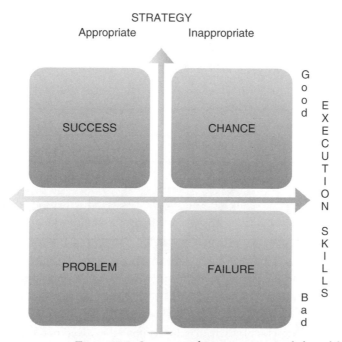

Figure 12.3 Strategy and execution matrix (adapted from Bonoma, 1984)

sport product/service not being available. Alternatively, a well implemented, but inappropriate sport marketing strategy only has a small chance of success. As a sport marketer, do ensure that you take the time and trouble, utilising all available information and data analysis tools and techniques, to create a sound sport marketing strategy in the first place to give yourself an even chance of success, and then implement it thoroughly and with conviction.

Sport marketing implementation brings the focus to the initial phase of strategic implementation – tactical implementation. The sport marketing tactical implementation plan has a focus for activities that occur in the first 12 months of the strategic sport marketing plan. Sport marketing tactical implementation relates directly to the actions to be performed and the timeline against which their implementation occurs, thus creating a schedule of activities. In effect, the sport marketing implementation schedule:

- identifies the sport marketing tactics to be deployed;
- determines the time required to complete each sport marketing tactic;
- determines which sport marketing tactics precede others;
- arranges the sequence and timing of all sport marketing tactics.

Figure 12.4 identifies one approach that sport marketers utilise to present a sport marketing tactical implementation plan – a GANTT chart. This is a very visual way of indicating the type and nature of sport marketing tactics to be implemented across the timeframe of the sport marketing programme. A chart such as this can present further detailed actions to address more specific tactical implementation (see Figure 12.5). Don't forget to assign responsibility to an individual who oversees the process of sport marketing tactical implementation. The budget made available is often limited and therefore must be used very wisely. It can be determined in one of three ways:

- as a percentage of sales;
- whatever the sport organisation can afford;
- based on the sport marketing objectives to be achieved.

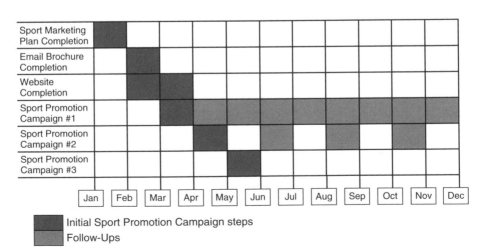

Figure 12.4 GANTT chart sport marketing tactical implementation

ACTION	2011 March	April	May	June	July	Aug	Sept	Oct
Media day for sport media representatives	Week 13							
Send out emails to potential sport customers		Week 15 & 16						
Presentation at the ... during their monthly meeting			Week 18					
Monthly sport media updates		Week 17	Week 22	Week 26	Week 31	Week 35	Week 39	Week 44
Monthly direct mail to interested sport customers (Newsletter)				Week 23 & 24		Week 32 & 33		Week 40 & 41

Figure 12.5 Sport promotion tactical implementation

The most suitable approach for any sport organisation to utilise would be the latter, that is, set with the specific sport marketing objective to be achieved in mind. This approach establishes which strategic and tactical activities are feasible. For example, the use of an e-database through which to communicate with the sport target market rather than incur the additional costs of a hard copy direct marketing approach. A sales-related approach pre-supposes a link between sales and sport marketing (the sport promotion component specifically) instead of considering the philosophy that sport promotion influences sales. Sport organisations that do not define a budget are likely to be replicating their broader deficiencies in applying a marketing orientation to their business. Thus they will probably struggle to identify where best to invest their sport marketing spend.

Sport marketing control

Sport marketing control is an on-going monitoring and review process that seeks to keep the strategic sport marketing plan on track during its implementation. Its basis is one of measurement: to establish whether what it set out to achieve has been successful – if it is not successful, why not; and if successful, what in particular made it so. Sport marketing control is a pro-active measure that can identify whether the strategic sport marketing plan is still appropriate in the ever-changing external environment. If it is not, then corrective action is necessary to put the plan back on track (see Figure 12.6).

Sport marketing control is dependent upon accurate and timely feedback on sport consumer reactions to the sport marketing mix. The MIS provides the necessary data to evaluate success. This process can begin during sport marketing tactical implementation (iteratively), but really should occur at the end of the implementation phase (post hoc) thus enabling the complete picture to emerge. This is a feed-forward process to enable lessons learnt to be included in future plans.

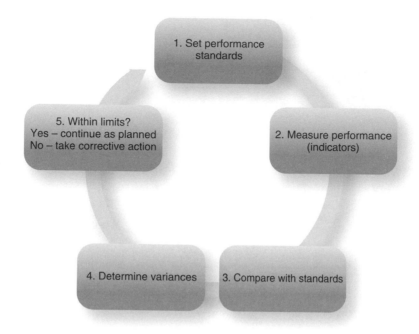

Figure 12.6 The control process

A strategic perspective

Kotler (1997) and Shank (2009) each consider the control of sport marketing activity from a strategic perspective. Shank (2009) identified three types of strategic control:

1 Planning assumptions control – assumptions made in the planning phase of the strategic sport marketing process, e.g. a competitor's reaction to sport pricing strategy is monitored for accuracy.
2 Process control – assesses the actions implemented to determine whether they are still appropriate in the changing sport environment, e.g. sport sponsorship monitoring of sales.
3 Contingency control – to account for the 'bigger picture' and expect the unexpected, such as a negative news story requiring a sport PR crisis management response.

Kotler (1997) provides a little more structure to the process of sport marketing control, through a broad and specific focus (see Table 12.1). The purpose of the control is identified; specific data forms that can provide the level of detail to determine success. Lines of responsibility are also indicated to identify who in the sport organisation should be performing such evaluation. To enable you to grasp more firmly the nature of sport marketing control, some examples of format and types of data will be outlined and examples from sport industry agencies that perform such functions will be provided.

Sport organisations sensibly keep a watchful eye on their expenditure, as well as their revenues through financial analysis. Many of the performance measures utilised for sport marketing control purposes are quantifiable, that is, reduced to numbers, but increasingly the research data derived from sport consumers is of a qualitative nature, that is, opinions and perceptions, although confusingly, the number of respondents in such research activity can provide a basis for quantitative insight. While it is easy to identify total sales,

Type of Control	Prime Responsibility	Purpose of Control	Approach
I. Annual-plan control	Top management; middle management	• To examine whether the planned results are being achieved	• Sales analysis • Sport market-share analysis • Sales-to-expense ratios • Financial analysis • Sport market-based scorecard analysis
II. Profitability control	Sport marketing controller	• To examine where the company is making and losing money • To evaluate and improve spending	Profitability by: • Sport product • Sport territory • Sport customer • Sport segment • Trade channel • Order size
III. Efficiency control	Line and staff management; sport marketing controller	• Efficiency and impact of sport marketing expenditures	Efficiency of: • Sales force • Sport advertising • Sales promotion • Sport distribution
IV. Strategic control	Top management; sport marketing auditor	• To examine whether the company is pursuing its best opportunities with respect to sport markets, sport products/services, and channels	• Sport marketing effectiveness rating instrument • Sport marketing audit • Sport marketing excellence review • Company ethical and social responsibility review

Table 12.1 Types of sport marketing control (adapted from Kotler, 1997)

the challenge in evaluating profitability performance for merchandising is assessing which channel provides the best net profit. While one distribution channel may reach the mass sport market place, it may require extensive spending in advertising and delivery costs to ensure sales are achieved. Nevertheless, financial analysis presents key feedback about the broader performance of the sport organisation, e.g. gross profit margin, return on capital employed (ROCE) and a whole range of liquidity and leverage ratios. For example, adidas Group in 2009 generated net sales of €10.4bn with a gross profit of €4.7bn and a ROCE of 11.3 per cent – but go see your sport finance class for more detail. Yes, these are important measures for sport marketers, as the results can impact directly upon the sport marketing budget. A decrease in the budget may lead to a rationalisation of the number of sport products/services available to the sport consumer or to specific sport marketing expenses that need rationalisation, e.g. reduced/enhanced sport advertising spend or the need to bring in-house or outsource the ISMC campaign. But more pertinent to the sport marketer are the efficiency measures relating to particular aspects of the sport marketing mix strategy and its tactical implementation such as the sport sponsorship strategy, sport distribution strategy, sport advertising strategy or sales promotion strategy; all these in relation to each separate target sport market, segment or consumer.

For example, sport advertising efficiency can be assessed by the standard ratio of cost-per-thousand (CPT – the cost to reach 1,000 target sport consumers), the number of enquiries to a sport advertisement, and the cost per enquiry (divide the number of enquiries by the cost of the sport advertising campaign). Similarly, for sport sales promotion efficiency, the percentage of sales generated by the sales promotion or the number/percentage of coupons redeemed is easy to monitor. Sport direct selling efficiency can be judged by the number of calls/web enquiries, or the number of new sport consumers secured per period. This provides a sales force with a 'cost per unit' figure. The sport distribution strategy's level of efficiency can also be evaluated by the time taken to complete orders and the percentage of orders executed, thus giving an indication of supply chain efficiency.

Assessing sport sponsorship success

To assess the success of sport sponsorship Masterman (2004) suggests a response to three simple questions is required:

1   How clear was the sponsorship?
2   Who took notice?
3   Did it achieve the objective set, e.g. sales, market share, image, awareness?

Masterman (2004) goes on to suggest that sport sponsorship evaluation is difficult to perform, as isolation of a specific activation activity is not always possible. Sales as a result of a sport sponsorship component may not be immediate and further leveraged activity may be required to exact the final sale. Media equivalency methods are most frequently implemented for media coverage/exposure emanating from a sport sponsorship programme. For example, the number of sightings and length of time a sponsor's logo was seen on TV (such as Rainham Steel) or the number of hits on a website ad. However, equating such exposure to the equivalent cost of purchasing advertising space and time is flawed due to true equivalency costs (e.g. discount levels on advertising rates) not being factored into the equation. Attitudinal surveys, focus groups and interview methods are now more commonplace to assess the higher-order effects of sponsor awareness and image in the sport target market.

Sport Marketing Surveys identify the increasing impact of a sport marketing programme in relation to the level of exposure in the first instance, leading to association, image, and favourability to sales of the sponsor's product/service (see Figure 12.7). Sport Marketing Surveys use a series of techniques to measure the effects of the sport sponsorship programme. The following two extracts from two of the biggest sport marketing research agencies in the world provide insight into the specific nature and type of evaluation data available to assess the success of sport marketing strategic and tactical implementation.

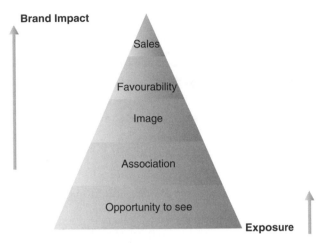

Figure 12.7 Sponsorship evaluation (adapted from Sport Marketing Surveys)

Example
Sport Marketing Surveys: sponsorship evaluation

Sport Marketing Surveys is an independent agency specialising in sports research with clients including adidas, Wilson, ECB and Sheffield City Council.

Valuation

Sports Marketing Surveys provides a range of services enabling the sponsor or rights holder to evaluate exposure to brand impact. Sports Marketing Surveys is able to measure time, activation spend, the property itself and the brand status in isolation or through a continuous programme for exposure and impact.

Exposure and collateral benefits

Sports Marketing Surveys has developed technologies to measure brand exposure through TV, print, radio and digital media. Sports Marketing Surveys evaluates brand exposure for specific events and properties and is also able to pre-test branding to help sponsors maximise their exposure in terms of positioning, wording, logos and colours.

TV. Access to the majority of sports coverage in Europe and are able to record any specific coverage on a global basis. The Mediatrak service provides transcripts of TV (and radio) coverage in key countries within 30 seconds of broadcast. The brand image recognition system measures the quantitative seconds of exposure that a brand receives during a broadcast and calculates an equivalent media value. QUALITY of exposure is measured through Visual Impact Methodology (VIM).

Print. Analysis of press cuttings is provided along with sponsorship and PR values for editorial and pictorial mentions. A qualitative analysis of cuttings is also undertaken in terms of key words, positive/negative comments and publication types.

···▶

Example continued

Radio. The Mediatrak tool enables monitoring of radio coverage of events and sponsors on key channels. Sports Marketing Surveys provide clients with links to the coverage, transcripts and an estimated value.

Digital. Sports Marketing Surveys has developed a number of methodologies to monitor digital media online and through mobile services. The Webtrak service searches for key words enabling evaluation of online mentions and exposure.

Collateral Benefits. Inclusion within the evaluation of benefits received from other contractual inventory such as ambient (spectators), advertising rights, corporate hospitality, ticket branding etc.

There isn't a sport or country that cannot be covered. Their Formula 1 evaluation programme covers over 60 countries for all Grand Prix; they have also covered football, cricket, rugby union, rugby league, tennis, golf, horse racing to name a few; others under their remit are snow golf, husky racing and snowboarding.

Impact

Sports Marketing Surveys works with its clients to develop a customised research programme for the brand, its target market(s) and objectives. By isolating the sponsorship they are able to measure:

- awareness of, and association with, the property;
- image transfer for key brand attributes;
- movement in favourability of the brand;
- shifts in brand consideration and loyalty.

The tailored research programme draws on a variety of quantitative and qualitative methodological options including:

- desk and client internal data such as brand trackers;
- syndicated sponsorship tracking using Sports Marketing Surveys in-house sponsorship brand tracker – Sponsatrak;
- sport event-based surveys for spectators and guests;
- targeted sports fan surveys accessing Sporting Insights, the in-house sports fan panel;
- bespoke client studies.

This information is combined with exposure data and analysed holistically to provide actionable findings enabling the client to improve and maximise their sponsorship return.

(www.sportmarketingsurveys.com)

Example
Sport und Markt

Sport und Markt is the leading research and consultancy company in international sport business, analysing advertising and sponsorship markets for over 20 years. Their clients include the Barclays Premier League.

Market research centre
- State-of-the-art telephone studio with over 70 CATI stations.
- Continual, domestic and international fundamental research on the most significant global markets with over 300,000 interviews conducted per year.
- In-house fieldwork department for face-to-face interviews and international event studies.
- 200 square-metre test studio for qualitative studies and focus groups.
- Analysis, interpretation and preparation of market research data obtained.

Comprehensive database with historical data from over two decades with relevant facts and information on more than 120 countries, 5,000 brands and sponsors, 500 events etc.

Media evaluation centre
- State-of-the-art 'Media evaluation centres' for global analysis and monitoring of relevant formats and content on TV, the internet, mobile content, radio, press etc.
- Global reception of 6,000 TV channels for recording of more than 1,500,000 hours of TV and analysis of approximately over 100,000 hours of TV accurate to the second annually.
- Global TV audience ratings via in-house connections and external service providers.
- State-of-the-art recording technology, analysis programmes and archiving systems with the most innovative system on the market: automatic image and logo recognition software based on reference videos (video recognition).
- Application of intelligent software for automatic media evaluation, e.g. automatic recognition, analysis and assessment of media content.

Internet monitoring centre
- State-of-the-art technology and the latest standards for global analysis and monitoring of relevant formats and content on the internet, live streams, mobile content etc.
- Comprehensive internet monitoring capacity with simultaneous recording and monitoring of up to 60 IP channels.
- Analysis of the exposure of global advertising messages and logos on the internet using state-of-the-art methods and standards (on-screen share calculation).

Implementation of advertising equivalency and CPT calculations as well as documentation of target group and coverage analysis in the digital media sector.　　　　···▶

Example continued

Press monitoring centre

- Comprehensive capacity for continual analysis of relevant content in print media in the significant European core markets.
- Broad media panel of approximately 50 print media from the marketing, advertising, economy, politics, law, sport sectors etc.
- Daily analysis and evaluation of domestic and regional newspapers, specialist publications, magazines, newsletters etc.
- Service, e.g. same-day provision of digitised articles via e-mail.
- Calculation of media value.

(www.sportundmarkt.com)

Learning Activity 12.1

Go to each of the websites of Sport Marketing Surveys and Sport und Markt to identify the following:

- The range of evaluation activity each company performs.
- The clients of each company.
- Case study archive material of previous studies.
- Any client feedback on the benefits of evaluation.

Case Study

Performance research

SPONSORSHIP: Snowboarding

CLIENT CATEGORY: Snack food

PROBLEM: A search for edgy, active sports that attract the youth market yielded snowboarding as a potential sponsorship opportunity. Available, 'pre-packaged' sponsorships, however, were scarce, and were limited to just a few single day events spread unevenly during a four-month winter season. It was thus concluded that the sponsor must design and create its own sponsorship programme for this sport.

METHODOLOGY: Focus groups were conducted among both new and veteran snow boarders in several snowboard target markets, and quantitative on-site research was implemented at key resorts.

INITIAL FINDINGS: Focus groups revealed that snowboarders are considered 'status leaders' among their peers, thus confirming them as an attractive target for product usage, particularly in teenage/young adult social settings. Other findings, however, revealed a sport marketing dilemma:

- *Mountain resorts are seen as catering to skiers, yet skiers are considered pompous, conservative, and contemptuous toward boarders.*
- *Participants view their sport as anti-establishment and perceive themselves as members of a separatist, radical 'club'.*
- *Big corporate brand names are viewed part of the establishment, and sponsorship is seen as 'mainstreaming' the sport, making it even more popular among the dreaded skiers.*

ACTION TAKEN: It was concluded that traditional sponsorships in snowboarding might actually weaken rather than bolster the brand positioning, yet the lack of commercial clutter and difficulty in reaching this market still made sponsorship a worthwhile pursuit. In response to snowboarders' needs and concerns, the sponsor built snowboarding 'clubhouses' at several resorts. These clubhouses were stationed mid-mountain, and were reserved for snowboarders only. They were equipped with appropriate music, real-time videos of boarders, benches for watching other boarders, tools, and snack food vending machines.

FOLLOW-UP RESEARCH: To verify the impact of the snowboarding programme on brand image and purchase intent, on-site quantitative research was conducted at several ski/snow boarding mountains. First, a simple record keeping of the number of participants entering the clubhouse, the average time spent in the facility, the activities engaged in, and the frequency of snack food purchase was recorded. Second, a pre-post methodology was used to measure incremental gains in specific product attributes and brand consideration, as well as solicit recommendations for improving the clubhouse design.

RESULTS: The quantitative research revealed that the clubhouse concept satisfied many needs of the snowboarders, supported their desire for segregation from skiers, and made a measurable difference in brand consideration. However, a detailed audit of the frequency and duration of exposure to the clubhouse revealed high visitation, but only among a small core group of boarders. Thus, because the sponsorship reach was too limited, the pilot programmes were discontinued.

(Adapted from Performance Research, 2010)

Learning Activity 12.2

Based upon the information about snowboarders in the case study, and from your own knowledge of this sport segment, or others like them, what type of snack food do you think would be a hit with snowboarders? What other type of company and/or product/service (sport/non-sport) do you think would be a good fit with the snowboarding fraternity?

Chapter Review

The success of the sport marketing strategy against sport marketing objectives is evaluated through a process of control. All sport marketing tactical implementation must be assessed and this now often requires third party expertise to perform this function. Increasingly, sport sponsorship agreements are placing the emphasis on the sponsee to identify the benefits accrued by the sponsoring body. When sponsorship dollars, euros or pounds sterling are 'on-the-line', the importance of valid and reliable analysis of 'what went on' is an important necessity, and this function falls to you the sport marketer.

Further Reading

Bennett, G., Cunningham, G. and Dees, W. (2006) 'Measuring the marketing communication activations of a professional tennis tournament', *Sport Marketing Quarterly*, 15: 91–101.

   The purpose of this study was to assess the marketing communication activations of a professional tennis tournament. Results indicate that respondents were satisfied with the marketing communications activations chosen by managers and marketers of the event. Most spectators (78.4 per cent) indicated that they intended to attend the tournament the following year.

Mullin, B.J., Hardy, S. and Sutton, W.A. (2007) *Sport Marketing*, 3rd edition, Champaign, IL: Human Kinetics.

   See Chapter 17 – a short one, but a good one that will get you thinking about all of the elements of the sport marketing mix in their implementation.

Chapter 13
Writing a sport marketing plan

Learning Objectives

This chapter is designed to help you:

- identify a suitable structure for a sport marketing plan;
- outline the key features of a sport marketing plan;
- provide 'live' examples of each section of the sport marketing plan.

Introduction

So we are almost at the end of the journey, in fact this is the beginning of the end. Actually it is the beginning of the beginning, as you now have to put all of the concepts and ideas considered in the previous chapters together in the shape of a *sport marketing plan*. This is the 'road map', the 'game plan', the document needed by every sport business. The sport marketing plan's strategic purpose is to document where the sport business wants to go and how it is going to get there. At the tactical level it details what sport promotional tools will be deployed to achieve its stated sport marketing objectives and bring to life its defined strategies.

This chapter will revisit many of the key principles and ideas from previous chapters and provide a structure to the development of the sport marketing plan. It will present an example, from a variety of sport organisations (UK and international), of each phase of the sport marketing plan, and culminate with a sport marketing plan from a named sports organization.

Components of the sport marketing plan

A sport marketing plan coalesces all of the key features from the analysis, planning, implementation and control phases of the sport marketing process. To co-ordinate this information a suggested template for a professionally presented sport marketing plan is:

1   Executive summary.
2   Background to the plan.
3   Environment analysis.
4   Sport marketing priorities and key assumptions.
5   Sport marketing objectives.

6   Sport marketing strategy and tactics.
7   Resource requirements.
8   Control and evaluation.

The overall plan should be sport consumer focused with a view to delivering on the objectives of growing sport product/service sales and/or participation.

1 Executive summary

The executive summary section of your sport marketing plan allows you to introduce your company and explain the major points of your plan in brief. Many people who need to be on board with the plan simply won't have time or interest to read it in its entirety. The executive summary is for them. You should write it after you've completed the other sections so that you already know what your major points are. Some of the key points to cover are listed below:

1   Introduce your company by briefly describing the nature of your sport business, the sport products/ services you offer, and the competitive advantage they hold in the sport marketplace.
    N.B. If your sport business is already in operation, state how long you've been in business and how long you've been at your current location. Describe your sport business activities, including sales and customers, and highlight your accomplishments and successes. If your sport business is not yet in operation, describe the experience and training you have that qualifies you (and key partners or managers) to operate this kind of sport business.
2   State your founding philosophy (the mission statement) and company objectives.
3   Describe the organisational structure of your sport business. Is it a sole proprietorship, partnership or corporation? List key management personnel. List the members of the board of directors (or equivalents).
4   Close the executive summary with a brief statement of the main sport marketing objectives and strategies contained in the plan. Include a financial overview.

The summary should compel the reader to continue their interest in the remainder of the sport marketing plan. The Cyclist Repair Centre example below illustrates each of the criteria for inclusion in an open and straightforward manner.

Example
Cyclist Repair Centre: executive summary

Cyclist Repair Centre (CRC) is a cycling specific sports clinic serving the Manchester, and broader North West community. Founded in January 2011, Cyclist Repair Centre is expected to quickly gain market penetration through a focused strategy, doing what it does best, serving cyclists.

Cyclist Repair Centre has identified two distinct sport customer segments that they will target. The first segment is the competitive cyclist. There are a total of 4,500 potential competitive   ···▶

Example continued

cyclists with an annual growth rate of 4 per cent. This group is seeking therapeutic repair/recovery services or training services to make them more competitive in their races.

The second group is composed of recreational cyclists. This group has 32,090 potential customers and a 5 per cent growth rate. These cyclists may race occasionally, but generally they are just people with a passion/enjoyment for cycling. The demographics for the recreational cyclist indicate an affluent (ABC1) group, many 'cash rich but time poor'.

Cyclist Repair Center has chosen to locate their centre in Manchester as it is renowned as the centre of cycling in the UK. Manchester has the premier indoor velodrome in the country and offers hundreds of miles of road cycling immediately as you head out of town. British Cycling has its training base located here.

Cyclist Repair Centre offers a wide range of cycling-specific sports medicine and training services that range from sports massage, injury diagnosis and repair, personal training, bike fit and fitness assessment.

Cyclist Repair Center will have on staff an accredited personal coach/trainer, a sports medicine physician, massage therapists, as well as a wide range of cycling specific equipment to assist these service providers.

By locating in Manchester, a cycling town, and offering focused services targeting different types of cyclist, the Cyclist Repair Centre will quickly generate customers and revenue. Targeted revenue for years two and three is £369,000 and £443,000 respectively.

1.1 Objectives
- To reach profitability by the end of year two.
- Generate revenue exceeding £400,000 by year three.
- Achieve a net profit of at least 10 per cent by year three.

1.2 Mission
The Cyclist Repair Centre will provide clients with individualised, cycling specific assessment, diagnosis, treatment, and training programmes.

1.3 Keys to Success
- Maintain our focus on cycling specific injuries and training.
- Offer a wide range of services meeting all of the cyclist's needs.
- Design and employ strict financial controls, a requisite for an efficiently run sport organisation.

(Adapted from www.bplans.co.uk)

2 Background to the plan

This is the context to the sport marketing plan. The vision and/or mission statement is stated, followed by an outline of the purpose of the sport business; the sport products/services offered, and their unique features with reference to the sport consumer. An overview of 'fit' in the sport market identifies what is going well, badly, and/or in need of attention.

The following example from the FIFA U-17 Women's World Cup held in New Zealand in 2008 provides a back-drop to activity levels, the potential to grow participant numbers and to encourage the wider support of the public to spectate during the event.

Example
FIFA U-17 Women's World Cup 2008

Globally women's football is experiencing a huge growth in popularity, participation, and technical standard. Every country in FIFA's family now has women playing, with the total number participating in the game now approximately 40 million, making it the largest sport for women.

Some 150 million people in 150 countries watched the last Women's World Cup in 2007, with games drawing an average attendance of 38,000. The 1999 Women's World Cup final also drew the largest crowd in history to watch a women's sporting event, with over 90,000 present at the Rosebowl. With growth in technical development of the women's game, FIFA decided to introduce an U-17 Women's World Cup in 2008. Expressions of interest for the U-17 and U-20 events were placed in February 2006. In September 2006, New Zealand was awarded the rights to host the U-17 event, reflecting the strength of both the women's game and the grass roots level of football in the country. This is the second time New Zealand has hosted an age grade FIFA event. The last was the U-17 World Cup (for boys) in 1999. Like the women's equivalent, this was also a 16 team event, with finalists coming from all of the six different FIFA Confederations. As host, New Zealand will qualify automatically for the tournament.

The New Zealand team's performance will be a crucial factor in generating support for the event, in particular bringing people into the stadium which is a key success factor for FIFA. FIFA will provide partial funding support in addition to marketing and operational guidance to the Local Organising Committee (LOC). To create a legacy for the development of women's football in New Zealand the NZF/LOC will look to link in competition objectives with those of their marketing, development, and media departments. NZ Football's key reasons in competing for the rights to host the tournament, were linked to the development of the women's game in this country. They were to:

- grow the game – increase player numbers (both boys and girls);
- increase awareness of football – raise the profile of women's football;
- improve the chances of New Zealand's success at a FIFA World Cup.

In terms of delivering a successful event for FIFA there are two guiding principles:

- the football must be given every chance to be good (the teams must be happy);
- the host country must be ready (FIFA must be happy).

For both points, full stadiums and the atmosphere of the tournament play a significant role. In addition to the satisfaction of FIFA's objectives and those of NZF, the fact that this is an inaugural global event adds to the responsibility of providing a solid foundation from which future U-17 women's competitions can build. We therefore hope to ensure that this event creates a legacy not only for New Zealand, but for the women's game internationally.

(Adapted from www.majorevents.govt.nz)

3 Environment analysis

The environment analysis describes and analyses the sport organisation's current and medium to longer-term situation (see case study on p. 200).

Customer analysis. Describe the catchment area for the sport organisation, the demographics of the catchment area, estimate the total market size, quantify and profile the sport target market(s) currently serviced in respect to their demographic, geographic, psychographic and behavioural characteristics. Describe the needs or benefits each sport market is trying to satisfy. Analyse the sport target market(s) in terms of growth potential, special needs, etc. Consider the reasons why potential sport consumers do not currently use the service or why existing sport consumers do not use it more. Extend the description and analysis of the sport consumers to include other stakeholders such as suppliers, paid and voluntary staff, funding bodies, media contacts, political or governing bodies, community action groups, local community residents and other relevant stakeholder groups. Identify organisations or individuals by name, describe what their stake is and what benefits they are seeking from the organisation.

Marketing analysis. Describe the sport products(s)/service(s) being offered and the existing pricing, promotion, place, physical facilities, personnel, and policy management strategies. Review the information and analyse it in terms of performance or effectiveness.

Competitor analysis. Identify the sport organisation's competitors, where they are located, and their relevant characteristics using the sport marketing mix variables. If possible, visit the organisations or talk with their customers to unobtrusively gather information. Analyse your competition in terms of their competitive position or unique selling point (USP). The USP is what sport organisation's use to differentiate and distinguish themselves from their competitors. Identify ways in which you might complement your competitors, such as through targeting different sport markets or through developing co-operative ventures.

External environmental analysis. Organisations do not exist in a vacuum free from the influences of their surrounding environment. Describe and analyse trends such as political, economic, socio-cultural, technological, environmental and legal forces. Get into the habit of scanning local newspapers, business magazines, professional and trade journals, government reports, seminars and other sources to obtain information.

The SWOT analysis summarises the environment analysis and you can see how an organising committee for a high profile sport event constructed a SWOT for the 2010 World Rowing Championships held in New Zealand.

Example
K2010 World Rowing Championships

Strengths	Weaknesses
• Popularity and standard of rowing in New Zealand	• International television coverage of major international rowing regattas in New Zealand
• Performance of the New Zealand rowing teams in the Olympics and previous World Championships	• Drop off in secondary school rowers participation to club registrations
• Strength of New Zealand secondary school rowing	

···▶

Example continued

- Marketability – cost effective access to personalities within rowing
- Rowing New Zealand's growing international reputation
- Access to marketing knowledge from previous World Championships held
- Fan base loyalty in New Zealand
- NZ Diverse culture
- New Zealand's International reputation as a tourist destination (TNZ 100 per cent pure campaign)
- International television coverage
- International media coverage.

- Distance to travel to New Zealand
- Availability of sponsorship dollar in New Zealand
- Timing of the regatta
- Accessibility of Karapiro
- Availability of accommodation especially 4 and 5 star accommodation in the Waikato region for international and national tourists.

Opportunities

- Transference of a potential fan base to a participation base within the rowing community
- Attracting ethnic markets
- Endorsement from VIPs (FISA, New Zealand government and the New Zealand national team)
- Commercial investment for national sponsors
- To promote rowing in New Zealand at a level that will capture the nation's imagination
- Exposure for Rowing New Zealand internationally and domestically
- Attract future sponsors to the sport.

Threats

- Rugby World Cup 2011 – attention and subsequent funding
- Weather
- Exam time conflict with secondary school students
- Potential poor performance of the New Zealand rowing team
- Current economic environment
- Perceived value of the product
- New Zealand public's lack of affiliation to international teams or team members.

Reflection Point 13.1

In view of the severe austerity measures (e.g. government spending cuts) it is interesting to note here that the threat of losing funding is not identified in this SWOT analysis. But, in relation to this, how important is this funding stream to sport events, and should it be reflected in the sport marketing plan?

4 Sport marketing priorities and key assumptions (or opportunity analysis)

This section requires a strategic focus in which the information from the situation analysis is used to identify opportunities, problems or gaps that need to be addressed. This is the second level of analysis that identifies assumptions about the issues faced in the immediate future, especially capability and resource issues. The Critical Success Factors are summarised, that is, the actions that the sport organisation must address to be able to achieve the plan. It is conceived with the key sport target markets in mind. A simple way to write an opportunity analysis is to identify three to six of the most important points that emerge from the situation analysis. These are the aspects that are focused on in the action plan and should be thought of as being most critical to the sport organisation's success.

The K2010 World Rowing Championships organising team identified five priority areas for further address in the remainder of the sport marketing plan. For each, a key question was reported that exposed the direction of the sport marketing strategy to follow.

Example
K2010 World Rowing Championships

Economic climate	What will encourage people to attend this event, rather than alternative events and activities?
Awareness	How can we ensure exposure of the event both nationally and internationally?
Accessibility	How can we ensure potential ticket holders can get to the venue and can purchase tickets with ease?
Affordability	How can we ensure that there are no sectors (family, students) that are priced out of attending K2010?
Perceived value	What will make the event an experience of value?

---

5 Sport marketing objectives

Sport marketing objectives often get confused with sport marketing strategies. Sport marketing objectives state what the sport organisation wants to achieve! They are concerned with the Ansoff matrix, and must be sport product/service and market focused:

- Selling existing sport products/services to existing sport segments.
- Developing new sport products/services for existing sport segments.
- Extending existing sport products/services to new sport segments.
- Developing new sport products/services for new sport segments.

Sport marketing objectives should be *quantitative* in nature, therefore, avoid using terms such as *increase*, *penetrate*, *maximise* in a general sense. Give them a numerical value in statements which relate to a sport organisation's market share, sales volume, profit margins, and sport product/service positioning, for example:

- Increase participation by 1 per cent each year for 3 years.
- Increase the percentage of the 'Paula' segment doing 3 × 30 from × to × by y.
- Increase sales by x per cent by y.

Example
Sport marketing objectives adapted from K2010 World Rowing Championships

- To attain a crowd attendance of 80,000 for the 2010 World Rowing Championships.
- To deliver a world-class event that exceeds FISA and world rowing expectations.
- To establish a financial (capital and revenue) legacy for Rowing New Zealand.
- To create a legacy and inspire future generations to continue their pursuit in rowing from secondary schools through to club and national representation.
- To raise the profile of Rowing New Zealand.
- To develop a database of demographic information for Rowing New Zealand.

Example
Sport marketing objectives for FIFA U-17 Women's World Cup

- To implement an innovative sport marketing and media/PR campaign that engages New Zealanders.
- To achieve 200,000 spectators during the U-17 WWC.

Additionally, specific sport development objectives are identified for associated and legacy-related activity.

New Zealand Football's development objectives

- To increase the number of women and girls involved in football by 25 per cent.
- To raise the profile of women's football nationally.
- To raise the acceptance of women's football in NZ, but particularly in school-aged children.

In both cases it appears that not all of the sport marketing objectives conform to the SMART principle. However, with baseline research data in existence, that is, the current profile level of women's football in NZ (and this is not a fact that can be taken for granted), it is possible through primary research to determine whether an improvement in the profile of the game has occurred as a result of the tournament. Similarly, creating a legacy or delivering a world-class event do have criteria that can be used to assess their achievement.

6 Sport marketing strategies and tactics

Sport marketing strategies refer to 'what' sport marketing activities a sport organisation plans to undertake, and sport marketing tactics refer to 'how', specifically, the sport organisation will achieve the sport marketing objectives. Sport marketing strategy can focus on penetrating the sport market; diversifying the sport product/service and the sport market; new sport product/service development; expanding market share; entering into niche sport markets etc. The sport marketing strategy will consider a combination of approaches to utilising the sport marketing mix prior to giving greater detail to these functions in the tactical implementation plan. The 12-month sport marketing tactical implementation plan states the precise means by which the sport marketing objectives are to be achieved. The objectives and strategy keep an eye on the longer-term, that is, overall aims of the sport marketing function within the organisation and the broader business objectives of the sport organisation itself.

Sport marketing strategies relate to the components of the sport marketing mix, and include:

- Sport product/service mix – quantity, range, quality, differentiation, positioning, add/delete service components.
- Sport ISMC mix – advertising approaches, overall sport promotional campaign, sales promotions, develop a sales force.
- Sport price – to attract new customers, new pricing policies for target sport groups.
- Sport place/distribution – develop new locations, improve supply chain.
- Sport PR – building long-term sport customer relationships.

TaylorMade-adidas has the following sport marketing strategies identified for implementation in their 2015 strategic business plan.

1 Re-launch the Ashworth brand with a focus on reconnecting the relaxed, lifestyle-oriented apparel with all golfers (professional and non-professional).
2 Extend the market leadership position through the introduction of one major product innovation each year.
3 Attract the most talented professional tour players to increase brand exposure and traction.
4 Explore and execute new and innovative ways to promote products using social media (Facebook and Twitter), online and product seeding initiatives.
5 Showcase the performance advantages and design credentials of products by creating state-of-the-art retail floor displays.
6 Extend market share by delivering best-in-class lines of products at multiple price points.

Each strategic thrust will enact its own sport marketing tactical implementation plan. Manipulation of each of the components of the sport marketing mix delivers the sport marketing strategy towards the attainment of the sport marketing objectives. Crucially, the integrated nature of the tactical implementation plan comes to the fore, as the sport marketer ensures a seamless delivery of the sport communication message to the sport target market(s). Remember that multiple sport target markets are the norm and so care must be taken to place the correct sport communication message in front of the correct sport target market. This is demonstrated by Figure 13.1 as it identifies internal messages to members of the organising committee, the social media savvy participant/spectator, and to both domestic and international journalists to help promote the event. Each has multiple update opportunities across the timeline of the plan to ensure a regular drip-feed of information to each of these important stakeholder groups.

Twelve-month sport marketing tactical implementation plan

The timeframe of 12-months available to the K2010 Rowing World Championships organising team created a tactical, rather than a strategic, focus to the implementation of the sport marketing mix. The communication timeline presents an overview of sport communication activities for implementation across this period. However, an innovative ISMC strategic approach was adopted by the organising team to move towards the achievement of multiple sport marketing objectives within multiple sport target markets. This was the use of the K2010 'RowBox', as follows.

The 'RowBox' is a 20-foot container providing an exhibition and 'on water' virtual experience. The 'Rowbox' toured international and national club regattas and secondary schools. The concept created a competitive environment for a National 'RowBox' Inter-School Tournament and corporate challenge events. Sport promotional activity of the World Championships surrounded the tour with posters, DVDs, flyers, merchandise and advertising (billboards, staff, e.g. branded cars, business cards, badges, uniforms; provided in-kind via print, radio and broadcast partners). Sport target markets that were reached included rowing clubs, primary and secondary schools, universities, sport fans, ethnic groups, and the international rowing community. As a result of this one initiative, all sport marketing objectives, except the specific delivery of the world champs themselves (see section 5, 'Sport marketing objectives', above), were touched. This is clear evidence of an integrated sport marketing tactical approach.

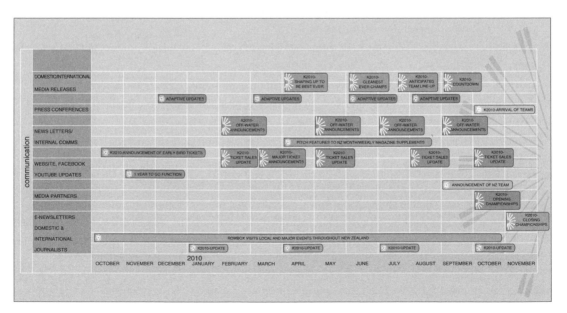

Figure 13.1 Communication timeline for K2010 Rowing World Championships (www.majorevents.govt.nz)

7 Resource requirements – revenue and capacity

Resource requirements are identified for all sport marketing-related activity across the period of the tactical implementation. This provides interested parties/publics with clear and unambiguous information about financial requirements. It also acts as an indicator for the control and evaluation phase of the plan. The sport marketing plan budget is either set in advance by the sport business and the plan works within its constraints or the budget is borne out of the plan. The latter course is the most effective as it allows the sport marketing function to propose what is really needed financially to realise the vision and objectives of the business. However, in reality, the sport marketing plan, more often than not, has to work within the financial constraints imposed on it by the sport business as whole.

Example
The marketing budget of the 2010 Vancouver Winter Olympics marketing and communications expenses

Sponsorship, Sales and Servicing	$21,184,000
Licensing and Merchandising	$7,225,000
Commercial Rights Management	$4,035,000
Ticketing	$9,083,000
Communications	$6,393,000
Community Relations	$10,619,000
Editorial Services	$10,442,000
Media Relations	$3,613,000
Internet Management	$7,446,000
Brand and Creative Services	$15,588,000
Torch Relays	$30,799,000
Total	$126,427,000
	(www.vancouver2010.com)

---

8 Control and evaluation

It is important to describe the processes and procedures to be used to monitor the tactical implementation and report on progress towards the achievement of the sport marketing objectives. Arrangements should be included for evaluation of all specific actions especially effectiveness of sport communications. Key performance indicators such as sponsorship recruitment rates, website hits, image enhancement/awareness increases in target sport consumer markets, financial analysis etc. are all important to this stage of the sport marketing process.

Example
Key measurables for the FIFA U-17 Women's World Cup tournament

Crowd attendance
- Ticketing receipts of all stadiums on match days.

Satisfaction levels of FIFA, LOC staff and volunteers, and teams
- Survey administered by email to sample of FIFA and LOC staff, and all team managers one week after the event.
- Focus to be on whether a fun experience was delivered to these sectors, and areas of success and improvement required.

Satisfaction levels of fans
- Volunteers to collect emails of as many consenting attendees at pre-designated matches (including opening, finals, NZ, and key games) as possible.
- Undertake in all venues.

Sponsorship revenue
- Cumulative value of National Supporter and Media Partner packages.
- Include the value of contra-based packages (for example, free advertising space or mobile airtime).

Ticketing receipts
- To be supplied by ticketing agency.

Furthermore, sport marketing plans should identify procedures for tracking each type of sport marketing activity being used. Tracking helps monitor the effectiveness of sport marketing tactical implementation and is especially helpful with overall programme evaluation. Here are some types of media along with ideas for tracking their effectiveness. The techniques will vary depending on your sport product/service and sport target market.

Display advertising. Tracking can be done through the use of different phone numbers, special offers (specific to the advertisement or publication), or reference to a specific department to call for information. When calls come in, staff must be prepared to record the information so the results can be tallied for that publication.

Direct marketing. With postal mailings, tracking is relatively simple. Include on the mailing label a code (called a key code or a source code) that corresponds with the mailing list so you know which list is producing the best results, and instruct your staff to record the information by asking the sport consumer for the code. You can also include sport consumer numbers here and record repeat orders without the problem of re-entering their information into your database. For telemarketing campaigns, tracking is also relatively simple since a live person is communicating with the sport consumer throughout the entire process, in most cases.

TV or radio ads. These can be tracked through the use of unique phone numbers, special offers (specific to that advertisement) or reference to a specific department to call for information. Again, when those calls come in, staff must be prepared to record the information so the results can be tallied for that particular spot. Another less exact method, if you're advertising on a very large scale, is to track immediate sales along with the timing of the advertisement.

Internet marketing. Usually, this is easily tracked because it is based on click-throughs or page impressions. Your web administrator should be able to provide reports that indicate the number of click-throughs that actually led to the purchase of your sport product/service. Also unique URLs that direct to your website to track user response to a specific promotion or campaign. You may also experience call-in sales as a result of your website activity.

Sales promotions. Most 'closed' sales promotions are basically 'self-tracking' because they require the sport consumer to do something, such as fill out an entry form (trackable), turn in a coupon, return a rebate slip (trackable), or log-on to a website to claim a prize (also trackable). 'Open' sales promotions, such as clearance sales, require a little more work to track, although they can be tracked in a general way by noting increased sales for that time period, store, region, or whatever the parameters of the sale.

Sport events. A sport event is also tricky to track. You know how many people attended, but do you know how many sales occurred as a result? You can issue coupons at the sport event that can be tracked, offer other special deals, or even allow attendees to join a special club. You have to be creative in order to track the true sales results of a big sport event.

Trade shows. A trade show's effectiveness can be tracked by collecting the right information at the show and following up on it. These results must also be tallied and recorded. The success of trade show attendance can be measured by the number of sport consumers who request information from your stand.

Reflection Point 13.2

Before the sport marketing plan kicks-off, make sure you have the database (MIS) structure in place to record this information. Use codes for every level of information so that you can sort by various specifications. This takes a lot of planning, as well as training for staff. What might be a consequence to the sport marketing plan if information is not recorded in an MIS?

A complete sport marketing plan

To bring this chapter to a crescendo the case study below presents an example of a sport marketing plan in its entirety. As is customary, the summary of the plan is presented in the executive summary. The backdrop to the plan identifies the current issues for address and the strategic direction to be taken in the remainder of the plan. The SWOT analysis summarises the environment audit and helps to identify priorities that act as opportunities for exploitation by the sport marketing strategy. Sport marketing objectives across three years are outlined and two of these from year one are developed into a tactical implementation plan. The budget for implementation activity is determined and control and evaluation techniques are suggested. These need some further detail attaching to them to provide a greater level of feedback on plan performance. One further critical point to note is that specific lines of responsibility should be identified in the tactical implementation plan to add that very important component of accountability.

Case Study
An adaptation of the Shropshire and Telford & Wrekin Sports Partnership marketing plan
1 Executive summary
Where are we now?

Current situation

> *Previous sport marketing and communication activities undertaken by the partnership have been limited and ad-hoc. There has been no systematic approach to communication and sharing of information. As a result, there is no existing identity or strong awareness of the partnership to the wider audience.*

Opportunities

- *Shared ownership, commitment and support from partners.*
- *Good relationships and existing links.*
- *Network for greater consultation and sharing best practice.*
- *Framework for improved, co-ordinated reporting procedure leading to increased funding.*

Areas of concern

- *Lack of systematic two-way communication channels.*
- *Poor links with non-competitive sports, private sector and the media.*
- *Different demographics and working practices of partners.*
- *Continuation of funding.*

What do we want to achieve?

Overall aim

> *Improve the communication of opportunities, successes and best practice across the county to successfully support the partnerships' overall aim of enabling sport and physical activity to be a part of everybody's everyday life in STW.*

Year 1 goals

> *Launch a branding campaign and presence for the partnership and introduce effective communication channels through which awareness of the partnership can be established. Year 1 will introduce a central database/management information system to support effective performance measurement.*

Year 2 goals

> *Develop positive brand recognition and greater awareness of SPA (sport and physical activity) opportunities across the county. Partners will be encouraged to share information and best practice through the development of effective two-way communication channels and regular*

consultation and feedback opportunities. The database will also be extended to include wider groups and increased input and use from partners.

Year 3 goals

Create ownership of brand by partners and establish the partnership as a flagship CSP (County Sport Partnership) for its achievements and working practices. The partnership will be in a position to react efficiently to the needs of partners through on-going consultation, monitoring and evaluation. Successful promotion of SPA opportunities to wider, harder-to-reach groups.

What do we want to say to whom?

Target groups

The sport marketing plan will provide a framework for co-ordinating communication efforts across the county and therefore strengthening the message to target groups – active and non-active participants and organisations from the following sectors: public and private sectors, sport, education, youth, equity and inclusion groups.

Messages

- Active Everyone – you don't have to be sporty to be active.
- Active Life – a little everyday goes a long way.
- Active Voice – one voice for sport and physical activity.

What are we going to do?

Year 1 actions: priorities within the action plan include the creation and launch of a brand, development of a new website and electronic partnership news service, establishing positive media relations, production of promotional literature, reports and newsletters, marketing support for events and the development of a central data management system.

What are the resource implications?

Marketing budget: £24,500 (as identified in the action plan).

How will it be measured, monitored and evaluated?

Criteria

- Annual partnership survey and focus groups.
- Online feedback form.
- Positive media coverage, monitoring and evaluation.
- Online registration for website and partnership.
- E-news service.
- Participation figures.
- Delivered within budget.

2 Background to the plan

Introduction

The Shropshire and Telford & Wrekin County Sports Partnership (STW CSP) is a partnership of key agencies committed to establishing a sustainable infrastructure to provide an integrated and unified system for all the community to benefit from sport and physical activity (SPA).

The simple principle of effective sport marketing and communications – knowing what you should be saying, to who and how – is fundamental to the work of the STW CSP. Marketing and communications is recognised by Sport England as being one of the three key strategic areas that CSPs need to focus on to deliver their goals and objectives. With the overarching aim of striving towards a single, coherent system for sport in the UK and increasing participation in SPA by 1 per cent, promoting this message and communicating the benefits of SPA to improve uptake and involvement is essential.

Our aim is to build a strong partnership that moves towards these goals. The creation and successful implementation of an effective sport marketing communications plan forms the basis of ensuring our partners and key target groups know:

- What the STW CSP is.
- What it does.
- Who it works for, and with.
- How it can service, inform and support SPA in the county.

Integral to this plan is the creation of a partnership management information system.

Current position

Where are we now?

Previous sport marketing and communication activities undertaken by the partnership have been limited.

- Brand identity – STW CSP currently has no logo, strap line or widely recognisable identity of its own. This presents an opportunity for developing and promoting a new, all encompassing identity for the partnership.
- Website – www.shropshiresport.gov.uk is hosted by Shropshire County Council. The statistics show that the site is not used to its full potential in terms of users and search engines. It also appears visually inconsistent and parts of it are not updated on a regular basis. The website feedback report rated the site's accessibility very high (9.7 out of 10), but found user satisfaction to be very poor with scores below 2.5.
- @ction Replay magazine – this has a circulation of 10,000 and is produced 3x per annum to coincide with the start of the new school term. It is aimed at young people, parents and clubs and is distributed to children (via a direct mail database) through schools, libraries, youth associations and leisure centres. The magazine is valued for its club contact information and details of upcoming coach education courses, but research has identified two areas of concern: 1) as the content is aimed at both young children and adults, the magazine is not 'owned' by

either group; and 2) a duplication issue, and different forms of communication that reach each target group with partnership news and messages are more effectively delivered and at a greatly reduced cost.

- *Communication – apart from @ction Replay, there is no systematic or regular approach to communications and information is shared on an ad-hoc basis across all target groups. There is the need to create greater reliability in sport communication links or new sport marketing vehicles.*

Vision and objectives

What do we want to achieve?

To deliver an effective sport marketing strategy and improve the communication of opportunities, successes and best practice between partners and target groups to successfully support the partnership's overall aim of enabling sport and physical activity to be a part of everybody's everyday life. The very essence of sport marketing is strategic planning and coordination. The STW CSP will have a yearly sport marketing plan that weaves together all activities and promotions in a considered and effective manner. A branding campaign needs to be the first stage of lifting the STW CSP to a new level giving us a springboard to engage with wider sectors.

Sport marketing and communication aims

1.0 *To achieve a strong corporate image and reputation for STW CSP consistent with its vision and values.*

2.0 *To develop and maintain a central database system to support an effective performance measurement structure.*

3.0 *To establish effective two-way communication with partners to promote STW CSP, share good practice and actively engage them in all aspects of the partnership's work.*

4.0 *To create positive communication with the public in order to raise awareness of the partnership, the benefits of physical activity and positively impact participation levels.*

5.0 *To raise the profile of SPA in Shropshire through use of the Olympic Games 2012, national campaigns and events.*

Strategic themes and objectives

The sport marketing aims have been developed from the partnerships' strategic themes and key communication objectives. The sport communication objectives within each of these themes are identified below.

Key messages

What do we want to say?

The sport marketing and communications strategy has identified the following key messages that all forms of communication should contain to ensure consistency within and across the partnership:

- *Active Everyone – providing sport and physical activity opportunities for everyone 'You don't have to be sporty to be active'.*

- *Active Life – enabling sport and physical activity to be a part of everyday life 'A little everyday goes a long way'.*
- *Active Voice – providing a single voice and system for sport and physical activity in Shropshire and Telford & Wrekin 'One voice for sport and physical activity'.*

3 Environment analysis

Strengths

- *Dedicated core team in place*
- *Shared ownership and commitment of partners*
- *National recognition through Sport England*
- *No competition*
- *Existing contacts and links with partners*
- *Success of Youth Games and DFest*
- *Depth and breadth of partners (LAs, SSPs, Police, PCTs)*
- *SABC & T&W beacon status for services in SPA*
- *Good links with LSPs in Shropshire and T&W.*

Weaknesses

- *Lack of identity*
- *Website*
- *Confusion between Active Sports & STW Partnership*
- *Two-way communications between partners*
- *Existing media relations*
- *Large geographical area*
- *Lengthy decision-making process*
- *Engagement of private sector*
- *Links with non-competitive sports*
- *Fragmented working – no collective approach across the county*
- *Links with HE & FE establishments*
- *Lack of central database or information system.*

Opportunities

- *Framework for greater consultation*
- *Evidence-based reporting and future investment*
- *Provide a network for sharing best practice*
- *No existing brand identity – blank canvas*
- *London Olympics 2012*
- *National campaigns and initiatives*
- *Ability to draw on national and regional funding*
- *Links with regional CSPs and SEWM*
- *Centralising information and data storage*
- *Lifestyle trend towards healthier living*
- *National surveys (e.g. Active People) to provide base-line data*
- *Diversify into other physical activity areas*
- *Attract wider participation – 16+ and inactive target groups.*

Threats

- *Confusion with role and perception of hosting partner*
- *Different demographics and working practices of partners*
- *Continuation of partnership funding*
- *Other short-term funding issues*
- *Difficulty accessing sedentary market*
- *Ageing population (in Shropshire)*
- *Expectations in terms of partnership functions.*

4 Sport marketing priorities and key assumptions (or opportunity analysis)

- *Developing sporting pathways – developing a simple, cohesive system for people to develop to the maximum of their ability according to their choice.*
- *London 2012 Olympic Legacy – using the Games to promote PA and tourism within STW.*
- *Corporate effectiveness and building the partnership.*
- *Education and lifelong learning – using SPA to promote academic attainment and adult education to benefit the individual and economy of STW.*
- *Community development and health improvement – using SPA to strengthen local communities to help people effect a positive and healthy lifestyle.*

5 Sport marketing objectives
What is our long-term vision?
Year 1 goals

- *Create distinction between Active Sports and CSP.*
- *Create awareness and establish a presence for the partnership through a strong image.*
- *Introduce effective communication channels to give a good springboard to further develop relationships and consultation.*
- *Implement a central database and management information system to support effective performance measurement.*

Year 2 goals

- *Create positive perception of partnership and develop brand recognition with a wider audience.*
- *Enable effective two-way communication and encourage sharing of information and best practice.*
- *Develop the database/management information system to include wider groups and greater input/ use from partners.*
- *Establish regular consultation and feedback opportunities to enable the development and continuous improvement of marketing and communication activities.*
- *Create greater awareness of SPA opportunities and benefits across the county.*

Year 3 goals

- *Sustain positive perception towards partnership.*
- *Create ownership of brand by partners.*
- *Gain regional/national recognition for partnership achievements and working practices – flagship CSP for SEWM.*
- *React efficiently and effectively to marketing and communications needs of partners through on-going consultation, monitoring and evaluation.*
- *Develop awareness of SPA opportunities and benefits to wider audience (e.g. sedentary groups).*

6 Sport marketing strategies and tactics

Key Actions	Target and Timescale	Measuring Success	Resource Implications
To achieve a strong corporate image and reputation			
Create distinction between the previous Active Sports Team and the new STW CSP.	Partnership team to meet all partners face-to-face before September. Press release to be distributed in August. Communication sent to schools and physical activity organisations, introducing the partnership team. Communication to schools to coincide with start of new school term and highlight the website for updated club contacts in light of @ction Replay *discontinuing*.	Formal feedback obtained from partnership survey/focus groups in February to coincide with annual conference. Media coverage secured. Number of new relationships established with physical activity groups.	Staff time and postage. £1k for partnership survey/focus groups.
Develop new 'single' identity for STW CSP.	Design brief agreed by 13 September. Core team and partners to adopt new identity by November.	Number of partners using the new logo in their communication. Focus groups to be established one year after implementation of new identity to evaluate its success.	£1.5k

···▶

Launch new partnership brand to partners and public.	Brand to be officially launched at annual conference in February.	Number of attendees at conference.	Staff time.
Creation of new website, first issue of partnership newsletter and e-news to coincide with the launch of the brand.	Launch plan to be agreed by October.	Focus groups.	Launch costs included in promotional budget of £6k.
Promote the partnership – raise the profile of the core team and communicate their successes on a regular basis through the various marketing mechanisms identified: • Core team page on website • Press releases • E-news • Quarterly/annual reports and publications • Partnership awards and presentation evening.	Identify one internal good news story per month to promote across all communications.	Awareness and perception of the core team to be evaluated as part of the survey/focus groups. Commitment of partnership funding after Yr3.	Staff time. Costs to be taken from promotional budget.

···▶

To create positive communication with the public in order to raise awareness of the partnership, the benefits of physical activity and positively impact participation levels.

Establish media contacts database and develop media relations with local, regional and appropriate national press, radio and television. Partner publications and specialist sport and physical activity publications to be included.	*Media database to be complete by September.*	*Establish internal press cuttings system to monitor media coverage.*	*Staff time*
Identify and proactively promote news stories that support the partnership's key messages and objectives and the following priority groups: • *Girls and women* • *BME groups* • *Disability groups* • *Those on lower incomes* • *Over 45s and over 60s.*	*Distribute at least one press release per month to sustain a presence for the partnership and its work.*		*Staff time.* *Printing and postage costs part of promotional budget.*
Work with partners to ensure existing and new websites and literature is fit for purpose – public-facing and user-friendly in terms of content and accessibility.	*September for existing website.* *December for new partnership website.* *On-going monitoring of sport literature and guides.*	*Website usage and feedback. Consultation on sporting literature.*	*Part of website development budget.* *Staff time.*

···▶

Develop links with private organisations/main employers in STW to encourage active lifestyles in the workplace.	Five companies to be identified by December.	Positive coverage secured in internal communications. Number of organisations signing up with intention of introducing new SPA initiatives for employees.	Part of promotional budget.

7 Resource requirements

Resources

What are the resource implications?

- In terms of staff time, delivery of the STW CSP sport marketing and communications plan is the responsibility of the Information and Communications Officer with support from the core team.
- Funding to deliver the sport marketing and communications plan has been secured as part of the establishment and development of the partnership through Sport England. The total sport marketing and communications budget is £24.5k, and the breakdown of this budget is as follows:

Sport marketing and communications activity

Partnership survey and focus groups	£1000
Creation of new brand/identity	£1500
Annual report	£1000
Management information system	£10000
Website and e-news creation	£5000

Breakdown of £6k promotional budget

Press releases and photo-calls	£800
Launch of new brand	£1000
On-going website development	£700
Newsletter – issue one	£1300
Promotional literature, flyers and adverts	£1000
Media (newspaper and magazine) subscriptions	£200
Promotion of Olympic Games, other national campaigns and county events (e.g. SYG, DFest and coaches conference)	£1000

8 Control and evaluation

How will it be measured, monitored and evaluated?

- *We have established measurement criteria for each action to ensure that the campaign delivers against its objectives and provides a tangible return on investment.*
- *Measurement criteria as detailed in the sport marketing and communications action plan include:*

  - *focus groups;*
  - *annual survey;*
  - *online feedback form;*
  - *positive media coverage and evaluation;*
  - *online registering for website and e-news;*
  - *participation figures – internal and external events;*
  - *delivered within budget.*

Targets and timescales for each key activity will be regularly monitored by the Business Development Manager, who reports directly to the Partnership Manager. Progress will be reported at each Management Board meeting and shared to the wider partnership on a quarterly basis.

Reflection Point 13.3

Since the Comprehensive Spending Review (2010) of the new coalition government, County Sport Partnerships appear to be a thing of the past and no longer will receive their funding. This reminds us that even the best sport marketing plan is not a panacea and cannot save a sport organisation if its external environment becomes so hostile. Do you think it is possible to foresee such political manoeuvres, and if so, at which point of the sport marketing process should these be identified?

Learning Activity 13.1

There really is only one suitable learning activity for you to perform at this point, can you think what it is? Yes, go and construct a sport marketing plan of your own. This could be for a project you are undertaking with your colleagues on your course or with a sport organisation of which you are a member.

Chapter Review

The sport marketing plan outlines what a sport organisation wants to achieve, how it can make efforts to achieve its aims, and whether it actually achieved them. It brings together all of the concepts, ideas, tools and techniques of the sport marketing discipline and enacts them for real. This chapter has suggested a format and provided insight into the key sections of a sport marketing plan – remember the four stages of analysis, planning, implementation, control – and it just leaves you now requiring to 'go do it!' for real.

Further Reading

Stotlar, D. K. (2005) *Developing Successful Sport Marketing Plans*, 2nd edition, Morgantown: Fitness Industry Technology.

This is a practical text that runs you through each of the stages of constructing a sport marketing plan. It gives valuable insight into the process and has lots of practical activities for you to perform.

Stotlar, D. K (2001) *Developing Successful Sport Sponsorship Plans*, Morgantown: Fitness Industry Technology.

Securing sponsorship is extremely important, so this text takes the same path as the one above to help a sport organisation construct a successful sponsorship offering.

References

adidas Group (2010) www.adidas-group.com

adidas Group investor relations www.adidas-group.com/en/investorrelations/strategy/reebok/default.aspx

adidas Group '2015 Strategic Plan: Reebok Strategy' available at http://www.adidas-group.com/en/investorrelations/strategy/reebok/default.aspx

Armstrong, G. and Kotler, P. (2005) *Principles of Marketing*, 14th edition, London: Prentice Hall.

Beech, J. and Chadwick, S. (2007) *The Marketing of Sport*, London: Prentice Hall/Financial Times.

Bell, B. and Blakey, P. (2010) 'Do boys and girls go out to play? Women's football and social marketing at Euro 2005', *International Journal of Sport Management and Marketing*, 7, 3/4: 156–172.

Bennett, G. and Lachowetz, T. (2004) 'Marketing to lifestyles: action sports and generation Y', *Sport Marketing Quarterly*, 13: 239–243.

Beverland, M. and Ewing, M. (2005) 'Slowing the adoption and diffusion process to enhance brand repositioning: the consumer driven repositioning of Dunlop Volley' *Business Horizons*, 48: 385–391.

'Big Goals, Big Game, Big Records' available at http://blog.twitter.com/2010/06/big-goals-big-game-big-records.html (accessed 4 November 2010).

Black (1993) *The Essentials of Public Relations*, London: Kogan Page.

Blakey, P. A. and Chavan, R. (2011) 'Twenty20 Cricket sport sponsorship management strategies: a comparison between India and the UK', *International Journal of Sport Management and Marketing* (in press).

bplans (2010) 'Cyclist Repair Centre', available at www.bplans.co.uk/sports_therapy_business_plan/executive_summary_fc.cfm (accessed 15 December 2010).

BOA Athletes' Guide to Dealing with the Media (undated) available at www.uksport.gov.uk/docLib/.../Athlete.../BOA_media_training-handout.doc

Bonoma, T. (1984) 'Making your marketing strategies work', *Harvard Business Review*, 62, 2: 69–76.

Bovee, C, and Thill, J. (1992) *Marketing*, New York: McGraw-Hill.

Brand Finance (2009) 'The power of brands', Soccer Ex. Q1, available at http://www.brandfinance.com/knowledge_centre (accessed 20 September 2010).

British Olympics Association www.olympics.org.uk

Chavan, R. (2010) IPL Case Study, Personal Communication.

Chelsea FC (2010) www.chelseafc.com/page/Foundation_Charity/0,,10268,00.html (accessed 18 November 2010).

Collinson, P. (2010) 'Scots make the most of Europe's winter woes', available at www.smh.com.au/environment/scots-make-the-most-of-europes-winter-woes-20100109-lzvz.html (accessed 10 January 2010).

Condor de Paul (2008) 'Nike internal analysis', available at http://condor.depaul.edu/almaney/StrategicAnalysisofNike.htm (accessed 22 December 2010).

Cornwell, T.B., Weeks, C.S. and Roy, D.P. (2005) 'Sponsorship-linked marketing: opening the black box', *Journal of Advertising*, 34, 2: 21.

Costolo, J. (2010) 'Twitter now has 190 million users tweeting 65 million times a day', available at www.pressgazette.co.uk/story.asp?sectioncode=1andstorycode=46425andc=1 (accessed 14 September 2010).

Croteau, D. and Hoynes, W. (2003) *Media Society: Industries, Images and Audiences*, 3rd edition, Thousand Oaks: Pine Forge Press.

Curran, N. (2008) 'Targeted audience advertising will give platforms the edge', in Stuart, J. (ed) *Digital Sports Competition Strategies*, London: Inside Business Media.

Cutlip, S.M. Center, A.H. and Broom, G.M. (2000) *Effective Public Relations*, 8th edition, London: Prentice Hall.

Department of Culture, Media and Sport (2010) 'November London 2012 Olympic and Paralympic budget report published – Anticipated final cost down £29m', available at www.culture.gov.uk/news/media_releases/7555.aspx (accessed 10 November 2010).

DiFonzo, N. and Bordia, P. (2000) 'How top PR professionals handle hearsay: corporate rumors, their effects, and strategies to manage them' *Public Relations Review*, 26, 2: 173–190.

Dionisio, P., Leal, C. and Moutinho, L. (2008) 'Fandom affiliation and tribal behaviour: a sports marketing application', *Qualitative Market Research: An International Journal* 11, 1: 17–39.

Direct Marketing Observations (2008) 'Sports and Social Media', available at http://directmarketingobservations.com/2008/11/30/sports-and-social-media/ (accessed 23 October 2010).

Dobersek, U. and Bartling, C. (2008) 'Connection between personality type and sport', *American Journal of Psychological Research*, 4, 1: 22–28.

Dorna Sports www.dornasports.com (accessed 15 December 2009).

Drummond, G. and Ensor, J. (1999) *Strategic Marketing: Planning and Control*, Oxford: Butterworth-Heinemann.

Durchholz and Woratschek (2010) 'Benefit segmentation of women's soccer spectators regarding FIFA Women's World Cup 2011 in Germany', European Association of Sport Management Conference 2010.

Eagleton, J. R., McKelvie, S. J. and de Man, P. (2007) 'Extraversion and neuroticism in team sport participants, individual sport participants, and nonparticipants', *Perpetual and Motor Skills*, 105, 1: 265–275.

Energy Saving News (2010) 'The carbon footprint of the World Cup: Blame FIFA, not South Africa', available at www.energy-savingnews.com/2010/06/carbon-footprint-football-world-cup-fifa-south-africa/ (accessed 23 October 2010).

England Netball (2010) 'Strategic vision', available at www.englandnetball.co.uk/About_Us/FAQs/miscellaneous.php (accessed 12 September 2010).

ESPN cricinfo (2010) 'Durham announce profit for financial year', available at www.espncricinfo.com/durham/content/story/465025.html (accessed 15 November 2010).

Fahy, J., Farrelly, F. and Quester, P. (2004) 'Competitive advantage through sponsorship: a conceptual model and research propositions', *European Journal of Marketing*, 38, 8: 1013–1030.

Fawkes, P. (2007) 'Nike cricket ad', available at www.psfk.com/2007/02/nike_cricket_ad.html (accessed 23 September 2008).

Feldt, T., Metsäpelto, R., Kinnunen, U. and Pulkkinen, L. (2007) 'Sense of coherence and five-factor approach to personality', *European Psychologist*, 12, 3: 165–172.

Fenn, D. (ed) (2008) *Keynote Sports Market Review*, 12th edition.

Forrester Research (2007) www.forrester.com/rb/research

Fullerton, S. (2007) *Sports Marketing*, Boston: McGraw-Hill.

Gigsport www.gigsport.com

Giulianotti (2002) 'Supporters, followers, fans, and flaneurs: a taxonomy of spectator identities in football', *Journal of Sport and Social Issues*, 26, 1: 25–46.

Gladden, J.M., Milne, G.R. and Sutton, W.A. (1998) 'A conceptual framework for assessing brand equity in division I college athletics', *Journal of Sport Management*, 12, 1: 1–19.

Glanville, T. (2010) 'World Cup: 15.4m viewers watch England beat Slovenia on BBC One', available at www.beehivecity.com/television/world-cup-15–4m-viewers-watch-england-beat-slovenia-on-the-bbc130502/ (accessed 14 September 2010).

Gratton, C. and Solberg, H.A. (2007) *The Economics of Sports Broadcasting*, Abingdon: Routledge.

Gratton, C. and Taylor, P. (2000) *The Economics of Sport and Recreation*, London: Spon Press.

Griffinyorkkrause.com, (2010) 'Case study: beer sponsors grab social media by the Vuvuzela at World Cup' available at http://blog.griffinyorkkrause.com/beer-sponsors-grab-social-media-by-the-vuvuzela-at-world-cup/ (accessed 23 October, 2010).

Golvin, C.S. (2007) 'The State of Consumers and Technology: Benchmark 2007', Cambridge, MA: North American Consumer Technographics, Forrester Research

Gonzalez-Herrero, A. and Pratt, C.B. (1995) 'How to manage a crisis before – or whenever – it hits', *Public Relations Quarterly*, 40: 25–30.

Goodman, M.B (1998) 'Corporate communications for executives', Albany, NY: State University of New York Press.

Greaves, A. (2008) 'Sponsorship of sports events is big business', available at www.business24–7.ae/articles/2008 (accessed 16 July 2008).

Grewal, R., Clive, T.W. and Davies, A. (2003) 'Early entrant advantage, word-of-mouth communication, brand similarity, and the consumer decision-making process', *Journal of Consumer Psychology*, 13, 3: 16–23.

Grunig, J.E. and Hunt, T. (1984) *Managing Public Relations*, Orlando, FL: Holt, Rinehart and Winston.

Hamill, S. (2007) 'Manchester United: the commercial development of a global football brand', in Chadwick, S. and Arthur, D., *International Cases in the Business of Sport*, Oxford: Butterworth-Heinemann.

Hopwood, M., Skinner, J., Kitchin, P. and Chadwick, S. (2010) *Sport Public Relations and Communication*, London: Butterworth-Heinemann.

Hopwood, M.K. (2005) 'Public relations practice in English county cricket', *Corporate Communications: An International Journal* 10, 3: 201–212.

Hunt, K.A., Bristol, T. and Bashaw, R.E. (1999) 'A conceptual approach to classifying sports fans', *Journal of Services Marketing*, 13, 6: 439–452.

IEG/Performance Research Sport Sponsorship Survey (2006) and IEG/Performance Research Sponsors Survey (2007), available at www.sponsorship.com (accessed 3 September, 2008).

Irwin, R.L. and Sutton, W.A. (1996) 'Roles, responsibilities and effectiveness of urban community relations programs within professional sport franchises', presented at *Sport in the City: An International Symposium on Cultural, Economic and Political Considerations*, Memphis, TN cited in Mullin, B.J., Hardy, S. and Sutton, W.A. (2007) *Sport Marketing*, 3rd edition, Champaign IL: Human Kinetics.

Janssen, I., Katzmarzyk, P.T., Boyce, W.F., et al. (2005) 'Comparison of overweight and obesity prevalence in school-aged youth from 34 countries and their relationships with physical activity and dietary patterns', *Obesity Reviews*, 6, 2: 123–132.

Kay, T. (2009) 'Ruff guide to sport and the family' available at www.sportdevelopment.info/index. php?option=com_contentandview=articleandid=619%3Aruff-guide-to-sport-a-the-familyandcatid= 47%3AruffguidesandItemid=1 (accessed 4 October 2010).

Kotler, P. (1997) *Marketing Management: Analysis, Planning, Implementation and Control*, Englewood Cliffs, NJ: Prentice-Hall.

Kotler, P., Keller, K., Brady, M., Goodman, M. and Hansen, T. (2009) *Marketing Management*, Harlow: Pearson Education.

Kotler, P. and Armstrong, G. (2005) *Principles of Marketing*, 11th edition, London: Prentice Hall.

Krautman, A.C. and Berri, D.J. (2007) 'Can we find it at the concessions? understanding price elasticity in professional sports', *Journal of Sports Economics*, 8, 2: 183–191.

Lamb, C.W., Hair, J.F. and McDaniel, C. (2009) *Essentials of Marketing*, 6th edition, Mason, OH: Cengage Learning.

Lawn Tennis Association (2010) www.lta.org.uk/Articles/About-Us/The-Tennis-Foundation/ (accessed 18 November 2010).

Levitt, T. (1960) 'Marketing Myopia', *Harvard Business Review*, 38, 4: 45–56.

Loos, J. (2008) 'Content delivery will become easier', in Stuart, J. (ed) *Digital Sports Competition Strategies*, London: Inside Business Media.

Manchester United FC (2010) www.manutd.com http://www.mufoundation.org/Charities.aspx (accessed 18 November 2010).

Martin, J.H. (1994) 'Using a perceptual map of the consumer's sport schema to help make sponsorship decisions', *Sport Marketing Quarterly*, 3, 3: 27–33.

Masterman, G. (2004) *Strategic Sports Event Management: An International Approach*, Oxford: Butterworth-Heinemann.

Masterman, G. (2007) *Sponsorship for a Return on Investment*, Oxford: Butterworth-Heinemann.

McDonald, M. (1994) *Marketing Plans: How to Prepare Them, How to Write Them*, Oxford: Butterworth-Heinemann.

McDonald, M. (2007) *Marketing Plans: How to Prepare Them, How to Write Them*, 6th edition, Oxford: Butterworth-Heinemann.

McDonald, M., Sutton, W.A. and Milne, G. R. (1995) 'TEAMQUAL TM: measuring service quality in professional team sports', *Sport Marketing Quarterly*, 4, 2: 9–15.

Merriam-Webster (2010) Merriam-Webster Online Dictionary, available at http://www.merriam-webster. com

Miller, C.C. (2010) 'Sport' fans break records on twitter' available at http://bits.blogs.nytimes.com/2010/06/18/sports-fans-break-records-on-twitter/ (accessed 4 November 2010).

Milne, G.R., Sutton, W.A. and McDonald, M.A. (1996) 'Niche analysis: a strategic measurement tool for managers', *Sport Marketing Quarterly*, 5, 3: 17–22.

Mintel (2009) 'Sponsorship UK', available at http://academic.mintel.com/sinatra/oxygen_academic/search_results/showand/display/id=1736 (accessed 12 August 2010).

Mitchell, J. (2010), Warrington Wolves Case Study, Personal Communication.

Mueller, S. and Peters, M. (2007) 'The personality of freestyle snowboarders: Implications for product development', *Original Scientific Paper,* 56, 4: 339–354.

Mullin, B.J., Hardy, S. and Sutton, W.A. (2007) *Sport Marketing*, 3rd edition, Champaign, IL: Human Kinetics.

New South Wales Sport and Recreation (2010) 'SWOT analysis', available at www.dsr.nsw.gov.au/assets/pubs/industry/ryc-swotanalysis.pdf (accessed 16 October 2010).

North West Development Agency (2010) 'Major sport venues and professional sport clubs: SWOT', *North West Region: Sport Sector Strategy*, available at www.nwda.co.uk (accessed 21 September 2009).

NZ Major Events (2008) 'U-17 FIFA Women's World Cup' available at http://majorevents.govt.nz/upload/72651/Marketing-Plan-Example-FIFA-U17-WWC-2008.pdf (accessed 17 December 2010).

NZ Major Events (2010) 'K2010 World Rowing Championships' available at http://majorevents.govt.nz/upload/72651/Marketing-Plan-2010-Rowing-World-Championships.pdf (accessed 17 December 2010).

Office for National Statistics (2010) 'General Lifestyle Survey 2008', available at http://www.statistics.gov.uk

Parasuraman, A., Zeithaml, V.A. and Berry, L.L. (1988) 'SERVQUAL: a multiple-item scale for measuring customer perceptions of service quality', *Journal of Retailing*, 64, 1: 12–40.

Pederssen, P.M., Miloch, K.S. and Laucella, P.C. (2007) *Strategic Sport Communication*, Champaign, IL: Human Kinetics.

Performance Research (2010) http://www.performanceresearch.com/snowboarding-sponsorship.htm (accessed 12 December 2010)

Picasso Enterprises (2010) 'The origins of sport marketing', available at http://www.picassoenterprises.com/2010/04/05/the-origins-of-sports-marketing/ (accessed 6 May 2010).

Pickton, D. and Broderick, A. (2005) *Integrated Marketing Communications*, 2nd edition, London: Financial Times Prentice Hall.

Porter, M.E. (1980) *Competitive Strategy*, New York: Free Press.

Porter, M.E. (1984) *Competitive Strategic Management*, Englewood Cliffs, NJ: Prentice Hall.

Quester, P.G. and Lardinoit, T. (2001) 'Sponsors' impact on attitudes and purchase intentions: a longitudinal study of the 2000 Olympic Games' available at http://smib.vuw.ac.nz:8081/WWW/ANZMAC2001/anzmac/AUTHORS/pdfs/Quester2.pdf (accessed 5 November 2010).

Red Bull www.redbull.co.uk/waybackhome

Rogers, E.M. (1962) *Diffusion of Innovations*, New York: Free Press.

Schwartz, P.J. (2010) 'The Most Valuable Sports Team Brands', *Forbes Magazine*.

Seital, P. (2001) *The Practice of Public Relations*, 8th edition, Upper Saddle River, NJ: Prentice Hall.

Shank, M. (2009) *Sports Marketing: A Strategic Perspective*, 4th edition, Upper Saddle River, NJ: Prentice Hall.

Shropshire and Telford and Wrekin Sports Partnership Marketing and Communications Plan http://www.shropshiretelfordwrekinsportspartnership.org.uk/downloads/STW-Marketing-Communication-s-Plan-Final.pdf (accessed 10 June 2010).

Smith, A.C.T. (2008) *Introduction to Sport Marketing*, Oxford: Butterworth-Heinemann.

Smith, F. (2010) 'Watford to re-evaluate plans due to season ticket sales' available at www.watfordobserver.co.uk/sport/8165236.Poor_ticket_sales_will_mean_re_evaluating_plans/ (accessed 16 November 2010).

Spicer, C. (1997) *Organizational Public Relations: A Political Perspective*, Mahwah, NJ: Lawrence Erlbaum Associates, Inc.

Sport Business (2009) www.sportbusiness.com (accessed 15 December 2009).

Sports Business Group (2007) *Sponsorship Works: Brand Marketer's Casebook*, London: Sport Business Group.

Sport Business International (2008) 135, available at www.sportbusiness.com/products/sbi/2009/feature-list (accessed 30 June 2009).

Sport England (2009) www.sportengland.org/research.aspx (accessed 18 December 2009).

Sport England (2010) 'Market segmentation', available at www.sportengland.org/research/market_segmentation.aspx (accessed 4 September 2010).

Sport Marketing Surveys http://sportmarketingsurveys.com

Sports Pro Media (2010) 'Global sponsorship analysis', *Sports Money Magazine*, available at www.sportspromedia.com/ (accessed 12 October 2010).

Sport Und Markt http://www.sportundmarkt.com/de/expertise/media-evaluation.html (accessed 14 December 2010).

St Helens Rugby League Club http://www.saintsrlfc.com/community (accessed 16 November 2010).

Strabane Golf Club www.strabanegolfclub.co.uk (accessed 1 August 2010)

Street Games (2006) 'Do disadvantaged young people participate less in sport?', available at http://www.streetgames.org/drupal-5.0/files/SG_briefing_paper_11_SOCIAL_CLASS.pdf (accessed 10 October 2010).

Stuart, J. (2008) 'Compelling insights and encapsulating change', in *Digital Sports Competition Strategies*, London: Inside Business Media.

Tapp, A. and Clowes, J. (2002) 'From "carefree casuals" to "professional wanderers": segmentation possibilities for football supporters', *European Journal of Marketing*, 36, 11/12: 1248–1269.

Taylor Report (1990) *The Hillsborough Stadium Disaster Final Report*, London: HMSO.

Tripodi, J.A. (2001) 'Sponsorship – a confirmed weapon in the promotional armoury', *International Journal of Sports Marketing and Sponsorship*, available at http://web.ebscohost.com (accessed 15 August 2008).

VANOC (2010) 'Vancouver Winter Olympic Games 2010 business plan', available at www.vancouver2010.com/dl/00/08/84/07–05–08-vanoc-business-plan-en-e_14d-dW.pdf (accessed 2 August 2010).

Verity, J. (2002) 'Maximising the marketing potential of sponsorship for global brands', *European Business Journal*, 14, 4: 161–173.

Virgin London Marathon www.virginlondonmarathon.com Press Releases (accessed 18 December 2009).

Volunteering Case Study www.hackney.gov.uk/sarah-m-salem.htm (accessed 12 December 2010).

Wann, D.L. (1995) 'Preliminary validation of the sport fan motivation scale', *Journal of Sport and Social Issues*, 19, 4: 377–396.

Wann, D.L., Grieve, F.G., Zapalac, R.K. and Pease, D.G. (2008) 'Motivational profiles of sport fans of different sports', *Sport Marketing Quarterly*, 17: 6–19.

Wells, W.D. and Tigert, D.J. (1971) 'Activities, interests and opinions' *Journal of Advertising Research*, 11, 4: 27–35.

Wikipedia http://en.wikipedia.org/wiki/Manchester_united (accessed 18 November 2010).

Wikipedia http://en.wikipedia.org/wiki/advertorials/featurearticles/spokespeople/directmail/newsletters/wordofmouth (accessed 30 November 2010).

Wimbledon (2010) www.wimbledon.org, www.aeltc.com/cms/media/pressreleases/2010queen_17_05_2010.aspx (accessed 18 November 2010).

Woodside, F. (2005) 'Consumer response to sponsorship leveraged packaging (SLP) – a FMCG context', unpublished master's thesis, available at www.anzmac07.otago.ac.nz/doctoralcolloquium.aspx (accessed on 23 September 2008).

Young, D. (1995) 'Looking at your company's fragile reputation', *Public Relations Quarterly*, 40, 4: 7–14.

Zhang, J.J., Pease, D.G. and Hui, S.C. (1996) 'Value dimensions of professionals sport as viewed by spectators', *Sports and Social Issues*, 20, 1: 78–94.

Zuckerberg, M. (2010) '500 Million stories', Facebook (accessed 21 July 2010).

Index

Active Learning in Sport – titles in the series

Coaching Science	ISBN 978 1 84445 165 4
Critical Thinking for Sports Students	ISBN 978 1 84445 457 0
Personal Training	ISBN 978 1 84445 163 0
Research Methods in Sport	ISBN 978 1 84445 261 3
Sport and Exercise Psychology	ISBN 978 1 84445 839 4
Sport and Exercise Science	ISBN 978 1 84445 187 6
Sport Management	ISBN 978 1 84445 263 7
Sport Sociology (second edition)	ISBN 978 1 84445 464 8
Sport Studies	ISBN 978 1 84445 186 9
Sport in the UK	ISBN 978 1 84445 383 2

To order, please contact our distributor: BEBC Distribution, Albion Close, Parkstone, Poole, BH12 3LL. Telephone: 0845 230 9000, email: learningmatters@bebc.co.uk. You can find more information on each of these titles and our other learning resources at www.learningmatters.co.uk.